"The workings of a criminally disordered mind has always been a fascinating subject for experts and lay persons alike. What causes someone such as Clifford Olsen to become probably the most evil serial murderer in Canadian history? How do trials play out for these individuals? Does our prison system simply throw away the key after they are incarcerated or is it worthwhile to attempt to rehabilitate such persons? Canadian and international psychiatrists and psychologists answer interestingly such questions in *Shrunk*, through their writings of true cases."

*Earl Levy QC, Barrister, Toronto, Ontario*

"This highly readable and fascinating book provides unique and personal insights into all-too-real instances in which unbridled mental disorder resulted in tragedy and loss, and wreaked havoc in the lives of perpetrators, victims, and their families. The book provides a glimpse into the often-hidden, troubled, and dark side of human behaviour. The compelling accounts of crimes committed by mentally ill offenders are told by experienced and highly respected psychologists and psychiatrists on the front-lines of the highest-profile mental disorder cases. *Shrunk's* authentic portrayal of what mental illness is really like, and what it can do to people, sets it apart from any other book of crime stories."

*Dr. Hy Bloom, LLB, MD, FRCPC*
*Consultant in Forensic Psychiatry, Psilex/Workplace.Calm*

"Scholarly inquiries into discrimination in Canadian society tend to concentrate on race and ethnicity, with occasional reference to physical disability. This traditionally narrow focus eclipses the legacy of systemic discrimination experienced by persons with mental disabilities, particularly those accused of a crime. Skewed public perceptions and social prejudices about mentally ill offenders have resulted. In turn, justice for such offenders is at risk. The practical experiences of the contributors to *Shrunk: Crime and Disorders of the Mind,* told in an easy-to-read format, go a long distance to correct those perceptions and mitigate those prejudices, particularly for the average citizen. This book should be on everyone's must-read list."

*John Rosen, Rosen Naster Barristers, Toronto, Ontario*

"Experiencing an enduring mental illness is a profound personal struggle that I would not wish on anyone! *Shrunk: Crime and Disorders of the Mind* promotes awareness, knowledge, and understanding of the complexities in diagnosing, treating, and supporting the recovery of those living with a mental illness who come in conflict with the justice system. *Shrunk* contains true and painful stories of lives tormented by mental illness and criminalization, their victims, and the families who suffer alongside them. And yet, this volume offers the hope that therapeutic jurisprudence works and that recovery is possible in living beyond the limitations of mental illness with meaning and purpose. But it takes the support of a caring community. A caring community that is informed and knowledgeable. Shrunk takes the reader behind the scenes of disordered minds, disabling mental health systems, and despairing families and victims by dispelling myths and misunderstandings. For many this will be a distressful and uncomfortable read, but for every reader an illuminating and elucidating one."

*Chris Summerville*
*CEO, Schizophrenia Society of Canada,*
*Winnipeg, Manitoba*

"The psychological and psychiatric forensic experts I encountered over decades of criminal law practice, both as Crown prosecutor and defence counsel, whether consulted by myself or by opposing counsel, were invariably highly qualified, experienced, principled and objective. *Shrunk: Crime and Disorders of the Mind* describes the diligence and commitment of these forensic experts who intervene before and at trial on the issue of fitness to stand trial, possibly providing evidence that the accused is not criminally responsible. It was gratifying to work in many cases with such exemplary professionalism."

*C.D. Evans QC, Barrister, Calgary, Alberta*

# SHRUNK

## CRIME and Disorders of the Mind

## Other Books by J. Thomas Dalby and Lorene Shyba

By J. Thomas Dalby

Williams, R. & Dalby, J. T., (Eds.) 1989. *Depression in Schizophrenics.* New York: Plenum Publishing Corporation.

Dalby, J. T. (Ed.) 1997. *Mental Disease in History: A Selection of Translated Readings.* New York: Peter Lang Publisher.

Dalby, J. T. 1997. *Applications of Psychology in the Law Practice: A Guide to Relevant Issues, Practices and Theories.* Chicago, Illinois: American Bar Association.

Nesca, M. & Dalby, J. T. 2013. *Forensic Interviewing in Criminal Court Matters: A Guide for Clinicians,* Springfield, Illinois: Charles C. Thomas Publisher.

White, J., Day, A., Hackett, L. & Dalby, J.T. 2015. *Writing Reports for Court: An International Guide for Psychologists who work in the Criminal Jurisdiction.* Sydney, Australia: Australian Academic Press.

*By Lorene Shyba*

Shyba, L. 2009. *Beyond Fun and Games: Interactive Theatre and Serious Videogames with Social Impact* Saarbrücken, Germany: VDM Verlag Publisher.

Evans, C.D. & Shyba L. 2012. *5000 Dead Ducks: Lust and Revolution in the Oilsands* Calgary: Durvile (formerly Durance Vile) Publications.

*The 'True Cases' Series*

Evans, C.D. & Shyba, L. (Eds.) 2014. *Tough Crimes: True Cases by Top Canadian Criminal Lawyers* Book One in the True Cases Series Calgary: Durvile (formerly Durance Vile) Publications.

*Forthcoming*: Perkel, Colin & Shyba, Lorene (Eds.) 2017. *Journo Tales: True Cases of Covering Crime* Book Three in the 'True Cases Series' Calgary: Durvile Publications.

# SHRUNK

## CRIME and Disorders of the Mind

EDITED BY

Lorene Shyba MFA PhD and J. Thomas Dalby PhD RPsych ABN

WITH A FOREWORD BY

Lisa Ramshaw MD DPhil FRCPC

DURVILE PUBLICATIONS

Durvile Publications Ltd.

Calgary, Alberta, Canada
www.durvile.com

(formerly Durance Vile Publications Ltd.)

National Library of Canada
Cataloguing in Publications Data
Shyba, Lorene and Dalby, J. Thomas
Shrunk: Crime and Disorders of the Mind
Issued in print and electronic formats
ISBN 978-0-9947352-0-1 (print pbk), ISBN 978-0-9947352-3-2 (epub),
ISBN 978-0-9947352-4-9 (audiobook),

1. True Crime —collections
2. Canadian Psychology
3. Canadian Psychiatry
4. Canadian Law
5. Canadian Essays—21st Century

I. Shyba, Lorene Mary, editor
II. Dalby, John Thomas, editor

*Book Two in the 'True Cases' Series.*

*Cover Illustration by Melanie Cook*
*Book and cover design by Lorene Shyba*
*Printed by Houghton Boston Printers, Saskatoon, Saskatchewan*
*Durvile is a member of the Book Publishers Association of Alberta (BPAA)*

First edition, first printing. 2016.

*To my dear family and friends, some of whom drift into mental disorder moments but I love you anyway.*

*Lorene Shyba*

*To my wife, Sue, and an amazing and talented group of women who happen to be my daughters.*

*J. Thomas Dalby*

# FOREWORD

Dr. Lisa Ramshaw

*Lisa Ramshaw MD DPhil FRCPC is the Forensic Psychiatry Subspecialty Program Director and an Assistant Professor at the University of Toronto. She is a staff psychiatrist in the Forensic Service at the Centre for Addiction and Mental Health in Toronto and has been a consultant psychiatrist in Nunavut for more than ten years. Her clinical practice includes assessments of criminal responsibility, fitness to stand trial, risk of violence and sexual violence, and assessments and care of individuals under the jurisdiction of the Ontario Review Board. She is also a member of the Ontario Review Board.*

*Everything can be taken from a man but one thing: the last of the human freedom—to choose one's attitude in any given set of circumstances, to choose one's own way.—Victor Frankl,* Man's Search for Meaning (1946)

As Shakespeare wrote, "There is nothing either good or bad, but thinking makes it so." These are words my mother shared at the right moment when I was an undergraduate at McGill University in Montreal. These insightful words from *Hamlet* allowed me to see the world a little differently. The ideas conjured by these words also happen to be fundamental to forensic psychiatry and psychology, a world where mental disorders and the law intersect.

A few years ago, a Toronto man ran over a police officer with a snowplow, killing him. The day before the jury began to consider its verdict, Rob Ford, the infamous then-Mayor of Toronto, called in to a local radio show to complain about the 'not criminally responsible on account of a mental disorder' (NCR) defence. Ford talked about how it hurt to see the guy go scot-free and asserted that if you killed someone and acted mentally disturbed, chances of freedom were pretty much assured. After the man was found NCR, and was to be sent to a forensic psychiatric hospital instead of to prison, the hockey commentator Don Cherry echoed Ford's thoughts, posting on Twitter that "it seems if you kill someone and act mentally disturbed then you can be let free." But people with psychotic disorders do not 'act' mentally disturbed; they *are* mentally disturbed. John Kastner, who produced and directed the documentaries of tragic crimes and forgiveness *NCR: Not Criminally Responsible* (2013), and *Out of Mind Out of Sight* (2014), put it well by asking, "Do we punish anybody else for an illness? A truck driver has a heart attack and kills ten people. Is he a criminal?"

In addition, mentally ill offenders certainly don't get off 'scot-free'. In Canada, those found NCR are detained in forensic hospitals —usually for many years, and somees more than thirty years—to protect the public and for rehabilitation.

Forensic psychiatry and psychology are extraordinary fields. Until recently, our professional work has been largely hidden from the public except for sensationalist and negative portrayals. Beyond the intrigue, those who we assess and treat are often shunned based not only on their admittedly destructive behaviour, but due to bias and stigma. The harm they cause makes the public angry; false stories are dreamed up about offenders' behaviour because better stories are not available to help explain. Imagination fills in the gaps in understanding. At times, interpretations can be debilitating. The person behind the label of 'accused' or 'mentally disordered offender' often becomes their disordered behaviour in the eyes of the world—as in *Hamlet*, the "thinking makes it so." Curiously, some of our non-forensic colleagues also find what we do mystifying and somehow wrong. We all see what we know, not what we don't know … yet.

In my fifteen years in forensic psychiatry, I've seen many sides of the profession: in assessments of risk of violence, in assessments of criminal responsibility, and in treatment and risk management. Working in a maximum secure forensic hospital in Penetanguishene, Ontario, I've met people who have lived in the hospital for many years after committing extreme offences: psychopaths driven by a need for dominance and instant gratification; serial murderers driven by narcissistic rage and sexual deviance; grievously ill people who had a delusional need to defend themselves from being killed. Working in a minimum secure forensic hospital with those who are transitioning to the community at the Centre for Addiction and Mental Health in Toronto, and in conducting forensic assessments in Ontario and beyond, I have witnessed many more stories—the man who murdered his mother because he thought she had been replaced by an alien who was going to kill his entire family and who is later forgiven by all except himself; the sex offender driven by desires and perceived needs; and the self-described 'unique' terrorist who really is like no other and is driven by a religious conviction that in his case became delusional. The varieties and motivations for criminal behaviour are vast. The challenges in our privileged world are like no other.

Strangely, fears that I had from childhood of the 'dangerous man' have softened. Over time, I have become less, rather than more, fearful of 'the accused'. Understanding lessens the mystery. I am more at ease with what is out there and I know that most people are remarkably good. Their stories have expanded my world.

Hearteningly, society is learning to respond with a greater openness and a desire to understand people who suffer from debilitating untreated mental illnesses. Thanks to treatment and compassion, some of these sufferers are making remarkable recoveries. Recent studies have shown that when released after their treatments, mentally disordered offenders are less likely to commit new crimes than inmates released from prison. As the Honourable Mr. Justice Richard D. Schneider notes, crimes in this population are the result of "untreated mental illness rather than deliberate criminality." Longer incarceration in prison actually results in poorer outcomes for them.

The personal and moving stories collected in this book will draw you in and allow you to look through a small window into the vast field of forensic psychiatry and psychology—into the experiences of those who have shared a part of the world in which they are fortunate to work. It will make you feel. It will allow you to see others and possibilities in a new way.

*— Lisa Ramshaw MD DPhil FRCPC*
*Founder, Forensic Psychiatry,*
*Assistant Professor, University of Toronto*

# CONTENTS

# Introduction

*Jim: Can you remember back that far? I can't remember what happened yesterday. (He laughs) I can't. How do you do it?*
*Plato: Oh, I had to go to a head-shrinker. Boy, he made me remember.*
*—Rebel Without a Cause, (Ray 1955)*

As editors of this book we auditioned a great many titles before settling on *Shrunk*, but how better, we reckoned, to write about the worlds of mental health and the law than to find a word used to describe the act of shrinking heads, or trying to understand the workings of a disordered mind. From the legal side, criminal defence lawyers use this term after meeting clients for the first time and assessing the circumstances of the crime. C.D. Evans QC, for example, recalls from his experience defending accused murderers and violent offenders that "If the crime is bizarre or absurd, it is a wise precaution to get the client's head shrunk." In *Tough Crimes: True Cases by Top Canadian Criminal Lawyers*, the first book in this 'True Cases' series, we discovered that lawyers such as John Rosen had similar thoughts when first encountering Paul Bernardo's disturbed mind, as did Joel Pink QC when unravelling the Antigonish Beech Hill murders.

From the mental health side, psychologist Dr. Lawrence Ellerby entices us to enter his *Shrunk* story about a journey from deviance to rehabilitation by promising to share the "contributions we shrinks can make in this difficult and complex social problem." And the informed general public, who make up a valued sector of our readership, might be of a mind to help out friends the way Plato, Sal Mineo's character, did when explaining his new-found clarity of mind to James Dean's character Jim Stark in *Rebel Without a Cause*, "Oh, I had to go see a head-shrinker." After all, who is there among us who hasn't been touched by mental illness among friends or family.

When we first started working on *Shrunk*, our idea was to create an anthology that would interface between the legal, the medical, and the behavioural by focussing on cases where judges and juries have called upon mental health experts when faced with the mentally disordered criminally accused. We assembled a list of eminent forensic psychologists and psychiatrists who we thought might be motivated to help build a solution to the problem of understanding mental illness in the criminal justice system. We asked them to consider their own involvement and how being exposed to people with mental health disorders affected them personally. Among our questions were: What were the outcomes in terms of your personal reflections? Was there a case that altered your perspective on humanity?

The original, previously unpublished stories that emerged from our invitations brilliantly illuminate a wide range of topics. These include Personality Disorders in the various *Diagnostic and Statistical Manual of Mental Disorders* (DSM) clusters, unlawful behaviour due to delusions and psychopathy, the criminal responsibility of accused persons, fitness of accused to stand trial, posttraumatic stress disorder (PTSD), wrongful convictions, and treatment and social consequences. We are in awe of the intense effort shown by our authors to inject their hearts and souls into explaining their experiences.

Our international contributors, Dr. Louise Olivier from South Africa, Dr. Jack White from Australia, and Dr. Sven Å. Christianson from Sweden revealed unique legal situations in their countries, as did Dr. Donald Dutton when describing a remarkable case in the United States. Their stories resonate with interesting terminology and turns of phrase that we edited only gently; in fact, we allowed individual voices to come through from all of our authors, whether Canadian or from countries beyond our borders. Within the editing process, we occasionally nudged writers to identify and focus on the heart of the story but we never had to ply their enthusiasm. Unlike any other book within the genre of True Crime, *Shrunk* presents the work of forensic professionals who have delved deeply, and with great commitment, into the disturbed human psyche.

'Forensic.' The word evokes images of crime scene tape or a cold corpse on the stainless steel autopsy table but its real meaning is much broader and simpler. Forensic is derived from Latin and literally means 'in the forum' or in modern terms 'in the court'. The forum in ancient Rome was the centre of most social debates and although the legal structure of the Romans did not have the same structure as in modern times, it was understood that the forum was where problems were formally and finally settled. When the word is added as a qualifier for psychologists and psychiatrists, it denotes that the focus of the work has a legal purpose. As such, many of the expectations or assumptions that might be made of other medical and behavioural science professionals cannot always be applied to the forensic breed. Forensic experts have, as a primary client, the courts or, indirectly, society even above the needs of the individual or patient being seen. A 'helping' role is not always assumed for the individual being examined, and when this is done, it is so that they may not harm other members of our society.

Most 'patients' do not come to forensic experts voluntarily but are often mandated to undergo assessments. And while forensic experts consider information that patients provide, this information is not accepted at face value; other data is often sought from multiple sources in due diligence. Very often confidentiality is not offered to patients as forensic experts give opinions in the public forum of the court system, in both written reports and oral testimony. These opinions are often repeated in the popular press, although not always accurately or comprehensively. Thus, in this book our contributors can freely give commentary on their public statements about specific cases, although several of our authors explicitly did obtain consent from the subjects of their chapter as a matter of their professional courtesy. Most of the cases contained in this book identify the individuals at the centre of their story, as they are historically important cases. But when identity did not matter to the narrative, pseudonyms were employed.

Forensic psychologists' and psychiatrists' roles in law can be as scientific commentators on mental health issues, evaluators of specific legal questions such as fitness for trial or criminal responsibility, or as advisors on appropriate sentencing/treatment alternatives. With some offenders, court-ordered treatment is necessary and this responsibility also falls to forensic mental health professionals.

Many lay persons confuse psychologists and psychiatrists and in the forensic area there are more similarities than differences. Both professions have the legal authority to diagnose and treat mental disorders and both are involved in almost every component of the legal system. Psychiatrists are firstly physicians undertaking the same training as every other medical doctor and then gaining specialized training with mental disorders. They can prescribe medications if that is deemed appropriate for the care of patients. Psychologists are trained as behavioural scientists with a strong research base and then gain clinical experience in assessing individuals with specialized psychological tests and treating patients using behavioural methods. Coordinated involvement of both professions is common. Allied professionals such as social workers and psychiatric nurses also can play key roles in forensic work.

One of the purposes of *Shrunk* is to let readers inside the work done by forensic mental health experts. Misunderstandings about 'insanity' cases abound among the general public. Legal systems like Canada's, which are descended from English common law, use precedent as the guiding principle where older established legal judgements guide modern court decisions. For insanity verdicts, a single case from London in 1843 has had continuing world-wide impact in courts. The case of *The Queen against Daniel McNaughton for the Wilful Murder of Mr. Drummond*[1] is arguably the most impactful of any in the history of forensic psychology and psychiatry (although these two professions did not formally exist at that time). A delusional man, Daniel McNaughton, shot the Secretary of the Prime Minister of England in the back in broad daylight in central London. The ensuing legal battle ended with a jury finding McNaughton not guilty by reason of insanity.

The public was outraged and the press indicated that all one had to do to escape justice was to feign madness. Young Queen Victoria, who had already survived several assassination attempts by 'mad' men, suggested to her Prime Minister that guidance from the House of Lords was needed. This body in turn asked the twelve judges of Queen's Bench to craft rules to be used in later insanity cases. The McNaughton rules survive to this day in little-changed form and pronounce that a person labouring under a mental disease that impairs their ability to distinguish right from wrong cannot be held legally responsible for their act—although this often meant long tenures in mental hospitals.

Finally, while forensic experts can offer the courts expert 'opinions' they are just that—views which may or may not be used by the

1 Dalby, J.T. (2006) The case of Daniel McNaughton: Let's get the story straight. *American Journal of Forensic Psychiatry, 27*, 17-32.

trier of fact (the judge or jury) in reaching legal judgements. Not every opinion offered turns for the benefit of the accused. Forensic experts also make it clear in the work that explanations of behaviour are never to be automatically converted to legal 'excuses'.

As seen in the various biographies of our contributors, they are an august group—leaders in their professions and most have multiple roles as clinicians, educators, and researchers. Many of our authors examined patients linked to the ultimate crime of homicide, but in everyday practice, psychologists and psychiatrists see patients charged with everything from shoplifting to exhibitionism to hit and run driving offences. While most of these stories have adults as the central character, adolescents also receive scrutiny and interventions.

There are many writing styles, as well as themes, represented in the book; from the academic, as reflected by the work of Porter & Dilley, and Cooper & Kanipayor with their comprehensive references and footnotes, to the flights of metaphor and creative non-fiction in the work of Dr. David Dawson and criminal defence lawyer William Trudell. In whatever style told, sober as well as enlightened thoughts and reprimands are exposed. We feel that however one decides to read the book, starting front to back for legendary tales of criminal evil, back to front for glimpses of optimism, or inside out to begin with stories of our day, *Shrunk* is worthy of a close read.

*— Lorene Shyba MFA, PhD &*
*J. Thomas Dalby PhD, R. Psych, ABN*
*Editors*

# PART ONE

# Legacy Cases

*Until we have the courage to recognize cruelty for what it is—whether its victim is human or animal—we cannot expect things to be much better in this world.*

*—Rachel Carson*

***J. Thomas Dalby** PhD, R. Psych, ABN has been a forensic psychologist for thirty-eight years and has been a Diplomate of the American Board of Professional Neuropsychology since 1984. He is a Professor (Adjunct) in the Department of Psychology at the University of Calgary and was also a member of the Faculty of Medicine at this university for twenty-six years. He has held a continuous appointment with Athabasca University since 1977. He was formerly administrative head of psychology departments at two Calgary hospitals.*

*Dr. Dalby is a Fellow of the Canadian Psychological Association, and in 2013 received the highest honour for professional psychologists in Canada—CPA award for Distinguished Contributions to Psychology as a Profession. He also is a recipient of the Dick Pettifor Memorial Award for exceptional career achievements from the Psychologists Association of Alberta. He has published over a hundred professional books, chapters and articles in medical, psychological and legal forums. He has conducted over fourteen-thousand forensic evaluations and provided courtroom testimony on over nine hundred occasions. His clients have included the National Hockey League, the United Nations, and police services, insurance companies, and law firms across North America.*

# Dr. Thomas Dalby

## Clifford Olson Unplugged

THE SUMMER OF 1981 was one of public terror in the greater Vancouver area. What began slowly as separate missing child or runaway cases turned into one of the most shocking series of murders in Canadian history. In July alone of that summer, six children went missing and were later revealed as brutally murdered. At least eleven children and teenagers, eight girls and three boys, would be killed before the murderer was placed in custody. The drama of this case however, had just begun with the murderer's arrest and the case quickly spun out of control of the authorities. The suspect, Clifford Robert Olson, was only one of three suspects during the period of the slayings, and the evidence gathered by the RCMP was minimal. There was certainly insufficient evidence to initiate an arrest for first-degree murder. While police had discovered several of the children's bodies, there was no evidence pointing to a specific perpetrator. Olson had been arrested and released over that summer on suspicion of a rape of a sixteen-year-old girl and had other allegations regarding children thrown his way, but, as always, charges were not pursued or were dropped because of flimsy evidence from a minor. When meeting with the RCMP at that time, Olson offered himself to the police as an informant for cash; he had in the past been instrumental in this role in the successful conviction of another criminal. He would accept cash for information relating to the disappearances of the missing children. Shortly after that, Olson was cornered by police after his car had been trailed to Vancouver Island with two women and he was charged with impaired and dangerous driving. In his car, investigators found an address book containing the name of one of the missing girls—this was all the evidence they had on the man who would become known as the 'Beast of B.C.' Olson would have to confess if the case was to go any further—but why would he? He was out of prison on mandatory supervision and was about to be prosecuted for other offences including sexual ones, so he was headed back to jail. Police indicated to him that there were pools of cash for informants but he knew using money to get information was a common practice anyway. What authorities had never done before in any open fashion was to give money to a criminal for self-incrimination.

That summer, my sister and her husband, reporter Ian Mulgrew, then-Bureau Chief of *The Globe and Mail*, had just moved to Vancouver with their young children, which intensified my concern and interest in the case. Ian became a key reporter of the Olson case, writing frequently in *The Globe* and finally penning a captivating book of the entire saga: *Final Payoff: The True Price of Convicting Clifford Robert Olson* (McClelland-Bantam, 1990).

The criminal trial with Olson in Vancouver was truncated by his guilty plea to eleven counts of first-degree murder on January 14, 1982. His sentence was eleven life sentences to be served concurrently in federal penitentiary and the judge recommended that he never be released. Olson had crafted a deal with authorities to receive one hundred thousand dollars from the RCMP, and approved by the federal Solicitor General, which would be placed in trust for his wife's and his infant son's support. In return, Olson would disclose the location of seven bodies of the missing children that had not been found and give details of the murder of those four youngsters whose bodies had already been discovered. Many of the facts of the murders slowly leaked out despite the guilty plea. Olson would typically cruise the streets or video game hang outs looking for naïve children or adolescents and, under the guise of running a construction company, ask if they would like a job with his company at a good wage. Those who agreed would be later offered a drink—alcohol or soft drink—that had been laced with the powerful sedative, chloral hydrate. This Mickey Finn would render his victims helpless. Olson was then free to sexually abuse or 'experiment' with the bodies of his victims and eventually bludgeon, stab, or strangle his prey. Some victims he buried in shallow graves in the forests, others he left in the open in the city. As a counter measure, Olson would frequently use rental cars when out on the prowl. One victim was even abducted immediately after Olson's meeting with the RCMP.

### *Payout to the Family*

The payout to Olson's family was obviously a source of much controversy across the country immediately following release of these facts. If looked at in a pragmatic way, the payment was logical as the bodies of those children hidden in the bush would never have been found otherwise and a criminal prosecution for these offences on what evidence the police had might have been unsuccessful. At an estimated ten-thousand dollars a day for such a complicated trial, the public purse would have paid even more if the trial had gone ahead, so the deal was a true devil's pact. But to many, the payoff did not pass the sniff test—it offended our sense of propriety that any money would go to the offender, even if it was only indirect payment. Later, legal attempts to have the money returned or given to the victims' families and attempts to sue those who had put the deal together were all unsuccessful. The reputations and careers of some of the professionals on both sides of this deal were nonetheless damaged beyond repair. It is unfair years later to second-guess authorities as they acted with a strong sense of urgency to resolve the crisis.

In my initial lecture to undergraduate students in Forensic Psychology, I dispel the myth that the field is driven by a hunt for serial killers. Forensic Psychology is very broad and encompasses a wide interaction between the disciplines of psychology and law, yet television crime fiction seems to suggest that there is a serial killer in every neighbourhood requiring psychological investigation. Early on a morning in October 1995, as I sat in my office at the Calgary General Hospital, I received a phone call from an official with the Department of Justice in Ottawa. Would I consider being retained to provide expert evidence for the Crown in a matter involving Clifford Olson and perhaps a separate, but similar matter with Paul Bernardo, recently convicted for serial sexual assaults and two murders? Well, once in a while I suppose we forensic psychologists and psychiatrists do focus on serial killers. I was cautioned by the federal official that Olson may sue me and asked if I had proper liability insurance. Apparently, Olson was consumed with making mischief by flinging frequent legal suits, all unsuccessful, against any opposition to his actions. Why not, he had nothing but time sitting in front of his typewriter in his small penitentiary cell.

With Olson ensconced in prison serving multiple life sentences, what did the Federal Government want me to do for them? As it was, Correctional Service of Canada (CSC) in August 1993 completely removed Olson's right to contact external parties other than his legal counsel, and particularly forbade contact with any mass media reporter. Olson's letters to media representatives would forthwith be destroyed and all mail received from them reviewed. Olson was transferred to the Special Handling Unit (SHU) in the Saskatchewan Penitentiary at Prince Albert, Saskatchewan from Kingston Penitentiary (he had threatened escape from the Kingston Pen and was found with a broom handle and handcuff key while there). Olson sued the CSC after this censure, claiming that this government agency had infringed his rights as a Canadian citizen as guaranteed by the *Canadian Charter of Rights and Freedoms*. These rights included fundamental freedoms to associate with whomever one wished and freedom of thought, belief, opinion and expression, including freedom of the press and other media of communication. While incarcerated, persons still had certain rights regardless of their criminal status. There was little doubt that his captors had removed these fundamental freedoms, but were they justified under law to do so? That was the legal question that I was asked to examine.

### *Direct Media Contact*

The whole issue of Olson's freedoms and his public profile came to a head when an article in *Saturday Night* magazine was published in the summer of 1993. Now defunct, *Saturday Night* was Canada's oldest national magazine with a circulation then of approximately 650,000, due to the publication being inserted in some of the country's biggest newspapers. Veteran conservative journalist Peter Worthington, in his article, summarized a number of personal interviews he'd had with Olson over an eighteen-month period at Kingston Pen, entitling the piece "The Journalist and the Killer." An informal and decade-old ban on direct media contact with Olson had apparently been ignored or forgotten. Worthington widely criticized the Canadian correctional system in his article, indicating that Olson seemed to be running his area of the penitentiary. Olson wrote an unpublished letter to the magazine's editor, John Fraser, after the article in *Saturday Night* appeared noting it was "an excellent and exceptionally first-rated article. Ninety percent was all true." He then went on for several pages in augmenting the other ten percent and that "Peter Worthington should get his facts in order when writing." Despite Worthington's claim that he lacked such, Olson asserted that he had a conscience, like everyone else and had remorse for his crimes. Elsewhere in Olson's official record are frequent acknowledgements of his pride in the brutality released on his victims and his subsequent, and easily obtained, notoriety. Why would he try to convince anyone he had remorse? Indeed, Worthington should have checked some of the facts in the article as Olson was unquestionably a pathological liar. Worthington praised some of Olson's opinions as "surprisingly sensible and astute," when everything I read and heard from him was obtuse and lacking any insight or the faintest glimmer of intelligence. Worthington claimed in his piece that Olson had some twenty-four cases reach the Supreme Court of Canada (SCC) when in reality only two matters of Olson's manifestos were ever considered by the SCC—one the year before he was arrested on the murders. Filing a legal suit does not mean it 'reaches' the court or consumes anything but a few minutes of clerical time as it is disposed of. In 1994, a federal court declared Olson a "vexatious litigant," barring him from launching any more lawsuits that complained about his prison treatment without special permission to do so.

Worthington reported that any imposed restrictions on communications with Olson seemed to quickly vanish in the prison and Olson was reportedly calling anyone he liked from his cell phone without any knowledge by the authorities. A radio personality in Toronto was reportedly in regular contact with Olson. Worthington constantly fed into Olson's self-importance with some hyperbole regarding his intelligence and knowledge—could someone as astute as Worthington really be drawn in by Olson's obvious bull? There was little doubt that Olson's façade, as I saw it, was as a lovable and perhaps mistreated nuisance, but he was highly skilled in manipulating others and an inveterate liar. His 'intelligence' was constantly overestimated (especially by himself) and any attempt to show sophistication of knowledge was undercut by his almost constant malapropisms and illogical arguments. His cognitive abilities had only been once estimated by an out-dated type of cognitive test, and his formal scores from this were in the low-average range. His reading levels were at Grade Five or Six. When I asked to conduct a series of cognitive tests on him, Olson refused, stating that his "own doctors" would do it. He obviously didn't have this crack team of experts standing by. On the other hand, why wouldn't Olson feel important when he had leading lawyers like Melvin Belli of San Francisco and nationally acclaimed journalists vying for time with him?

So who was Clifford Olson? Many of my undergraduate university students recently could not answer this question and were not even born when his crimes were taking place. I sifted through Olson's entire criminal file which sat on my desk—officially starting at his first incarceration at age seventeen but beginning much earlier than this. His school record was replete with teacher observations of manipulating other children, physically assaulting them and even targeting adults, for example, stealing vegetables from the backyards of citizens and brazenly selling them back to them at their front door. He was often absent from school and left school after Grade Eight. At the time of his final arrest, Olson had escaped seven times from various penal institutions. Already at the age of twenty-one, his correctional file indicated that he was "always acting the fool" and was a maximum security risk with an extensive criminal history. He was deemed "not a hopeful prospect for successful rehabilitation at this time"—or as it turned out, any time. Even in his twenties he presented himself as superior to others and constantly rationalized his criminal behaviour. His criminal record before the murders included eighty property offences, one armed robbery, two parole violations, and five mandatory supervision violations. These convictions were only a sample of the criminal behaviour he later acknowledged. He would later boast that of the eleven murdered youngsters, he was only charged with their murder, not for sexually violating them or their bodies even though the evidence was clear that he had. In total, Olson spent less than four years of his adult life outside of prison. Most law enforcement professionals who viewed the case believed that Olson had killed before the series of eleven victims in the Vancouver area. It would have been extremely unusual for a serial killer to begin his evil odyssey at the age of forty. Olson later claimed various numbers of murders in Canada and the United States and once took police on a wild goose chase in a bogus search for more bodies for simply the opportunity to be out of prison for a period. By the time I testified against him, he claimed to have killed over two hundred persons.

### *Olson's 'Literary Works' and Public Notoriety*

Olson wanted desperately to be the most notorious serial killer of all time and had registered the titles of two books by himself; "Profile of a Serial Killer," and "Inside the Mind of a Serial Killer—A Profile." Official copyright certificates were issued with these titles despite the fact that there were no books written and thankfully there never would be. This self-delusion, that he was an 'author' and uniquely tainted criminal was just another clue to his aberrant personality. He claimed that he was negotiating a publication contract in the range of three and a half million dollars for his literary works. Even in prison, Olson continued his constant antisocial behaviour and was proud of the fact that for five years he had purchased postage stamps and altered them to appear to be of greater value. He continued to taunt other inmates about his special privileges. When I went through some of his confiscated correspondence, Olson had enticed young schoolgirls, who apparently wanted the excitement of corresponding with a serial killer, to send Polaroid pictures of themselves in various stages of undress.

One of the reasons set out by the authorities to reduce Olson's notoriety was ironically for his own safety. With his continued-deviant aura in prison, he was a target by the rest of the prison inmates and it would have brought high praise to an inmate it he were to kill Olson. With Olson's reduced visibility, he would eventually be forgotten and may even be allowed to intermingle with other inmates rather than remain in protective custody. When offered treatment, Olson would be cooperative up until the time he actually had to participate and then he declined. He wrote, "Let me make myself clear, I'm having problems for the murders I have committed. What is going to be done for me?" He wanted individual therapy as he was in protective custody and repeatedly became uncooperative as soon as any efforts were organized, as they were not up to his standard.

Did this trial really matter—wasn't it just a small administrative issue? A line had been drawn by the Federal government that made it much more. This psychopath would not again dupe the government into paying out more taxpayer money for his deviousness and every public statement he made was with the goal of making himself look superior to the inept government and his gaolers. The stakes were high—Olson wanted to slap the establishment in the face again and there was sufficient anxiety among officials that he just might do it! If Olson won judgement from the Courts—he was seeking fifty-thousand dollars in damages as well as a lifting of the gag order—confidence in the Federal government and the entire cast involved in the administration of justice was going to take a direct and substantial hit. It was a tipping point but the public knew little about it, just as they had lacked information about the initial payoff. However, with a legal victory by the Department of Justice, the precedent would be used to handle Paul Bernardo and his contact with media and any other psychopathic inmate who wanted to gain notoriety with the public and continue to poke the wounds of victim's families with interviews or books about their deeds.

The lawyer I would be working with was Bruce W. Gibson of the Saskatoon office of Justice Canada. Bruce had been busy dealing with Olson's numerous hijinks ever since Olson had been placed in the Saskatchewan Penitentiary. Bruce was amazingly patient with Olson, not allowing him to see the frustration that the entire justice and correctional system was experiencing with his constant absurd claims. Bruce was a calm and highly focussed man who never lost his cool even though Olson took up a good chunk of his professional time.

The trial on this matter took place in the cafeteria of the SHU, which had been converted to a Federal Court for the duration of the hearing. As I walked through two levels of electronic scrutiny in the SHU, I reached the main conference room. There on the board were listed eighteen of Canada's most violent men—I had met ten of them. It would have been too much of a security concern and media circus if the trial had moved to the old brick Court House up on the hill overlooking downtown Prince Albert. The press were kept a block away by a police barricade. Our lunch that day—all of us—consisted of baloney sandwiches that were being served in the entire prison. Duty counsel for Olson, Garth Bendig, a sharp lawyer only two years at the bar, quipped with me that his baloney sandwich was likely to be his full payment for his representation of Olson. The idea that inmates in Canadian prisons have some sort of 'cushy ride' on the taxpayers' dime has always been a fiction proffered by the 'get tough' conservative movement who had no clue about what federal prisons were like. This approach has never shown any appreciable decrease in recidivism and some have even concluded that it can increase the probability that offenders will commit new crimes.

### *The Trial and Olson's Disorders*

The trial between Olson and Her Majesty the Queen (*Olson v. Canada*) took place on January 11, 1996. Olson shuffled into the temporary courtroom with his hands and feet in heavy chains and with two massive, bald guards flanking him. He was a short, rumpled man with a Cheshire grin—a dishevelled troll, revelling in being the centre of attention once again. With his chains removed, he sat directly looking at Justice Darrel Heald, a Saskatchewan native son who had previously been Attorney General of the province and who had been on the Federal bench for twenty-five years. When giving testimony, I sat at right angles on Olson's right, about ten feet away. He often frowned at me during my testimony or avoided eye contact when I spoke about him.

The oral evidence began with Acting Deputy Warden Thomas Taylor giving the background to Olson's obsession with notoriety for his murders and CSC's steps in curtailing his access to media. I then was called to provide the Court with a clinical analysis of Olson, the disorders from which he suffered and why the decision to stop his contact with the media was appropriate and necessary.

I began outlining the multiple mental disorders with which Olson had been diagnosed. The first and obvious one was an Antisocial Personality Disorder. A personality disorder is according to DSM-5 (the current diagnostic system for mental disorders) "an enduring pattern of inner experience and behaviour that deviates markedly from the expectations of the individual's culture, is pervasive and inflexible, has an onset in adolescence or early adulthood, is stable over time, and leads to distress or impairment." Essentially, Antisocial Personality Disorder (APD) is a pattern of disregard for, and violation of the rights of others since age fifteen. It includes repeatedly committing crimes, repeated lying and conning others, impulsivity, aggressiveness, recklessness for the safety of self and others, and consistent irresponsibility. Lack of remorse for their actions is common. This official diagnosis overlaps with the idea of what a 'psychopath' is, although the term is not listed separately in DSM. Many forensic psychologists and psychiatrists feel that psychopathy is a small subset of Antisocial Personality Disorder but still recognize that a few psychopaths may not fall in the category of APD, for example, workplace psychopaths. Most criminals, even those with APD, are not psychopaths. The accepted standard for measuring psychopathy is the Psychopathy Checklist—Revised, initially constructed by Dr. Robert Hare of the University of British Columbia. It contains twenty descriptive items including superficial charm, conning/manipulation, shallow affect, lack of empathy, impulsivity, irresponsibility, failure to accept responsibility, and criminal versatility. A score ranging from zero to two points is given for each rating item. The maximum is therefore forty points—the score I gave Olson. I had seen many psychopaths in my career but never one who had every element in spades. Psychopaths are not rare in the Federal correctional system so this diagnosis was not the important aspect of his rehabilitation or 'treatment' in prison.

While many psychopaths have some sense of grandiosity, Olson's sense of his self-worth was off the chart. This made a second personality disorder diagnosis obvious—narcissistic personality disorder. In my analysis, this was absolutely key and only about one percent of prison inmates carried this diagnosis. Narcissistic personality disorder is a diagnosis rendered when there is a pervasive pattern of grandiosity in fantasy or behaviour, need for admiration, and lack of empathy. Olson met the description perfectly—he constantly exaggerated his achievements and talents and always expected to be recognized as superior. He was preoccupied with fantasies of unlimited success, power, or brilliance. He was thoroughly convinced that he was special and unique and could only associate with other special or high-status people. He sought admiration from wherever he could get it and had an extreme sense of entitlement. His arrogance, however, arose from no earned accomplishments. I explained to Justice Heald that the core of CSC's plan was that he not have contact with the media, as this contact was reinforcing his narcissism and making it worse, if that were even possible. I indicated that his prohibition from media contact was in his best interest, as well as that of the institution, and the general public.

I continued his diagnostic analysis by pointing out that Olson had some alcohol- and substance-use issues in the past but had no access to these substances in the prison and this was not a substantive issue requiring attention by the correctional authorities.

Finally, I labelled Olson a pedophile and a sexual sadist and on hearing this he tried to stand up to object but his counsel quickly laid a hand on his shoulder and scolded him to shut up. Olson would interrupt occasionally and was often complaining to his lawyer during my testimony. His form of pedophilia—sexual attraction to both girls and boys—was quite uncommon and was simply another element of his criminal versatility. There was no crime that he would not commit, no boundaries that he did not cross. His sexual sadism indicated his sexual arousal could come from the physical or psychological suffering of another non-consenting person and was evident in the forensic evidence I reviewed. He had no rebuttal to this diagnosis.

### *Why Provide Treatment?*

The public may wonder, why provide any treatment at all to this undeserving man? Just lock him away and throw away the key! The Canadian federal correctional system has, as one of its entrenched mandates, to 'correct' or rehabilitate offenders. Other goals include, of course, deterrence from further crime and protection of society. Correctional Service of Canada has an envious international reputation of very successful rehabilitation of offenders. Less than two percent of federal offenders released on parole commit another violent offence. CSC is the largest federal employer of psychologists; a fact which contributes to the success of their many treatment programmes. Ten percent of male offenders and twenty percent of female offenders have a diagnosis of a mental disorder on admission to the federal prison system in Canada. While in prison, inmates participate in educational, employment, and treatment programmes—all addressing factors identified as contributing to their offending.

There is no process where CSC gets to decide whether an inmate gets treatment; if they need it, they get it or at least it is offered to them. Inmates, of course, have the right to reject treatment and just sit in their cells. So our federal correctional system is obligated to develop an individualized 'correctional plan' and in Olson's case it was deemed that restricting access to the media was in his best interest and that by reducing his notoriety he may eventually be transferred to general population in a correctional institution. Of course, another goal was of restricting his contact so that he would not further inflict pain on the families of his many victims. CSC had an obligation to stop him from accruing gratification from the fact that he murdered and sexually assaulted those children and teenagers. Even though he was deemed "untreatable" by nearly every forensic professional who examined him, efforts had to be made to at least manage his conduct regarding his narcissism. There was no realistic hope of him ever being released from prison. Worthington described the ban on contact "bizarre" and suggested, in a column in *The Sun* newspapers on January 19, 1996, that it would be best just to let Olson have contact with any media he wanted and the public would grow weary of him, and therefore the media coverage of him. He also indicated that Olson would get around the ban somehow, as he was a psychopath.

Justice Heald rendered his written decision in less than a month following the trial and ruled in favour of the Federal Government. Olson was indefinitely prohibited from media contact and was allowed only very restricted general access to anyone else, such as his lawyer. The case was immediately used as precedent to ban three other federal prisoners from talking to the media. The Canadian Association of Journalists denounced the gag order as an infringement on their access to news, but victim rights groups applauded the decision. Olson served the rest of his sentence in this imposed silence. Mr. Worthington's predictions were wrong—Olson could find no way around his ban. His only public showings were at occasional parole hearings, to which he had a right, but at which he had no realistic hope of ever being released. He died of cancer on September 30, 2011 at the age of seventy-one.

It might be argued that we should just forget all about men like Olson as any discussion gives them some status that they never deserved. This is faulty thinking. By examining the case, we do not provide accolades but we are forced to examine our system of criminal justice, corrections, and even investigative tactics. The police investigation system and cross-referencing of offenders is far more advanced now than when Olson was skulking around the streets and he would very likely have been arrested sooner if such technology had been available. The Canadian criminal justice system has also evolved since

Olson. It is very likely that Olson would have been tagged as a Long Term Offender (LTO) had such legislation been in place at the time. The LTO designation was created in 1997, primarily targeting sexual offenders, that is, those at high risk for committing further offences, like Olson. These individuals can be supervised by authorities even after their entire criminal sentence has expired, and further incarceration of up to ten years in prison can be imposed for breaches. Olson's case caused many changes in the criminal justice system. Victims groups arose and victims' rights were entrenched in sentencing; a missing children's registry was established; the *Criminal Code of Canada* was amended barring multiple murderers from applying for early parole under the 'faint hope clause', and Olson's pension and old age income supplements were suspended, as were the benefits of other federal inmates while incarcerated.

I am often asked what causes men like Olson to commit the offences they do. Much Canadian research has contributed to answering this question. When asked, Olson would always say that it was the alcohol and drugs he took as well as the correctional system that warped him from an early age. Of course, this response was absurd. Olson was a bad seed—a psychopath who was trouble right out of the gate and he remained so despite the efforts of the 'system' to correct his tendencies. While psychopathy is a mental affliction, it has never been a candidate for mitigation consideration or legal excuse for any offence such as an 'insanity' case—that other major mental disorders such as schizophrenia or other psychotic disorders might be. While there is strong genetic evidence for psychopathy being passed through generations, there were no other examples in Olson's immediate family. He killed because he wanted to and he could get away with it, he thought. Of course, his motivations for the murders were multiple; sexual, sadistic, power-driven, curiosity, avoidance of detection; and, in addition, his general disregard for anyone other than himself. He was not complex or difficult to predict—but as evil as they came.

***Sven Å Christianson** PhD is a Professor of Psychology, and Chartered Psychologist at the Department of Psychology, Stockholm University, Sweden. He has authored or co-authored over one hundred scientific papers and a number of books, for example* Handbook of Emotion and Memory; Traumatic Memories; Advanced Interrogation and Interviewing Technique; Offenders' Memories of Violent Crimes; Inside the Head of a Serial Killer; and Psychological Myths in the Legal System. *The objective of his research programme is to gain an understanding of the relationship between emotion and memory, with a specific focus on victims' and offenders' memories of violent and sexual crimes. Dr. Christianson has been a consultant in numerous murder, rape, and child sexual abuse cases, and he is often used both as a speaker and as a psychological expert witness.*

# Dr. Sven Å. Christianson

## A Cat-and-Mouse Game

Just before Christmas in the year 2008, a tearful voice delivered a news bomb in front of Swedish television cameras, "I have not committed any of those murders I've been convicted of and I have not committed any of the other murders I have admitted. That's how it is."

The convicted serial killer Sture Ragnar Bergwall (also known as Thomas Quick) whom the Swedish people had followed in the media for fifteen years as the personification of evil, suddenly declared himself innocent of eight murders he had been convicted of in six separate trials held between 1994 to 2001. The genesis of Bergwall's retracted confessions was his association with Hannes Råstam, an investigative journalist whose specialty was tracking down false confessions of convicted offenders. Two to five years after Bergwall and Råstam first met, and with massive media support, decisions were made to refer each of the cases to the Swedish Court of Appeal. Prosecutors decided to withdraw public prosecution in all of these cases, and subsequently, in 2014, Bergwall was released from a high security clinic as a free man. The television, radio and Sweden's leading print media touted the whole matter a 'legal scandal', portraying Bergwall as an innocent victim of cynical forensic psychiatric care and an incompetent justice system.

Sture Bergwall played a cat-and-mouse game with justice where he provided two different versions of the truth. In the first version, he admitted to many murders, claiming at one time to have committed as many as twenty. In the second version, he took back these confessions. No matter which version he represented, signs of a psychopathic personality, sexual deviation, and sadism were obvious in his makeup. Bergwall's case analysis is based on my own interviews and how he presented himself for over twenty years in connection with litigation, forensic psychiatric care, and in the media.

### *Sture Bergwall's First Version of the Truth*

Bergwall's first version, as callous murderer, began in the summer of 1992 when he was at Säter high security forensic clinic about two hundred kilometres north of Stockholm, where he had been treated for several periods since the age of nineteen for various crimes including rape of young boys, attempted murder, and robbery. As an example, he had once held a bank official, his wife, and their nine-year-old son hostage in their home while an accomplice held up a local bank branch.

During his stay at Säters, Bergwall told medical staff that he might have killed a boy. This was a completely voluntary statement. The boy was eleven-year-old Johan Asplund who disappeared on a November morning in 1980 when he was on his way to school. Bergwall says he molested the boy, killed him, and then cut up the body. The attending physician, Kjell Persson, and his colleague medical doctor Göran Fransson, found this story so compelling that they contacted the police. A preliminary investigation was initiated by the regional prosecutor Christer van der Kwast in Norrland (a northern region of Sweden), and it turned out that Bergwall was willing to reveal information about several other unsolved murders of young boys. "Forty-two-year-old admits…" read the headline that would soon become a recurring notice in the media.

Prosecutor van der Kwast believed, however, that Bergwall's information regarding Johan Asplund was not sufficient to prosecute at that time (the case was resumed and heard seven years later). This led Bergwall to tell of the murder of another young boy, fourteen-year-old Tomas Blomgren who had disappeared on his way home from an amusement park in 1964, the body later being found in a shed.

Although the murder of Blomgren was time-barred, that is outside the statute of prosecution limitations, Bergwall's factual details corresponded so closely to actual findings that further questioning about the other murders was justified. He next confessed to the murder of a fifteen-year-old boy, Charles Zelmanovits, who had disappeared on his way home from a school dance in Piteå, in November

1976. Parts of the body were found seventeen years later, in September 1993, buried in a wooded area a few kilometres from the boy's home. Bergwall provided facts that had not been publicly released including the location of the dumping site. Van der Kwast decided to go ahead with prosecution of Bergwall. The year was 1994.

### *My Role in the Case*

When the investigation began in the Charles Zelmanovits case, prosecutor van der Kwast requested that I "assist in an investigation where a man told of repeated murders he committed over a long period of time." Since my academic research relates to what victims, witnesses, and perpetrators remember from violent crimes and trauma, I accepted this assignment. They wanted to know: Is Bergwall a possible/potential offender? Does Bergwall remember what he says he remembers? How should he be interrogated on the basis of scientific parameters of memory?

In assessing Sture Bergwall's background, I discovered his long history of violence and his repeated sexual offences against young boys, including the aggravated rape and attempted murder of a nine-year-old boy who had been admitted as a patient at the hospital where Bergwall had been employed as an orderly. Bergwall had also attacked a man in his home and left him dying, thinking, as the man lay bleeding on the floor, that he would never survive. (As it turned out, this man was able to later report watching the whole while, as a smiling Bergwall cleaned his knife and wiped down other traces on the site.) In addition, Bergwall told and wrote in detail about his sexual preference for young boys and of explicit sexual violent sadistic fantasies. My observation was that this culprit displayed a repetitive compulsion, symptomatic of serial rapists and serial killers. He also had forensic awareness of covering up evidence. In my opinion, Bergwall's history and lifestyle qualified him as a potential offender.

The prosecutor's second question was about Bergwall's capability to remember what he claimed to remember about the murders. He had used drugs during the earlier part of his life, and the killings were far back in time, so the question was justified. I had previously examined patients to study the impact of head injuries and brain diseases on memory, including in connection with neurosurgery. My practice and studies had been conducted at various university hospitals in Sweden, in Canada at the Montreal Neurological Institute, McGill University, and The University of Washington Medical Center in the United States. I had professional experience in this scientific domain to respond to this legal issue.

I met with Bergwall for the first time in autumn of 1994. He was a tall, thin, balding man with thick glasses. He gave a servile impression and the yellowish-grey teeth and vague smile revealed him as a heavy tobacco user. He claimed that he kept fit by running hundreds of laps on a patio, totalling a mile a day, several times a week. Bergwall was open in our contact and positive about the impending memory testing.

The assessment of Bergwall's memory capacity was based on standard evidence-based theory and research. He showed good intellectual and verbal skills, and memory testing revealed that he had generally normal memory function. Regarding the learning of new information, the results were in the lower part of the normal range. Regarding retrieval of older information, that is, general knowledge and autobiographical memories, however, he exhibited very good memory function. Bergwall had had no documented incidences of brain damage or dysfunctional memory. My expert opinion to the Court in the autumn of 1994 was that Bergwall had the potential to remember his autobiographical history and that he also, from this perspective, could be credible.

The third question regarded interrogation techniques. I began a series of interviews with Bergwall, which resulted in over a hundred hours of interview time between 1994 and 2000, the objective of which was to create a clinical profile of Bergwall and an understanding of his motivation for the murders. The objective of this profile was to help guide the police's interrogation of Bergwall by providing the best chance of interpreting his confession correctly, with minimal influences from other sources. The technique used in creating this profile is called a 'cognitive interview', based on the premise that the person who has the information should be mentally active during the interview, that is, the witness, rather than the interrogator should do the reconstruction of events.

An important aspect of extracting memories that are historic is to return both to the internal and external context of the informant at the time of the event (for example focusing on sensory context), which can be done either mentally or by reconstructions of the scenes of crimes. My experience is that it is easier for perpetrators to act out crime scenes rather than to than to tell about them. Furthermore, it is harder to lie during reconstruction dramas as opposed to providing verbal descriptions during a standard police interview. The reconstruction methodology was accordingly adopted by the police and the prosecutor in the ongoing investigation, with Bergwall willingly cooperating.

In meeting with me, Bergwall told of his upbringing and the development of his sexual sadistic behaviour. We did not talk specifically about the specific murder being investigated, but rather in general terms about how and where he sought his victims, his approach in killing, and his post-crime behaviour. We also talked about other offenders, including the serial killer Westley Allan Dodd, whose picture Bergwall had on the wall of his room in the clinic. He said he admired the way Dodd hanged a boy in a closet and then photographed the boy's agony. Bergwall told me that one of his aims of our talks was that the information he provided be used to capture prospective offenders and that I should spread this knowledge to health professionals, staff in schools, social services, the police, the judicial system, and the general public.

In Bergwall's first version of the truth, he had significant motive for his confessions to the murders. He said he wanted to participate in the police investigation so that the families of the victims could obtain knowledge about what happened to their children and relatives. He wanted to appear as good and do the right thing.

In order to better illustrate the manipulation capability of Sture Bergwall and his cat-and-mouse game, I want to put this in context, that is, to briefly describe his background.

### *Early Life and Criminal Behaviour*

Bergwall was born on April 26, 1950, one of seven children and grew up in Falun, a town of about 35,000 inhabitants, inland in Sweden. His father was a factory worker and his mother had various temporary jobs. The family belonged to a nonconformist church. At the age of seven, Bergwall contracted tuberculosis and was in a sanitorium for eight months. He left primary school without completing it and had no vocational training.

Previous to being convicted of eight murders in six separate trials between 1994 and 2001, Bergwall had already spent much of his time in various psychiatric facilities. His pathology and manipulation capability was evident as early as 1961. During talks with me, he said that he developed fantasies of attacking young boys when he was eleven-years-old and by the age of fourteen he was committing assaults against young boys who "looked good and were feminine soft." When caught, his school principal and the school physician would counsel him, but he carried on his clandestine assaults using money and threats. Bergwall told me that at sixteen, he also attacked a women and he watched the newspaper for information on the assault. His sexual preoccupation continued with his high school in Uppsala and he was suspended in his first semester for his repeated violence. Dr. Erik Brunnander, examining Bergwall in 1967, formally notes a deeply disturbed personality.

Bergwall was sentenced in 1970 for the first time for acts of abuse against several children, including rape, and molestation for which he was sent to Sidsjön forensic hospital in Sundsvall. As forensic psychiatric examinations by Dr. Otto Brundin, summarized in the verdict

> Bergwall suffers from a constitutional conditioned high-grade sexual perversion of type pedofilia *cum sadismus,* ... that Bergwall is not only dangerous, but under certain conditions extremely dangerous to the personal safety of life and limb, and therefore that closed psychiatric care is urgently called for.

Berwall had committed fornication with an eight-year-old boy and tried to strangle him and did not release him until he thought the boy was dead.

He was discharged from Sidsjön but was soon re-admitted due to his excessive use of alcohol and drugs. In January 1973, he was moved to Säter high security clinic. By March 1974, Bergwall was once again discharged and six days later, he tried to kill a thirty-two-year old casual acquaintance in Uppsala city. The attack was unprovoked and Bergwall struck him with a frying pan and stabbed the man twelve times leaving him for dead. He was returned to hospital rather than legally prosecuted.

Despite the doctor's judgement on re-admission that treatment was needed for some considerable time to come with regard to his "grave mental abnormality," Bergwall was fully discharged from Säter in June 1977. Had Sture Bergwall by this time been successfully rehabilitated from his pedophilic sexual sadistic addiction?

Although he kept out of forensic treatment centres for a number of years, 1976 to 1990 had been a time of escalating fraud and violence where Bergwall had just not been caught in the act. However, in April 1991, Bergwall was convicted for aggravated robbery, aggravated theft, arson, aggravated fraud and theft. The forensic psychiatric report stated at this time that Bergwall was in need of psychiatric care, since he had a "personality disorder with borderline personality organization level combined with a serious impulse control disorder, and sexually perverted behaviour with sadomasochistic traits."

In connection with the investigations and clinical assessments, Bergwall underwent different examinations over the years. He was given diagnoses of borderline schizophrenic, dissociative state, and personality disorder, pedophilia, and sadism. Clinicians pointed out that he was unusually difficult to assess.

After Bergwall returned to Säters high security clinic in 1991, he began to talk about his fantasies and the murders he committed. The staff writes at this time that "[He] has a certain pleasure to tell you about these fantasies." In talks with the attending physician in 1993, Bergwall gave sufficient information to justify police intervention throughout the 1990s. He was prescribed benzodiazepines — anti-anxiety medications which can sometimes be mildly disinhibiting but can also impair episodic long-term memory. Later Bergwall was to point at this drug for his confessions but any objective review of this possibility would have it quickly discounted as his stories did not match the timing of his medication use. In connection with the police investigations, Bergwall changed his name to Thomas Quick, originating from his mother's maiden name and used this for the following decade. The police investigation eventually resulted in District Court indictments where Bergwall was charged with eight murders. He was to confess to many other murders he also claimed to have been responsible for. He was sentenced for these separately in 1994, 1996, 1997, 1998, 2000, and 2001.

It was seven years before Bergwall broke his silence.

### ***Sture Bergwall's Second Version of the Truth***

In the spring of 2008, Swedish Television broadcast the Swedish journalist Hannes Råstam's documentary called *Why Did They Confess?* The program was about young people who had been accused of a series of arsons in Falun, Sweden in the mid 1970s, bringing their confessions into question. Råstam was now actively looking for other cases where he suspected that people had confessed to crimes they had not committed. In the same spring of 2008, Råstam phoned me, asking if I thought Thomas Quick's (Sture Bergwall's) confessions might possibly be false. Just as the young people who had admitted the arsons, Bergwall was also from Falun. I told Råstam that I did not have the full picture of the evidence relating to the murders for which he had been convicted, or for the other murders he claimed to have committed which had not been tried in court. Råstam made contact with Bergwall by letter anyway, and they began corresponding.

In his second version of the truth, Bergwall said that during the years after the convictions, he looked for an opportunity and a person to whom he could disclose his innocence. This was an interesting statement because various media had criticized his confessions throughout the 1990s and had led him to suspend cooperation with the police after the last sentence in 2001. He had only to pick up the phone and call one of the journalists, and tell them that he was innocent. But instead, he chose to sit quietly for seven years until journalist Råstam began courting him. Bergwall said

> When Råstam showed up, I was about to fade away and slowly die.I had seen a documentary *Why Did They Confess?* and I thought it had a very good tone. I then got a letter from Råstam and then lit a little thought that maybe I would not reject him, and I wrote that we could meet.

Several meetings resulted between Råstam and Bergwall and by the time of their third meeting in September 2008, Bergwall fully recanted his confessions. This resulted in three Råstam television documentaries: *Thomas Quick, del 1: Säters Hemlighet* (2008), *Thomas Quick, del 2: Berättaren (2009),* and *Thomas Quick: Så skapas en seriemördare (2010).* These documentaries offered a theory that Bergwall/Quick's confessions had no basis in fact and Råstam was fully convinced that Bergwall/Quick was a false confessor. In the media, Bergwall's psychotherapists, defence lawyers, prosecutors, and the police were ridiculed, whereas Bergwall was painted as a victim and presented as a good guy for having taken back his confessions he said he made. He said it was to give resolve to the families of the murder victims.

Predictably, the documentaries provoked a media storm. The same defence lawyer with whom Råstam had worked in previous so-called false confessions became involved and new trials were requested and granted for each of Bergwall's cases. Bergwall's new role in the media was that of a prophet. At the only hearing (2010) held with Bergwall during the years of appeal, it was clear that he lied freely about how he received the information about the various murders, but his new information was never questioned in the interrogation or checked. Later, in a hearing in 2014 (during the Bergwall Commission), he explained his earlier confessions by saying

> It is the context, the environment that started the whole thing. The ward I was on and the clientele that were on the ward and the therapy that was conducted in the ward…I wanted to get therapy. It was my dream and desire…I was about to be released ... how would I handle myself out there and not abuse drugs… I was plagued by benzodiazepines and therapy. At times, I knew that I was telling a lie, sometimes I did not know it and believed in it…I was an outsider, and wanted to become a part the community. There started the process.

He also stated that he wanted to create an image of himself as a person who lacked full understanding. He said, "I did not understand the consequences."

In his new version of the truth, Bergwall claimed that he never had any knowledge of the murders to which he had confessed. In this later version, psychotherapy allegedly encouraged him to make up stories of false memories and subsequently, he was painted as a serial killer. He stated that he wanted, but did not dare to, interrupt the therapy, "I have a hard time to describe the fear, but I was afraid." What this supposed fear was about never surfaced.

Bergwall says that he loaded up on facts about the murders through newspapers and by visiting libraries, but this would be an active process rather than passively being manipulated by therapy or police. Regarding two of the murder investigations, I was assigned by the prosecutor to examine whether the facts given by Bergwall in his confessions—facts that were not available in the press material—might be gleaned by reading newspaper articles about the crimes. Results from a test of ten people, reading all the news material available, clearly demonstrated that newspaper media could be ruled out as a source for the data Bergwall provided the police in their investigation. Regarding a third murder, Bergwall claimed that he learned of the circumstances by visiting the City Library in Stockholm. A check of this claim shows that the library in question, and other possible libraries in Stockholm, did not provide press clippings about the murder at the relevant time, yet this remained as a hypothesis in the popular press for his knowledge.

When Bergwall's second version of the truth was presented—the one where he is innocent of the murders—the media, prosecutors, and other representatives of the judiciary completely ignored his antisocial behaviour and his long history of pathology as a sadist and pedophile. The 'Bergwall Commission' was set up to investigate and report on the conduct of the judicial and health care systems in connection with the criminal proceedings that led to Sture Bergwall being convicted of eight murders. The Commission was also instructed to analyse any flaws in their conduct to determine whether changes needed to be made. A matter that both the Bergwall Commission and the media highlighted was that Bergwall had left sketchy and sometimes deliberately false information, which he called "conscious deviations." One could interpret this pattern as a psychological defence of a disturbed person—a defence that many offenders use to avoid pain and inner misery. However, an alternative interpretation is that he was conducting a deliberate cat-and-mouse game with those who were investigating him. He gave only the minimal amount of information during the questioning so that the prosecution could proceed with the investigation.

It should be noted that, in all verdicts, there were factual findings and circumstances supporting Bergwall's confessions that were later ignored in the popular press to support their proposition of false confessions. In this text, I refrain from discussing the evidence or guilt, but focus on Bergwall's approach to the truth, whether he is guilty or not of the murders he has told about. The mass media comments that Bergwall was convicted on no evidence strays far from the reality of the legal cases presented to the Swedish justice system.

### *The Forensic Science*

Serial rapists almost invariably develop a *modus operandi* early in life and the type of early sexual crimes that Bergwall committed paralleled other serial killers. For example, the abuse committed against young boys by 'The Clown Killer,' American John Wayne Gacy, was easily detected, and he was sentenced for these. After serving a three-year term, Gacy moved to another town and had time to kill at least thirty-one young men before he was re-arrested. Another American, Westley Allan Dodd, whose picture was on the wall in Bergwall's room at the clinic, had an early development that is strikingly similar to Bergwall's with early sexual assault of other boys

Moreover, some experts convey that it is unusual for serial killers to not have gender or age preferences. They believe that serial killers primarily stick to one or the other gender, and that they stick to victims within a certain age range. This information formed a major discrepancy between Bergwall and other serial killers because it was a possible contributor to his evasion of detection. Through this type of overt stereotyping, investigations may fail to discover links between various crimes and the correct, and more serious, perpetrator who has a greater criminal versatility with few boundaries. It is well known that many pedophiles assault children of both sexes. "If you turn them over, the butt looks the same," explained a serial rapist to me once in an interview.

Research shows that although unusual, some serial killers lack a specific victim pool, that is they kill people from both sexes and all ages, and commit murders with varying motives. For example, from 1974 to 1991, coincidentally coinciding in time with Bergwall, the American serial killer Dennis "BTK" Rader brutally murdered families, single people, children, and adults. Some victims were found in their homes, others had been removed. Another case is Israel Keyes, a rapist and robber who killed a couple, and both younger and older women across several U.S. states. Like Bergwall, Keyes provided clues in a cat-and-mouse game with the police when they went searching for missing victims, some of whom were never found. Regarding the murders to which Bergwall confessed in his first version of the truth, adult murder victims' bodies were found in open spaces while the bodies of the young victims were hidden in the forest. The bodies of two children, including eleven-year-old Johan Asplund, have never been found. One explanation for this may be that the murder of the adult victims were motivated by aggression and revenge, and bodies were therefore left to be found. The murder of the young people and children, on the other hand, may have been sexually motivated, something to which the offender would return to in his fantasies, or even by revisiting the crime scenes.

When a serial killer is arrested and investigated, they are using frequent attention as a way to be confirmed. Some serial killers admit guilt in order to appear as 'the worst of the worst'. In their quest for attention and admiration, some serial killers also admit to murders they did not commit. Henry Lee Lucas was convicted of the murder of an elderly woman in Texas in 1983. During the trial, he told the judge that he was convicted of only a small fraction of the murders he had committed. Lucas said that between his release from prison in 1976, where he had been incarcerated for murdering his mother, and 1983, he had killed hundreds of people across the United States. Based on Lucas' detailed confessions, which in most cases had been guided by the police by means of leading questions, the police 'solved' 201 previously unsolved cases, spread across thirty-five different U.S. states. Lucas got all the attention he could have wished for and instead of sitting on death row in Florida, he travelled to various crime scenes across the United States, was interrogated by police investigators, and testified in court. Many police officers saw it as a privilege to have a conversation with the worst of the worst. Later, more detailed examination of Lucas' involvements in the murders showed that he could not possibly have been in the place at the time the offence was committed. When the commotion subsided around Lucas, in what the FBI agent Robert Ressler come to call 'the Lucas fiasco,' Lucas admitted to Ressler that he had killed fewer than ten, maybe not more than five persons. Perhaps the case of Sture Bergwall is a Swedish example of the same thing. In his first version of the truth, he confessed to nineteen murders, but perhaps the number of victims is significantly lower.

### *A Profile of Serial Killers*

How should we look at these offenders? When they disclose information about unsolved crimes, it is not likely to ease their conscience, or to show respect to the victims and families of victims, or to atone for their crimes. They may confess because of a need to share experiences with someone, but mainly they try to elevate their status among the worst of the worse. Some offenders admit guilt, then take back their confessions, blame someone else, and then confess again. Serial killers have only their own needs in mind. They rape on the basis of sexual needs, and they mug on the basis of economic needs. They create alliances with the police, lawyers, and health professionals, and reject and vilify friends and relatives when they want to. When they return to their former habitual system of their perpetrator personality and deny crimes, health and investigative personnel are smeared, and alliances are recreated with relatives previously slandered, who now become allies in the denial.

Serial killers lie constantly, which is a prominent aspect of their personality. Bergwall is an example of an offender who admits and denies on the basis of his own needs, and there is only one thing that we know with certainty: that he is lying. First, he freely admits multiple murders of which he is convicted of eight, then he takes back his confessions and is acquitted of the earlier murders. The problem we are left with is to find out when Bergwall, or other serial rapists or serial killers, are telling the truth.

### *The Pathology*

Key factors in Bergwall's stories are the manipulation, the lies, and the cat-and-mouse game with both the judicial system and legal psychiatry. The Bergwall Commission reported that Bergwall had fabricated information, and manipulated others throughout his entire life. "Persons of the same extraordinary talent for the imaginative and manipulative as Sture Bergwall are rare ...," writes Professor Emeritus Kjell Asplund, member of the Bergwall Commission. Although there is substantial evidence of Bergwall's propensity to lie, the judicial system seemed to not want to draw the correct conclusions from this. In a general sense, his credibility was questioned, but in practice, he was treated as trustworthy. The Bergwall Commission noted that it was one person's word against the other regarding Bergwall's testimony, that he received help from the police, the therapist, and the coroner, yes, even by me, to shape a credible and informed narrative of false memories. This conclusion, however, ignored the knowledge of these cases labouriously built up by investigative and medical professionals as well as the by the three defence lawyers who represented Bergwall throughout the years of his confessions.

Bergwall can talk about his deceptive behaviour and his need for control, without there being any attempt, on his part, to change his behaviour. Asked if he had a special talent for deception, he answered, "I think I have that."

Bergwall writes under the heading "Alter-ego" in his autobiographical book *Kvarblivelse*: "I have been a double nature, where my ambivalence has been almost impossible for the people around me to see or discover." Under the same heading of Alter-ego, he writes about his good side: "... I want to show the good side of me that existed parallel and simultaneously with my destructive side, the side that has love and true empathy for other people."

No matter which version Bergwall wants to represent for the moment, his psychopathic personality emerges. One sign of this is, for example, he presents himself as a person with good intentions, and sees himself as the victim. Central in an individual with a psychopathic personality is a manipulative drive. Throughout his confessions in version one, he wants, he says, to give the families of the victims certainty and he wants to ease *their* guilt. Even his decision to take time out from the police investigation in 2001 was for the sake of the murder victims' relatives. He does not want them to hope in vain now and he cannot cope with the mistrust against him. And likewise in his second version, he wants to work for the families of murder victims, give them solace.

In one of the documentaries, Bergwall was asked by a reporter about his intentions:

> I want *[pause]* that attention should be directed to the forensic mental health services and what may be behind those walls of this therapy context and so on. I want my siblings to get redress. I want to *[attempting tears, he hastily covers his mouth with his arm]* that the alleged relatives of the victims also will be vindicated. I want people to be clear about that we actually do not live in a society with the rule of law. I want people to discover that the courts are manipulated by the police and the prosecution, and the actual forensic psychiatric care. That's what I want *[nodding and looking sideways]*. And I want for my own sake of peace to tell it like it is.

Research in the psychology of deception has shown that it is difficult to decide if someone is lying by observing body language and eye movements. But television is a very disclosing medium. Bergwall was not used to sitting with a camera in his face and to lie about something that was deeply rooted in his psyche. He did not have the same control as he was accustomed to, and he therefore exposed himself to risk. During the interview, Bergwall's talk was almost staccato-like. He pronounced a sentence at a time, but was not comfortably or naturally present. His eyes did not seek contact with others, he kept his eyes away from a conscious contact with the reporter and the camera as if he was separated from his message, that is, the message seemed not to be rooted in him. When the lie was abysmal, he could not control his facial movements, and he hid his face in his hands.

Compassion can be seductive and provides a great opportunity for psychopaths to be manipulative. In Version One of his truth, he wrote in his book, "... I am the Sture Bergwall that today takes responsibility for my misdeeds and who dares to remember my vulnerability as a child." In the second version of his truth, he wanted the authorities and the public to recognize that we do not live in a secure society. In both versions, Bergwall expressed with great sentimentality that he wanted to take responsibility and tell the truth—one of the psychopath's personality traits—but he showed no concrete action to fulfill this mission.

Bergwall's grandiosity was also evident. He wanted to be the centre of attention, to have power and control over others. He did not want to be questioned or exposed. When he was questioned during the years of confessions by some of Sweden's most celebrated journalists and spokespersons for the tabloid press, his first reaction was to write his own opinion articles. When criticism continued despite the convictions, he chose to discontinue contact with the police. He turned to Sweden's biggest newspaper, announcing that he had been betrayed by those who questioned his stories, and that he was a victim of their incredulity. Seven years later he retracted his confessions. A Swedish journalist saved him from the fate to "wither away and slowly die." Regarding his wait to disclose his innocence, he explained this by saying that he thought no one would believe him.

Victimization is also a recurring theme in both of Bergwall's versions of truth where there is a shifting of blame and responsibility onto others. In his first version, he talked about himself as a victim of his parents' and an older brother's sexual abuse. His mother, he indicated, had also tried to kill him on various occasions. According to him, his drug use in adolescence was due to homosexuals who abused drugs and alcohol, or because of his relations with fellow patients in health care settings, and he blamed the parents of his victims for not having protected their children from being murdered.

In the second version, victimization is likewise evident when he takes back his confessions and is granted stature of the innocent. In this version, he was a victim of psychotherapy and drug treatment in healthcare, as well as in the judiciary system, that is, police investigations, prosecutors, and courts. This was also to be the predominant view aped by the media. From being "Sweden's most dangerous man", he transitioned to being a victim of "Sweden's biggest legal scandal."

Power and control, and probably a sense of triumph, arose in the knowledge that so many people devoted time and resources to him. By taking back his confessions and once again becoming a victim, he kept the triumph, which is sweet reward to a sadist, that is he was able to have control and be the only one who owned the truth. Perhaps, in his mind, it might also be a sadistically pleasurable experience to ridicule all those who investigated him, the ones he had a prolonged contact with, and those he previously idealized. To idealize and then destroy people, either in fantasy or in reality, is a significant feature of a sadistic person.

In a television interview a few years ago, Bergwall explained with a smile on his face how he had tricked the staff with his "improbable and bizarre" stories about recovered memories of parental abuse and the murders of the boys. With that said, it is also important that therapists and investigators see their own professional responsibilities in the cat-and-mouse game, see the manipulation, and not be carried away by it. It is important to understand the diversity of the many nuances in a deeply disturbed person like Bergwall.

Bergwall was occupied with sexual fantasies. They constituted both the motive and the driving force for his actions, which, among other things, showed up in the macabre details that were reported during police questioning and in court. He plagued families with sadistic details, and said in a later phase, with dripping sentimentality, that relatives should have certainty when he takes back his confessions.

Detailed descriptions of how he sadistically tortured victims sexually, cut off body parts, and ate the parts of the bodies, was provided by Bergwall during police interrogations, trials, in letters, and in his book *Kvarblivelse*. In the telling of the crimes, he mixes facts with fantasies. Although family members learned about what happened to their children, it was terribly painful to re-visit the cruelties, especially the futility of re-living the events when he later claimed that he just made it all up. Courts sentenced him on the facts that linked him to the crimes. In Version Two, when he took back his confessions, they focussed once again on the macabre details and errors, as this allegedly proved his innocence. The judiciary and the media could not see that these were two sides of the same pathology.

When free, Sture Bergwall directed his sadistic sexual acts against children and adults. When in forensic psychiatry care, he directed hate in words and in writing to the parents and relatives. When he took back his confessions, his sadistic behaviour showed up in well-orchestrated media violence where he, with the help of journalists, ridiculed and vilified health professionals and investigators. In my interviews with Bergwall, before he retracted his confessions, he often commented on the media saying, "What I've learned over the years, is mainly how defenceless the public is when facing what is reported in the media."

The concluding question is whether history will be rewritten once again if Bergwall's sadistic violence is repeated. Which version of the truth will then appear? Another question is also how health professionals, investigators, and media would see and understand the manipulation by this man.

Sture Bergwall, aka Thomas Quick, was acquitted of the eight murders of which he was originally convicted. He lives with protected identity in an unknown location in Sweden.

***Patrick Baillie,*** *Ph.D., LL.B. is a forensic psychologist at the Peter Lougheed Centre in Calgary and a lawyer. Since 1995, he has also been a Consulting Psychologist with Calgary Police Service, Psychological Services Division. He has written hundreds of pre-sentence assessments used by all levels of courts in Alberta. For six years, he was a member (and for two years Chair) of the Accreditation Panel of the Canadian Psychological Association; and in 2007, he was named as a member (and, later, Chair) of the Mental Health and the Law Advisory Committee of the Mental Health Commission of Canada. In 2008, he received the John G. Paterson Media Award from the Psychologists Association of Alberta for his contribution towards keeping the public informed about psychological knowledge via the media. In the months after the tragic events of September 11, 2001, he served as a volunteer psychologist with New York Police Department and, in 2011, he travelled to Haiti to provide psychological services after that country's devastating earthquake. In 2014, he received the John Service Member of the Year Award from the Canadian Psychological Association, in recognition of his various volunteer efforts to promote the field of psychology.*

# Dr. Patrick Baillie

## David Milgaard
## Tunnel Vision and Wrongful Conviction

WITH ALL DUE RESPECT to Edward Bulwer-Lytton, it was a dark and very cold morning on January 31, 1969 as David Milgaard, along with his friends Ron Wilson and Nichol John arrived in Saskatoon, having driven overnight from Regina. The group was looking for the home of Albert 'Shorty' Cadrain, located at 334 Avenue O South. Although David and his travel companions had arrived around 6:30 a.m., more than two hours would pass before they located the desired residence. In the intervening time, the car they were in had become stuck in two snow banks, the group had driven up and down residential streets looking for that particular house, and David had run shoeless into a motel to ask for directions. The sun hadn't come up until close to 8:30 a.m.

Around 7:00 a.m., Gail Miller, a twenty-year-old nursing student, who also lived on Avenue O South, was sexually assaulted and murdered. Although an initial list of some 160 suspects was generated, all suspects were soon eliminated, leaving the police at a relative dead-end.

After meeting Shorty and having some minor repairs done to their car, David and his friends left Saskatoon later that day, heading for Edmonton, but made a wrong turn and ended up in Calgary. Just over four weeks later, Shorty, perhaps seeking some of the reward money that had been offered for information regarding the death of Ms. Miller, called Saskatoon police and told them that he had seen blood on David's clothing when the group arrived at Shorty's house that January morning. In the following days, investigators from the RCMP interviewed Ron and Nichol, who each said that David was never out of their sight for more than a minute or two that morning.

A few weeks later still, Ms. Miller's wallet was located, close to Shorty's residence. David was interviewed again in mid-April 1969 and, denying any role in the death of Ms. Miller, he voluntarily provided hair and blood samples to police. On May 23, 1969, Ron and Nichol were interviewed one more time. Ron told police that David had admitted to the murder; Nichol told police that she watched as David killed the young nurse. (A 1976 psychiatric assessment of David stated that "Witnesses to the murder were too terrified of Milgaard to testify for several months.") David was arrested a week later.

David's trial took place before a jury, presided over by the then-Chief Justice of Saskatchewan, the Honourable A.H. Bence. The prosecutor was T.D.R. Caldwell QC. During the trial, two other witnesses would testify that David, under the influence of drugs, had re-enacted the murder and had admitted to killing Ms. Miller. Nichol John testified, but did not say that she witnessed the murder. The Crown, though, read in her statement from May 23. Other minutiae that absorbed trial time included debates over dog urine and over antigen secretion. On January 31, 1970, precisely one year after Gail Miller's death, David Milgaard was found guilty of murder and sentenced to life imprisonment.

### *David's Early Years*

David was born in July 1952 as the oldest of four children to Lorne and Joyce Milgaard. When David's brother was born thirteen months later, he required considerable medical care and David was soon sent to live with relatives. During David's childhood, his family moved frequently, with eighteen different residences by the time David was fourteen years old. School problems started when David was in kindergarten and there are early reports of the involvement of social workers, psychiatrists, and psychologists working with David and his parents to address his restlessness, aggression, and impulsiveness. After being removed from multiple school settings, David's first criminal charge came at age fourteen, for auto theft. Various foster placements were attempted, as were placements in group homes. On occasion, David was detained in custody. Four days after being declared a ward of the court, at age fourteen, David was discharged from a psychiatric hospital for failing to meet "minimal standards." A December 1966 psychological assessment reported that David had an average IQ and had never failed a Grade, but suggested that he might struggle to verbalize frustrations and may feel "threatened, disapproved, rejected."

By age fifteen, David was using marijuana frequently and he had experimented with LSD. He drank alcohol only infrequently and may have had just a single episode of intoxication. David would often run away from whatever home or facility he was supposed to be residing in, heading to Vancouver, or Winnipeg, or Saskatoon. In the spring of 1968, David left the last of his foster homes and travelled first to eastern Canada and then to Oregon. He worked for a while as a magazine salesman. By late January, 1969, David was in Regina, hanging out with his friend, Ronald, and with a new companion, Nichol. During the drive to Saskatoon that cold night, the group stopped in Aylesbury and broke into a grain elevator, looking for money. Lost in Saskatoon, the group pulled Ronald's car alongside a woman and asked her for directions. According to Ron and Nichol's trial testimony, the woman might have been Gail Miller.

Clearly, with his childhood history, with even just a petty crime in the hours before the death of Ms. Miller, with evidence that he'd had a knife during the drive to Saskatoon, and with the possibility that he had spoken with Ms. Miller that morning, David was in no place to be able to testify at his trial without expecting a very difficult cross-examination. He had a very competent defence lawyer, Calvin Tallis, who would go on to be appointed to the Bench, eventually taking his seat on the Court of Appeal of Saskatchewan.

### *David in Jail*

Imagine being a seventeen-year-old young man, sitting in Saskatchewan Penitentiary, sentenced to life imprisonment for a crime that you did not commit. A report from a Classification interview in March 1970 described David as "a quiet, soft-spoken individual who impresses as being a person who is extremely depressed but hides the depression behind a smile. ... He repeatedly insists on his innocence and is convinced that the appeal court will verify that this is so." The report also mentioned "several older cons who are protecting him ... and helping him find his way around." David's appeals were not successful, being dismissed in Saskatchewan in January 1971 and by the Supreme Court of Canada later that year.

In June 1972, Mr. Caldwell, the trial prosecutor, wrote a five-page letter (with attachments) to the National Parole Board (NPB), expressing grave concern over the notion that David would ever walk out of prison. Mr. Caldwell reported that the head of psychiatry at University Hospital in Saskatoon was of the "opinion that Milgaard is suffering from a severe behaviour disorder best called a Sociopathic Personality." Mr. Caldwell concluded, "I have never had occasion to write in this manner during my thirteen years as a full-time Crown prosecutor, however, I feel very strongly about this case, and I would be horrified to think that Milgaard might some day be released from custody."

An inflammatory diagnosis and the related language from Mr. Caldwell's letter became quite common in David's institutional files. At a parole interview in September 1977, an NPB member wrote about David, "He is either completely psychopathic in that his behaviour before us was inappropriate; or he is so neurotically disturbed that he has built up a system of defences against the memory of his act." Another NPB member who interviewed David at that time commented that the Board "had some discussion ... as to whether (David) should be encouraged to enter into intensive psychotherapy which would attempt to destroy his defence pattern and confront him with his offence."

In fact, medical labels became so routine that during his time in custody, David was given a range of mental health diagnoses, including: Schizoid Personality Disorder; Psychopathic Personality type; Sociopathic Personality Disorder; Character Disorder with strong Antisocial features; Situational Psychotic Illness; Schizophrenia—acute reaction in a Psychopathic Personality; Prison Psychosis; Acute Schizophrenic Episode; Manic Depressive Phase, illness, disease, or disorder; Substance Abuse; Acute Psychotic Reaction; Personality Disorder, Other and Unspecified; Schizophreniform Psychosis; and, Major Affective Disorder. (Some evaluations did conclude that there was no evidence of any major mental illness.) The inconsistency of diagnoses must have concerned correctional officials who were continuously trying to determine whether or not David had a serious mental health problem. Still, a March 1981 psychiatric evaluation proffered a new theory of the homicide and David's role, commenting

> The crime was horribly vicious. It involved the rape and multiple

> stabbing of a young woman on her way to work as a nurse's aide in the early morning in a temperature of -40°. She had been asked the way by the subject but did not know it and that seemed to be the only provocation. It is reported that the subject showed little emotional change at the time. Such an event must surely have been the act of somebody who was mentally ill.

There is documentation about David describing some psychotic symptoms that arose periodically, including auditory hallucinations and "sense of bodily electricity." In October 1983, he lashed out at a staff member while behaving quite irrationally, leading to a referral for a comprehensive psychiatric assessment. However, most psychotic symptoms usually abated quite quickly. For example, in August 1984, David was admitted to the Regional Psychiatric Centre (Prairies) (RPC) "due to an apparent psychotic episode" in which he stated that he was the son of God and during which he often lay "catatonic like for hours," but that admission report also notes that the psychotic behaviour "was short lived, and completely disappeared within two weeks of his arrival at RPC" and that he was not taking any anti-psychotic medication. Multiple other reports suggested that when David displayed psychotic symptoms, these might have been entirely for manipulative purposes. In 1986, medication to treat an apparent psychotic episode was withheld for one week in order to allow for "better assessment" of the veracity of the symptoms.

I don't mean to be taken as doubting that David displayed bizarre, irrational, potentially psychotic symptoms on multiple occasions during his twenty-three years in custody. At times, his sleep was seriously disrupted by anxiety over his case; at times, he accessed prison brew or other substances that might have influenced his behaviour. Likely, at times, he was psychotic. My concern relates to how those symptoms were then viewed in terms of his risk for 're-offence', especially when the only delusion repeatedly cited was the one relating to David being wedded to his contention that he was innocent in the death of the young nurse.

Even as late as April 1992, almost twenty-three years after his arrest and within days of David receiving news of the Supreme Court of Canada's decision that led to him being out of jail, the NPB denied him any form of conditional release, again referring to mental health issues when they wrote:

> You have demonstrated, on previous occasions, your difficulties in coping with stressful situations. You have provided also evidence of your unpredictability when attempting to cope with anxiety and/or personal difficulties.

During his incarceration, David escaped on two occasions: once from Dorchester Penitentiary, and once while on an Escorted Temporary Absence (ETA). The Dorchester escape lasted only a couple of days before David and the other inmates, who had escaped with him, were returned to custody. Fleeing on the ETA, David remained at large for seventy-seven days and was shot by the RCMP upon his arrest. Additional concurrent sentences were given for offences related to these escapes.

Clearly, from mental health reviews that suggested David's belief in his innocence was delusional to NPB decisions that denied release because of a lack of remorse for the homicide, David's insistence that he did not kill Gail Miller cost him significantly. As a 1989 Progress Summary confirmed, "Due partially to the subject's refusal to admit guilt as to his original conviction, the NPB have been reluctant to grant a parole release." In part due to frustration over the continued expectation that he should admit guilt for something he didn't do (as if verbalizing guilt would, by itself, somehow reduce his risk for future misconduct) and over the helplessness of prolonged incarceration, David made several serious attempts at taking his own life early in his sentence. These attempts were often beyond being simply manipulative as David engaged in behaviours such as swallowing barbed wire, ingesting leather dye, and cutting his arms.

Late in his incarceration, David was referred for psychiatric treatment with Dr. Stanley Yaren, who, years later, assessed Vincent Li, discussed in this book in a chapter by Dr. Jeffrey Waldman. Dr. Yaren took the view that David was neither dangerous nor prone to violence, that he showed insight into his mental health challenges, and that he was likely to be able to maintain mental stability with suitable follow-up care. Dr. Yaren diagnosed David as having a manic-depressive illness and said that David was very compliant with pharmacological intervention, experiencing only "mild and brief depressive periods" and no "major episodes of decompensation." Dr. Yaren explained that manic-depressive illness "is a condition which renders (David) susceptible to the development of temporary states of psychosis." Dr. Yaren also suggested that media attention around David's case, legal arguments that boosted and then shattered his hopes for release, and tensions with other inmates over David's celebrity status "had a demoralizing effect upon (David's) mental condition" and "would have been difficult even for a person without David's psychiatric disorder to tolerate." Dr. Yaren generously conceded that his own previous diagnosis that David had a personality disorder "was an error," adding, "What was observed and interpreted as a personality disorder was a relatively mild form of manic psychosis. With treatment the problematic 'personality traits' have virtually disappeared."

During his time in custody, David became very active in a social justice group. After early outbursts that resulted in institutional charges, David seemed to settle into his sentence, with a 1978 psychiatric review commenting that the writer had learned that

> Milgaard had in recent months shown signs of maturity in that he had been working more steadily both at his academic work and his institutional employment, had played an increasing role in the social life of the institution, had managed to establish better relationships with his family, and had shown increasing willingness to discuss his various problems with staff of the Institution.

### *The Rest of the Story*

Living in the basement at 334 Avenue O South in Saskatoon was Larry Fisher and his wife, Linda. In September 1970, Mr. Fisher was arrested while sexually assaulting a victim in Fort Garry, Manitoba. He confessed to the crime and also told police of two previous sexual assaults committed by him in Saskatoon. Indeed, as was later discovered, in October and November 1968, Mr. Fisher had sexually assaulted three women in Saskatoon, causing police, who believed the three crimes to be related and who had, at the time, no suspects, to issue a public warning in December 1968, weeks before the murder of Ms. Miller. A fourth woman was raped in Saskatoon by Mr. Fisher in February 1970. Even if police drew no connection between Mr. Fisher and the sexual assault and murder of Ms. Miller when initially investigating her death, they certainly knew of the potential linkage in August 1980, when Linda went to them with her evidence against Larry.

From the time of his arrest, David and his mother, Joyce, both said that he had nothing to do with the death of Gail Miller. Joyce worked tirelessly to prove her son's innocence, offering a reward for information that might exonerate him, hiring lawyers and other experts, and, after learning in 1983 of the Larry and Linda Fisher connection, placing an advertisement to try to find Linda. In early 1986, Joyce retained Hersh Wolch, who assisted in making multiple applications to the federal Minister of Justice and who, beginning in January 1992, argued on behalf of David in a Reference Case before the Supreme Court of Canada. On April 14, 1992, the Supreme Court ruled that David had failed to establish his innocence, but the Court accepted that new evidence presented in the Reference Case might have affected the original verdict. The federal Minister of Justice directed that a new trial should be held. The provincial Crown opted to enter a stay of proceedings, meaning that no new trial would be held.

In December 1993—twenty months after the Supreme Court's decision and with the homicide charge stayed—the RCMP completed a Violent Crime Linkage System (ViCLAS) assessment on David, putting his name into a database that might match features of the death of Gail Miller with similar features in other crimes, all the while linking back to David, even noting which brand of tobacco he smoked (in case Export A cigarettes were ever found at a crime scene). While completing a ViCLAS assessment on someone wrongfully convicted is a tad bizarre, in fairness the assessment was completed before David had been entirely exonerated.

The ViCLAS assessment contains a reference to one of my favourite descriptions of David, albeit a tragic one: "A sixteen-year-old kid stuck in a forty-year-old body." Except for his two periods of being unlawfully at large, David was in custody from the age of sixteen until he was thirty-nine. How many important milestones in a typical life did David miss during those years? Finding new romantic relationships? Developing a productive career? Acquiring material possessions? Having children and being with his family? The list goes on and on and on.

In July 1997, using semen only recently found in Gail Miller's panties and dress, clothing that should have been destroyed long ago, but hadn't been due simply to an administrative error, a forensic lab reported that DNA results excluded David Milgaard and matched Larry Fisher. The federal Minister of Justice and the Saskatchewan

Minister of Justice each expressed their apologies to David and to his family. In May 1999, a compensation agreement was reached with David and his family. The lead negotiator for the Saskatchewan government was the Honourable Alan Gold, former Chief Justice of Quebec and my original legal mentor. David's team included Mr. Wolch and Sheilah Martin, my law school Ethics professor. (Sheilah was later appointed to the Court of Queen's Bench in Alberta.) The day after the announcement of the compensation package, I was scheduled to host a small gathering of friends to celebrate the conclusion of my first year of law school. Sheilah called that morning and asked if she could bring "a friend." Before the day was done, Joyce Milgaard was sitting on my living room floor, eating dessert and chatting with some of my classmates. Six months later, Larry Fisher was convicted of the murder of Gail Miller.

I recount this thumbnail version of the chronology because, as my former supervisor and gifted colleague Thomas Dalby writes in his chapter about Clifford Olson, for many people these days, stories of such historic importance are becoming increasingly forgotten. Sometimes, David is known simply as the man who spent twenty-three years in jail for a crime that he did not commit. But there is much more to him and to his story that makes this tale so very personal.

In 2004, the Saskatchewan government ordered a public inquiry into the wrongful conviction of David Milgaard. In late 2005, I wandered out of a lengthy speech at a fundraising dinner to take a phone call. When the call was done, I turned around to find myself face to face with Mr. Wolch. As I've said, we had met before, including one occasion on which Mr. Wolch kindly advised me that I was not being sued for my role in prolonging the incarceration of a man found guilty in a different case of wrongful conviction and wrongful imprisonment. Mr. Wolch asked if I would be interested in doing a psychological assessment of David. Because? David had recently indicated that he had no interest in appearing before the public inquiry and the Commissioner, the Honourable Mr. Justice Edward MacCallum, had indicated that, without a very good reason why not to—and given that the inquiry was taking place at David's request—the Commissioner would not hesitate to order David to attend and to answer questions. I was quite intrigued by Mr. Wolch's request. For me, forensic psychology has always been about making a difference, making a contribution, sometimes for an individual, sometimes for society. I knew that David had struggled, entirely understandably, after being freed from a flawed system that I was part of. If there was something that I could do now to assist him and the process, I was happy to have the opportunity.

The public inquiry had been presented with over three-hundred-thousand somewhat-unsorted pages of printed material. Buried in there were mental health assessments, decisions of the NPB, original police documents, and treatment program reports, along with countless pages of (for me) useless information. The public inquiry paid for me to spend time in Saskatoon, sorting through those documents and beginning an assessment of David. (When I first flew to Saskatoon, I arrived on a very cold, winter night. There was a significant amount of snow on the ground. Quickly forming an image of the early hours of January 31, 1969, I was tempted to ask the airport taxi driver to head over to Avenue O. I didn't.) I had contact with Joel Grymaloski, a mental health therapist who had met with David for years in Vancouver. Mr. Grymaloski was of the view, expressed in a report to Justice MacCallum dated November 4, 2005, that David met the diagnostic criteria for Posttraumatic Stress Disorder and that having him appear at the public inquiry "would most probably undo the last ten years of his work and effort to stabilize his life and move past his traumatizing past."

David, about to welcome his first child, had other priorities and, in addition to not wanting to testify, did not want to discuss the issues with me. Still, even without meeting with David, there was abundant evidence available to me to support a diagnosis of Posttraumatic Stress Disorder (PTSD), with symptoms likely to be exacerbated by being placed before the public inquiry—at which multiple parties (for example the police service, a specific detective, the Crown, federal corrections) each had their own lawyers who might wish to question David—and forced to recount the story of his wrongful conviction and prolonged incarceration. Commission Counsel (the very skilled and, in my view, compassionate Douglas Hodson) advised me that twelve subject areas were likely to be canvassed with David, including his criminal activity prior to 1969, his drug use, discussions with Nichol and Ron about ways to criminally obtain money when the trio were to arrive in Saskatoon, having possession of a knife during the drive to Saskatoon, changing clothes at Shorty's house, and being in a hurry to leave. Does that sound like questioning that might suggest to David that he had a role to play in his own wrongful conviction, effectively putting him on trial once again?

PTSD essentially involves three sets of symptoms that follow from exposure to an event involving actual or threatened death or serious injury: nightmares, flashbacks or other intrusive thoughts about the traumatic event; avoidance of thoughts or external stimuli (that is, the place, the people) associated with the traumatic event; and, hyper-vigilance, an exaggerated startle response, or other cognitive changes (for example difficulties with concentration). When I eventually testified at the public inquiry, I spoke about those symptoms and about how David's desire not to testify was consistent with avoidance. Mr. Grymaloski's contacts with David also made clear the presence of the other symptoms, with many examples.

I proposed—and all the lawyers agreed to the idea, some grudgingly—that Mr. Hodson travel to Vancouver and videotape a question-and-answer session of limited scope and duration with David, allowing Mr. Grymaloski to be present as professional support. What David had to say was clearly important to the public inquiry, but the less contentious atmosphere of a single, impartial lawyer asking pre-determined questions in a safe context with minimal disruption to David's schedule struck me as being a reasonable compromise.

During my testimony at the public inquiry, Mr. Wolch asked me if there was any "other rational conclusion" why David might not want to talk about his arrest, trial, and incarceration. I answered

> I think that there is likely to be a general sense of wanting to put it past him, wanting to leave it as history and not be constantly bringing it up. As you are well aware, Mr. Milgaard has moved to a different phase of his life and has recently become a father. I think that it's unfortunate, but when Mr. Milgaard's obituary is written, at hopefully a distant point in the future, the obituary will almost invariably start, "David Milgaard, who spent twenty-three years in jail for a crime that he did not commit ... ."
>
> His life has been defined on the basis of something that he didn't do and he's now in a position, like many of us, to be able to choose how his life, from this point forward, is going to be defined, and so he's very much focussed on the issues related to his fatherhood. Each of us wants to have some sort

> of a—I'm not going to use the term legacy—but we want to have our own reputation that's consistent with how we view ourselves, and so his reputation to this point has been largely defined by something over which he had no responsibility.... To go back to that is to distract him from the new focus that he has. He wants to be focussed on being a responsible father and looking to the future rather than dealing with these extremely difficult issues from his past.

***And Later***

In late 2011, David, who had moved to Calgary, was charged with offences arising from a domestic incident. Mr. Wolch stepped in, as he has with many clients, and the charges were quickly and appropriately withdrawn. With the agreement of the Crown Prosecutor, the judge who signed off on the withdrawal ordered that David had to participate in counselling with me. There was no physical contact in the alleged offence, being a simple disagreement over how to handle a family issue. Couples counselling and parental counselling were also ordered.

Since then, including long after the expiry of the order, David has been seeing me for individual counselling, through my role with a publicly funded, community-based forensic mental health program. When finally released from custody, David did not want further external constraints on him and his behaviour. Apart from the contacts with Mr. Grymaloski, David did not have significant counselling. Now, he is a sixty-three-year-old man facing health, financial, and other personal challenges; he works, because he wants to and because the compensation money from 1999 is gone (through basic costs of living and through bad investments, with no mansions, fast cars, first-class travel, or other sprees of spending); and, he spends time with his family. David is trying to define himself without looking backwards.

Everything that I have said about David so far is a matter of public record. You might have to do a little digging, but it's all there. David graciously consented to me writing this chapter and he reviewed it prior to publication. The one piece that I will share from my direct contacts with David over the past five years is that he has never shown or spoken of any animosity or vengeance towards Ron, Nichol, Shorty, the police investigators, Mr. Caldwell, the members of the National Parole Board, and anyone else related to his wrongful conviction and prolonged incarceration. Instead, David has put his focus on the present, on spending time with his wife and two children, on various social justice causes including both the plight of those wrongfully convicted and the need for better elder care. He has never shown any evidence of psychosis nor any propensity for violent misconduct. He has spoken publicly and with the media about issues that are important to him, but never about his own trial or the indignities of incarceration. In short, David has been gracious, generous, and committed to the welfare of others.

David's conviction arose from the tainted, false evidence reportedly uttered by Shorty, Nichol, and Ron. A degree of tunnel vision by investigators made David a suspect in a crime that he had nothing to do with. Early denials of opportunity and motive were brushed away when his friends, in questionable circumstances, gave him up as the supposed perpetrator. There never was any physical evidence tying him to the crime—how could there be, given that he had nothing to do with it?

In custody, though, the abuse of David continued, now being perpetrated by correctional authorities and by some mental health professionals. They said he needed treatment to overcome his denial; his periodic psychotic symptoms and suicide attempts were manipulative; his serious mental health issues made him a high risk for 're-offence'; and, stress made his behaviour unpredictable. Inconsistent diagnostic labels assisted in perpetuating a belief that David was unstable, beyond simply struggling under the enormous weight of being wrongfully incarcerated. The scientific method involves forming hypotheses and then looking for information to prove those hypotheses wrong. Far too often, we form hypotheses and then look for information to prove us right. It's easy to believe that a drug-using, non-compliant, knife-toting, aimless teenager could perpetrate an otherwise unsolved homicide, and to believe that his denials of doing so are simply part of a significant mental health problem. Just as overly invested police officers have exceptional power for changing the life of someone they believe to be guilty, so do mental health professionals who are unwilling to admit that the justice system makes mistakes. Our diagnostic labels, our new versions of the alleged crime, our commentaries on risk for re-offence all carry huge weight. We do our best, but sometimes we are wrong.

*Jack White PhD (Adelaide) FAPS is the principal psychologist at 'White & Associates Psychologists', a forensic psychology practice based in Adelaide, South Australia. In 2008 he received the Award of Distinction from the Australian Psychological Society for his outstanding contribution to forensic psychology. He has a Doctorate Degree in Psychology from the University of Adelaide and is a Fellow of the Australian Psychological Society. Academically he has published widely in areas that include: report writing, psychometric assessment, Indigenous neuropsychology, mental impairment, intellectual disability, and criminal behaviour in athletes. Together with Andrew Day, Louisa Hackett, and Thomas Dalby he authored* Writing Reports for Court: An International Guide for Psychologists Who Work in the Criminal Jurisdiction, *published by Australian Academic Press in 2015.*

# Dr. Jack White

## The Bodies in the Barrel Case
## Wagner, The Muscle Man

A FORENSIC PSYCHOLOGIST is trained to be observant, detached, and critically evaluative. Most times such an approach is automatic. This is a case that challenged those attributes. It involved Robert Joe Wagner, one of three people charged with eleven murders in South Australia. The case became known as the 'Bodies in the Barrel' case. There were four books published on the crime and the 2011 feature film, *Snowtown*. Each of those versions was based on a reconstruction of prosecution evidence.

This account is from the offender's perspective. It shows how a relationship grew between the psychologist and the defendant in the midst of Australia's most notorious criminal trial. It details Wagner's history and his psychological profile. It explores the mind of a man who killed many people.

Between August 1992 and May 1999 eleven people were killed in South Australia. The crimes were uncovered when the remains of eight victims were found in barrels of acid located in a rented former bank building in Snowtown, South Australia on 20 May 1999.

Three days later, two more bodies were found buried in an Adelaide suburban backyard. By the end of June 1999, nine of the ten victims had been identified.

There were four people charged with their murder: John Justin Bunting, Robert Joe Wagner, Mark Ray Haydon, and James Spyridon Vlassaksis. On 21 June 2001, after a series of pre-trial hearings, Vlassakis pleaded 'guilty' to four murders and was given four life sentences. Bunting, Haydon, and Wagner each pleaded 'not guilty' to eleven counts of murder. Their trial began on 14 October 2002—the longest and most expensive criminal trial in South Australian history.

### *The Psychologist's Involvement, Part One*

My first meeting with Robert Wagner came after a phone call from his legal representative, Bill Morris, six months into the trial.

"Jack, we need your help."

"What's the problem, Bill?" I asked

"It's Wagner, he's very distressed," replied Morris.

"The press have been hounding his family. They showed film of the family on the television news the other night. His kid's only five and is copping heaps at school. Wagner's livid. He said he want's to sack us too 'cause we didn't get it suppressed."

I now realized Bill was very serious. He and the other members of Wagner's legal team were being well paid and the trial had many months more to run. This was Australia's biggest serial murder and not only had the court rooms been specially adapted at a cost of several million dollars, but the unusual step of having fifteen jurors was included ... three more than the norm.

"I can see him at one o'clock. Is that okay?"

"That should be fine, Jack. They're keeping him in the cells in the basement of the court. I'll let the sheriff officers know you're coming. I'll meet you there."

### *Irony of Blocked Identities*

My office on King William Street was conveniently located only fifty metres from the court. In my upstairs room I had an excellent view of the police holding cells and the back entrance to the courts. It always intrigued me how the media assembled on ladders to take photos of offenders as they were led from the cells to the court. The irony was that they were usually unable to show the faces of the accused and pixelated the face to block the person's identity for the television news audience. No such protection was afforded the family of the accused. Although family members had committed no offence, the media lapped up any opportunity to show the world what they looked like and usually in the most unsympathetic light. A typical ploy was for the photographer to provoke a reaction and film the response. The image of abusive family members was likely to reinforce the accused's supposed guilt.

As I navigated my way through the labyrinth of corridors beneath the Sir Samuel Way Building, I finally came to the section where prisoners were held during trials. The connecting door was activated and I was greeted by a security guard who directed me to Wagner's legal men, Steven Apps and Bill Morris. They were both immaculately dressed in dark suits and looked worried and very serious.

"Afternoon, Jack," said Steve Apps, Wagner's Senior Counsel.

"I'm glad you could come at such short notice. I gather Bill has filled you in on what has happened?"

I nodded.

"We usually always see Wagner as a twosome," said Morris. "It's a bit of a self protection thing. Would you like one of us to sit in with you?"

"No, I don't think that will be necessary, but why don't you both introduce me? If there are any problems we'll see what course to take then."

"That sounds fine with me," said Apps.

### *First Impressions*

My first impression of Robert Wagner was that he was a very tall, solidly built man with a sad but pleasant manner. He had thinning light brown hair, a light moustache and goatee beard. His glasses gave him an intellectual look. He spoke in a slow, considered way, his voice deep and controlled.

"Robert, please call me Jack. Bill and Steve have spoken to me and have asked whether I might be able to help you as a psychologist. They tell me you've been very upset by the media?"

Wagner looked down, before his tearful eyes stared forlornly at me.

"Yes, Jack. I feel very angry and I have been shaking all morning. My son has got nothing to do with this trial and those press bastards are making his life hell. I spoke to him by phone last night and he was in tears. The kids at school are calling him names and he doesn't know what to do."

Wagner was visibly upset as he recounted the closeness he felt for his son.

"He's just like me—when I was a kid."

Wagner continued, "I'm also not too happy with Steve and Bill. The Judge said that the media should leave my family alone and they didn't do anything to stop it happening."

I understood the frustration in Wagner's tone.

"Well Robert, the media damage has been done and we can't turn back the clock to stop it happening now. We can't also do much for your son at the moment. I can, however, help you work on some ways of dealing with these stresses. How does that sound?"

Wagner nodded. I then proceeded with a brief explanation about the use of relaxation techniques and started with some practical breathing exercises. After half an hour of the exercises Wagner's external appearance appeared much more calm and his shaking had fully resolved. I experienced a strangely intimate bond with this intervention, and a positive feeling of general well-being.

Over the next five months, I continued seeing Wagner for regular relaxation sessions before or after court. We would talk about coping strategies and about his relationship with his family. I did not speak about the trial or matters related to the charges. It was an unusual bond that existed between us—one that was based around trust—and that was, for Wagner, the most important personal attribute. My inference here was based on his reaction to people in his life whom he had expected to be trustworthy—his mother, his psychiatrist, the police and Barry Lane—but who had let him down.

On 8 September 2003, the jury found both Bunting and Wagner guilty of multiple murders.

Bunting was convicted for eleven murders and Wagner was convicted for ten murders. The two men were each sentenced to imprisonment for life on each count to be served cumulatively.

Soon after the verdict, I received a phone call from Wagner's legal representative, Bill Morris. He thanked me for the support I had provided his client throughout the trial and then asked if I was happy to prepare a detailed psychological report on Wagner that may or may not be used at some time in the future, should he ever apply for parole.

"Of course, Bill. I'd be delighted."

### *The Psychologist's Involvement, Part Two*

On 7th October 2003, a month after the trial had ended, I sat in a private interview room within the eastern wing of B-Division, in Yatala Labour Prison.

"Robert, nice to see you," I said with some sincerity.

Wagner was dressed in a green prison t-shirt and blue denim jeans. He appeared much more relaxed now than he had been throughout the trial.

"Bill has asked that I prepare a psychological report about you. Are you happy to talk to me about your past?"

Wagner smiled and nodded his agreement.

"I'm not going anywhere, and time is something I've got plenty of."

Over the ensuing weeks, I scheduled a series of ninety-minute sessions at the prison. This was no ordinary assessment. I aimed to explore Wagner's life, his role in the offending, and administer a number of psychological tests to determine the profile of a man found guilty of ten murders. Ultimately, this report was an attempt to address the questions: Should this person remain in prison until his death? or Should he one day be released back to the community?

### *Wagner's Childhood*

Robert Joe Wagner was born in Sydney on the 28th of November 1971. His parents separated six months after he was born. He did not have any further contact with his biological father, and believed that if his father had wished to contact him, he would have done so. Wagner said his mother was born in the late 1940s and he described her as being "very strict." He said she regularly punished him and "hit me with a wooden spoon whenever I misbehaved."

Wagner had a maternal half-sister, who was six years older than he and a person with whom he had a good relationship. Wagner did not know anything about his sister's biological father. He said that she was now married with three children and worked as an age-care worker in a nursing home.

Wagner indicated that his childhood memories were "generally unhappy" and he felt "emotionally lost and confused" when he reflected on them.

Wagner described two significant life traumas that occurred in his childhood, the first when he was eight years old, the second, six years later.

At the age of eight years, Wagner stated that he was the victim of repeated sexual abuse that was perpetrated by "Mr H—a family friend." Wagner claimed that the abuse occurred over a twelve-month period and that his sister was also a victim. He said he perceived he could not escape the abuse which involved anal penetration and "probably occurred a hundred times or more." Wagner said that he was also required to masturbate H and perform oral sex on him. He said that when he protested, H would beat him—"but nowhere a bruise would show." Wagner said that H had also threatened to "kill my pet dog if I said anything … and made me feel I was a piece of shit."

Wagner claimed that he did not remain silent about the abuse.

He said that first, "I told my mother about the sexual abuse, but she did not believe me."

He said he then attended the local police station, where "the police did not believe me—and nothing happened as a consequence."

Wagner said he was directed to receive 'counselling'. He said, "I saw this male psychiatrist. I told him about the abuse and he told me it was probably all my fault and not to worry about it." Wagner indicated that he very quickly lost interest in the counselling process.

When Wagner turned fourteen years, his life took a further turn. That year Wagner's mother established a new relationship with a partner who Wagner described as being "very Victorian" and a person who believed that "children should be seen and not heard." Wagner did not get along with him and did not see him as a parental figure.

Wagner began running away and said that he did not want to be in the home environment. He said he left school. Wagner's schooling had been in Adelaide's northern suburbs, which was a low socio-economic area. He said that because of his sexual abuse victimization he was never able to concentrate on school work. He said he was frequently in trouble, and was always fighting. He said he suffered from dyslexia, and was unable to read or write. Wagner said that the education system did not seem to care about his limitations—"I just got passed no matter how badly I did."

After primary school, Wagner went on to secondary school, where he attended for a few months before dropping out. He said he was always getting into trouble for smoking and not wearing the recommended school uniform. He said the "school said I had to wear blue jeans and a blue t-shirt—so I wore black jeans and a black t-shirt." Wagner said he struggled with the school work because of his inability to read and write. He said "in the end it was easier to give up." He said, "the school was happy that I left."

Soon after leaving school, Wagner met Barry Lane who was then aged thirty years.

Wagner said that Lane was "friendly towards me, and gave me cigarettes." Lane was a tall, slender man with long shoulder-length brown hair and was recognizable by his loud, effeminate disposition. Lane was a renowned cross-dresser who also went by the name 'Vanessa' when he was exposing his feminine side. On one eventful day at the local railway station, Wagner was with Barry Lane when a gang of youths started calling them a pair of fags. Wagner said that he became incensed by the remarks and reacted. He said he targeted one of the youths and beat him up severely. The following day he met up with Lane who told him that the newspapers had reported that the youth had died. Wagner said that Lane then offered to help him and proposed that they move interstate to avoid the police. Because of his illiteracy, Wagner was unable to verify the claim and agreed to go with Lane to Melbourne. In fact, Lane's claim was false.

He said that for the next four years "I felt blackmailed by Lane, who threatened to tell the police about me if I returned to Adelaide." Wagner denied that he was ever a willing sexual partner of Lane's—a claim made by various media sources—but stated that on at least one occasion he had been drugged by Lane and that when he awoke "I had a sore bum and blood in my underwear." Wagner said that while living with Barry Lane, he witnessed Lane targeting young boys for sexual favours.

### *Wagner as an Adult*

When Wagner was aged twenty-four years, he met his life partner, 'Vicki'. He said she was "a very supportive and trusting person" and in 1998 they had their first child, a son who Wagner perceived had "many of my attributes." He said his son had "a very angry attitude and could be very violent … he says what he thinks without fear."

Wagner said he enjoyed the time he spent with his son who regularly visited him in prison. He said "it was sad when it was time to say goodbye but I taught him not to show emotion." Wagner said "I try my best to teach him what I know … they fear him at his school because I also taught him how to throw a proper punch!"

Wagner stated that his partner had three other children from previous relationships that included two daughters and a son. Each of Wagner's step-children exhibited behavioural problems around violence, while his step-son had been diagnosed as having an intellectual disability. Wagner said that he generally got on well with his step-children, but did not feel as close to them, as he was to his biological son. Prior to his arrest, Wagner and his partner lived with the four children in a three-bedroomed South Australian Housing Trust house in a poorer northern suburb of Adelaide.

Despite Wagner's lack of education, he prided himself on being "a self taught mechanic." He said "I can't read a book, but I can put an engine together blindfolded." Wagner indicated he'd had limited employment that included casual jobs spray painting cars, fixing cars, gardening, and selling newspapers. He said the longest job he had was for three years selling newspapers. He said he had also worked as a volunteer firefighter for the Country Fire Services.

Wagner said that among his few close adult friends was John Bunting who lived near to him. He said they had each come from disturbed backgrounds and were both interfered with when they were aged eight years. Wagner said that "our common experiences of being sexual abuse victims made us closer—we shared a bond." Wagner believed "we had an understanding and were on the same wave length."

### *The Murders*

Wagner was convicted for ten murders, but said he was only directly involved in the direct killing of one person by himself, that of "Barry Lane." He said the other murders were carried out by Bunting and others. Wagner said he was there for most of the murders, but his role was more as support and intimidation.

According to Wagner, the murder of Ray Davies was carried out in January 1996 by a female person from within their immediate circle. Wagner claimed that this woman strangled Davies to death with a pair of jumper leads. Wagner went on to say her three-year-old son had been sexually molested by Davies and that she herself had been a victim of sexual abuse as a child.

Wagner said the second murder victim, 'Suzanne Allen' was in fact found dead in the bath in December 1996 by Bunting and Vlassakis, after they had gone to her house with the intention of committing a robbery. Wagner said Allen was a large woman and her body was naked and very cold. He said that they cut her up and put her in garbage bags, before they buried her in the same hole that Davies was buried in.

Wagner said that Michael Gardener, a known homosexual child molester, was the third victim and his murder was carried out by Bunting and Vlassakis in September 1997.

### *The Fourth Murder Victim*

The fourth murder victim, in October 1997, was—Barry Lane. Wagner said that he had received a phone call from his sister who had told him that Lane had been ringing her and was causing her distress. Wagner said that at the time he'd had little to do with Lane for several years. Wagner said he and Vlassakis went to Lane's house, where they were greeted at the front door by a nineteen-year-old boarder, Thomas Trevillion. Wagner said that Lane was not at home, but on speaking with Trevillion they determined that the boarder had been sexually interfered with by Lane and that they were going to give Lane "a real belting."

Wagner said that when Lane returned to the house "we all enjoyed a cup of coffee together."

He said, "I then walked over to Barry Lane, grabbed him, put handcuffs on him and sat him on a chair." Wagner said he proceeded to question Lane about "what he had done to me when I was a child and whether he was still abusing children." Wagner said he did not need to hear Lane's pathetic responses—he knew what was going on and what Lane had been up to for many years.

Coldly he stated, "I then strangled him to death."

After a pause of what seemed an eternity, Wagner was in the zone. He provided a detailed description of the murder and mimicked his actions as he spoke. The account had Wagner emotionally aroused. As an observer it was cathartic. Wagner's teeth were clenched and his eyes wide open. His strong hands squeezed Lane's imaginary neck and as Wagner's energy dissipated, the imaginary body fell limp. That concluded our session. He had spent all he was going to that day. The next time I saw Wagner, he was full of energy and cheerful. He thanked me for listening and added, "it was something I had to do … I would do it again without any hesitation." Wagner also explained that they then put Lane's body in the car boot and drove it to the township of Murray Bridge where it was submerged into a drum filled with acid.

Wagner said that the fifth victim was Thomas Trevillion in November 1997, who had serious mental health problems and had become actively psychotic in the week following Lane's murder. Wagner said that Trevillion's death was in fact the result of a suicide, not a murder, and his body was discovered hanging from a tree in the Adelaide Hills.

Wagner said that Gavin Porter was the sixth victim, who died in April 1998. He was a friend of Vlassakis and a drug dealer. Wagner indicated that Porter had overdosed and that he was not involved with his death.

The seventh victim was Troy Youde, murdered in 1998. Youde was the older brother of Jamie Vlassakis. Wagner said that Youde had sexually molested Vlassakis when he was a child. Wagner said that Vlassakis was responsible for strangling Youde and that Wagner's involvement was as "the strong man." Wagner said he was not affected by Youde's death.

Wagner Brooks was the eighth victim, murdered in September 1998. He said he was the eighteen-year-old intellectually disabled son of 'Gail Sinclair', another of Bunting's girlfriend. Wagner said that Brooks had been accused of sexually abusing a young child. He said that Vlassakis, Bunting and himself took Brooks to Murray Bridge where they questioned him about his involvement with the child. Brooks was held in a bath and they recorded him saying "I am going to Perth" for later deception. He was then strangled. The basis of the recording was to indicate that Brooks was still alive and living in Perth, Western Australia, when, in fact, he was dead. They hoped to avoid closer police scrutiny if their victims were 'missing'—rather than fully off the radar. They were also collecting the victim's social security payments.

The ninth victim was Gary O'Dwyer, murdered by Vlassakis and Bunting in November 1998. Wagner said that he did not know very much about that murder.

The tenth victim was Elizabeth Hayden, murdered in November 1998. Wagner said that she was a friend who was married to Mark

Hayden. Wagner denied being involved with her murder, but assumed she was killed because "she knew too much about the killings."

The final victim was David Johnson, murdered on May 9th, 1999. Johnson was Vlassakis' step brother, and it was alleged that he had been picking up girls between the age of twelve and thirteen and sexually interfered with them. Wagner said that Vlassakis, he, and Bunting took Johnson to Snowtown where he was handcuffed and questioned. Wagner said that his responses were recorded on Bunting's computer. Wagner said that they also had Johnston count from one to a hundred, saying the names of people and common phrases. He said the purpose behind the recording was to collect verbal material that could be used to make others believe Johnston was still alive. Wagner said that either Vlassakis or Bunting had strangled Johnson with a belt.

Wagner stated that Bunting had been the primary organizer and brains behind the killings. He said the bodies were initially stored in barrels in Murray Bridge before being moved to Mark Hayden's house in Adelaide. Wagner said that the police investigation was beginning to cause them concern and so they moved the barrels then to Houghton, about twenty-five kilometres north of Adelaide, before finally moving them to Snowtown in January 1999 where they were stored in a disused bank vault that Bunting and Hayden had rented.

On 20th May 1999, police opened the bank vault and discovered eight bodies in barrels. On 21st May 1999, Bunting, Hayden, and Wagner were arrested and charged with murder of a person unknown between August 1993 and 20 May 1999. On 26 May 1999, two more bodies were found buried in the backyard of Bunting's former Adelaide address. Vlassakis was charged with murder on 2nd June 1999.

### *Wagner's Overview*

Wagner told me that he believed the world was now a safer place as a consequence of the murders. He said he did not know if he was happy or sad about his involvement in the murders. He said during the killing "I felt all these incredible emotions." He said that after the killing "I felt nothing." Wagner said that during the act of killing "I felt a release of intense emotion and anger that I associated with my own child abuse."

Wagner indicated that he always knew that he would get caught for the murders. He said that the killing had gotten out of control and those involved had become "cocky" as though it would continue forever.

Wagner said that Bunting was "the mastermind" and that he was the "muscle man."

He said that since having been found guilty of the murders, he regretted that he would not be able to share the pleasures of parenting with his son in a "normal way." He continued to stress that his actions were "for the right reason." He said "I think the justice system was the straw that broke the camel's back. I feel very angry at people who sexually abuse children and I feel it more intensely because of my own experience."

### *The Psychometric Assessment*

During the course of the assessment, Wagner completed a number of psychometric tests to provide further insight into his psychological make up.

An important assessment for any criminal matter is to measure an offender's cognitive functioning.

In this case it proved very instructive. Wagner had outlined in his history a limited education background, and the results from the intelligence tests showed his verbal skills, that is reading and writing, were very limited. The data were consistent with him having a significant dyslexic disorder that had likely been undiagnosed and untreated since childhood. His 'non-verbal' intellectual functioning was in the 'normal' range, such that his problem-solving skills placed him around the 37th percentile of the age equivalent population.

The next measure examined was Wagner's personality type.

Costa & McCrae's Five Factor personality model was used to examine his personality using a dimensional approach. Empirical research has demonstrated that the 'Big Five' personality model shows consistency in interviews, self-descriptions, and observations. For a forensic psychologist, the measure provides an indication of the person's long-term emotional stability, their risk of developing mental health problems and whether he or she might likely engage effectively in rehabilitation. People who successfully rehabilitate typically show a resilient personality that is co-operative and focussed on achieving a positive outcome. That is, from the models perspective, they are low on the 'Neuroticism' (N) factor score, and high on the 'Agreeableness' (A), and 'Conscientiousness' (C) factor scores.

Wagner's personality profile was within the average range for the 'Extraversion' (E), 'Openness' (O), and 'Conscientiousness' (C) factor scores; and within the low range for the 'Neuroticism' (N) and 'Agreeableness' (A) factor scores.

Such a personality profile indicated that Wagner was emotionally stable and able to deal with most of life stresses. He perceived he had good control over his emotions, but at times could be impulsive. He was a person who was generally friendly, but preferred the company of a few rather than many. He was attracted to excitement-seeking activities. Wagner was open about his feelings but conservative with his ideas and values. He had limited trust in other people and was often very stubborn and set in his ways. Wagner generally saw himself as being disciplined and organized, but lacked clear goals in life, and did not see himself as being overly competent.

As a measure of psychopathology, Morey's Personality Assessment Inventory (PAI) provided the ideal instrument to measure Wagner's clinical profile, treatment profile, and interpersonal style. This remarkably powerful clinical tool offers the clinician a wide range of diagnostic and rehabilitation information that can be interpreted with accuracy and reliability.

Analysing the results of the PAI showed Wagner's responses were consistent and that he did not show an overly negative or overly positive response set to the questions.

Wagner's clinical profile was elevated on subscales that included 'Traumatic Stress', 'Cognitive Depression', 'Affective Depression', 'Activity Level', 'Irritability', 'Hypervigilence', 'Negative Relationships', 'Self Harm', and all the subscales of the 'Antisocial Features' scale.

Such a configuration of clinical scales suggested that Wagner was a person with significant tension, unhappiness, and pessimism. Much of this had likely related to his exposure to past traumas of childhood sexual abuse. He indicated that his past trauma continued to cause him worry and anxiety. Wagner was also inclined to act out as a primary means for resolving his emotions. He was an impulsive person who could be hostile, impatient, and unempathetic.

The combination of impulsivity, resentment, and high energy

levels may result in him having limited consideration for the needs of others and lash out impulsively at those who may have crossed him. These same traits may also place Wagner at increased risk for aggressive acting out behaviours, and it was likely that such behaviours led to impairing his ability to maintain social role expectations in both formal and informal settings.

Wagner's substance use was not a significant problem, nor did he exhibit psychotic features.

On the treatment scales, Wagner was significantly elevated on 'verbal aggression', 'physical aggression', and 'stress'. His 'elevated aggression' profile indicated he was a person who felt in control of his anger feelings and impulses, but his behaviour would suggest this was not the case. In situations of conflict he was likely to express his anger directly both in a verbal and physical manner. Wagner reported that his level of stress was significant, and he indicated he felt life issues were troubling him considerably.

On the interpersonal scales, Wagner's responses indicated that he was 'very low' on 'Dominance' scale and within the 'average' range for 'Warmth' scale.

A person displaying this pattern would be characterised as self-effacing and lacking confidence in social interactions. Wagner had difficulty having his needs met in personal relationships, and would subordinate his own interests to those of others in a manner that may seem self-punitive.

### *Psychological Choices*

Understanding why a person kills another person usually involves examining the person's motivation and their psychological make-up.

Wagner, as a child, experienced the worst form of sexual abuse. Not only was he was repeatedly sexually abused by an older man, but when he actively sought help through his family, the police, and a mental health professional, no tangible assistance was ever provided.

At that point Wagner likely lost faith in the justice system.

Following his childhood abuse, Wagner became a further victim. On this occasion it was at the hands of an older man—again outside of his control. This abuse was perpetrated by Barry Lane, who was later to be his murder victim.

Wagner's motivation for wanting to kill people who abused children was self-evident. His psychological profile, however, was not suited to planning vigilante activities. To this end, Wagner needed a like-minded ally. Such an ally was Bunting, who, like Wagner had been a victim of childhood sexual abuse. Bunting was a planner and had identified relevant targets.

Wagner was a big man and demanded respect because of his physical size. Bunting was a short man who lacked a physical presence. Together Bunting and Wagner formed a liaison that was motivated to kill people who they believed abused children, a duo of 'brain' and 'muscle'.

Was Wagner an evil monster? No doubt the media portrayed him as such. The sentencing Judge showed little sympathy when he described him as a person "in the business of killing for pleasure" and "incapable of rehabilitation."

Wagner was a man who had never coped with the emotional pain of being a victim of abuse. With the support of a vigilante leader, he found an outlet to relieve some of his pain.

Were there a law of human behaviour (akin to Newton's third law of motion) that for every (human) action, there is an equal and opposite (human) reaction, then Wagner's behaviour can be explained and understood. His action of violent killing was a human reaction to his extreme suffering in childhood. This was certainly not how the Australian Courts viewed the behaviour, but it may be how many people who have been victims of child abuse may view it.

At his sentencing, Wagner spoke from the dock—the only words he spoke in court throughout his eleven-month trial

> Paedophiles were doing terrible things to children. The authorities didn't do anything about it. I decided to take action. I took that action. Thank you.

The question remains, was he evil and psychologically disturbed? Or was he a person who had no other psychological choice?

# PART TWO

# Current and Conundrums

*Life is infinitely stranger than anything which the mind of man could invent.*

*— Arthur Conan Doyle*

***Joel Watts,** MD, FRCPC, DABPN (Forensic Psychiatry) completed his medical degree at the University of Western Ontario in 2003, his Psychiatry residency at the University of Ottawa in 2008 and a fellowship in Forensic Psychiatry in Cleveland, Ohio in 2009. He practiced at the Institut Philippe-Pinel de Montréal (a maximum security forensic hospital) from 2009 to July 2015 doing assessments, treatment, and rehabilitation of mentally ill offenders. He also assessed and treated sexual offenders as part of a treatment program funded by the Correctional Service of Canada. He held a faculty appointment as an assistant professor in the Department of Psychiatry at the University of Montreal and was a site director for the General Psychiatry Residency Program. He was also the Program Director for the Forensic Psychiatry Residency Program from 2012 until July 2015. He has since moved to the Royal Ottawa Mental Health Centre (ROMHC) where he continues to work with and assess and treat individuals with mental health difficulties who have legal problems or an increased risk of violence. He is currently the president of the Quebec branch of the Canadian Academy of Psychiatry and the Law (CAPL) and is on the board of directors (secretary) of CAPL.*

# Dr. Joel Watts

## The Case of Luka Rocco Magnotta
## A Forensic Adventure Down the Rabbit's Hole

I HAD JUST FINISHED SWIMMING at the cottage near Calabogie, Ontario. It was a sunny afternoon when I received an unexpected phone call that was to have an enormous impact on my career as a forensic psychiatrist. Several hours later on that Saturday, June 16, 2012, I sat among five Montreal police detectives aboard a Canadian Forces Polaris jet as we took off from Montreal's Trudeau International Airport headed for Berlin. Our mandate was to pick up Luka Rocco Magnotta and bring him back to Canada. This rather extraordinary experience was just the beginning of an almost three-year journey for me, and my involvement in this fascinating and gruelling case.

As a forensic psychiatrist, people often ask me if I ever have an interest in sharing or writing about the experiences I have regarding the mentally disordered offenders I assess and the horrors of some of their cases. As a physician and a consultant to the legal system, confidentiality is an important principle that must be respected. Even in trials where an accused's personal information becomes public knowledge, professional ethics dictate that confidentiality should be respected as much as possible. I am very fortunate that Luka Magnotta consented to my sharing information I gathered about him.

Before May 2012, not many people had heard of Magnotta. Nonetheless, he already had somewhat of a following on the Internet. As an aspiring model who lacked a great deal of self-esteem, he had also worked for many years as a prostitute and escort. He was quite savvy about the inner workings of the online world. He had posted many photos of himself and comments about his life, in an attempt to gain positive attention and approval of others. Many of the photos were altered to make him appear as if he was in exotic locations. He was prone to striking dramatic poses and spent an inordinate amount of time and energy trying to appear like he was a wealthy celebrity. Having a positive, flashy image was very important to him.

There was also a darker side to Magnotta's online presence. This came to light in 2010 when a video of an individual suffocating kittens to death in a vacuum bag was posted online. Several other videos appeared about a year later. These recorded an individual feeding a cat to a python and someone drowning a cat in a bathtub. Different people and animal rights activists began to link them to Magnotta. He later admitted to me that he was involved in making the videos. At the time, he told a different story—that a man named Manny had instigated and pressured him to kill the animals and produce the videos. Being the only person visible in the videos, Magnotta became the object of online hostility. Groups attempted to track him down. A Toronto-area branch of the SPCA began investigating and tried to locate him.

His darker side was also seen in an online story posted about Magnotta dating Karla Homolka, the former wife and accomplice of notorious rapist and killer Paul Bernardo. Another posting, which he later admitted to writing himself, called him a dangerous 'psychopath.' Journalists from Canada and the United Kingdom sought him out. Interestingly, he sought journalists out, in an attempt to distance himself from these postings and deny responsibility in the cat killings. Magnotta later admitted to having fuelled the online fire by writing a sexually explicit and threatening letter to a journalist in the UK. In the letter, Magnotta stated that his next video would involve humans. All of the above served as a juicy backdrop to the next chapter in his life, the killing of Chinese national and Concordia University student, Jun Lin. Police and Crown prosecutors argued that this was Magnotta's ultimate attempt to gain fame and notoriety.

### *Horrifying Discoveries*

On a hot May 29, 2012, Montreal police were called to 5720 Decarie Street. A human torso had been discovered in a suitcase, which had been placed out amongst garbage, awaiting pickup. On the property, police discovered more remains in several garbage bags. These included severed legs, arms, and a dead puppy. The remains included no obvious identifying marks and did not include the hands, feet, or head of the victim. Later that same day, staffers at the Conservative Party of Canada headquarters in Ottawa made the gruesome discovery of a human foot. It had been mailed in a box containing a letter. In light of this, Canada Post employees were able to intercept another package mailed to the Liberal Party of Canada headquarters in Ottawa shortly afterwards. That package contained a human hand and a letter. Many days later, two similarly wrapped packages containing the other foot and hand of the victim arrived at two schools in the Vancouver area. Some of the letters that accompanied the body parts named and threatened then-Canadian Prime Minister, Stephen Harper, and his wife, Laureen Harper.

While the evolving crime was horrific enough, the first day of the investigation brought more. Magnotta had produced a now infamous video of Lin's death. A citizen had reported to police that they had seen this video, entitled "1 Lunatic 1 Ice Pick", on a little-known gore website. News of this quickly hit the airwaves. The video, produced in a similar way to the cat-killing videos, showed a naked and heavily sedated male tied to a bed. Magnotta was seen straddling him and asking if he was "okay," all the while holding an electric saw in his right hand. The film then cut to images and video of Lin in several states of dismemberment. It also showed Magnotta performing several degrading sexual acts on Lin's body parts. In the online video, it was impossible to clearly identify Magnotta. It *was* possible to do so, however, in the original source video, which police found in the trash. It was only discovered, a year later at the preliminary inquiry, that the naked man tied to the bed on the first part of the video was not Jun Lin. Instead, it was a still-unidentified Colombian man Magnotta met and had sex with on May 19, 2012.

Information about the discovery of Lin's body and parts, the threats to the political elite, the online video, and Magnotta's escape on a flight to Paris led to a media frenzy and international attention. Many conclusions were drawn about him. Most of the information available portrayed Magnotta as a cold and calculating murderer who sought fame by taunting the media and police. Police in Berlin eventually captured Magnotta on June 4, 2012. At the time he was in an Internet café, browsing news reports about the manhunt for him.

Several weeks of diplomatic and police work between governments ensued. On June 18, 2012, Magnotta was released to Canadian custody and brought back to Montreal aboard a Canadian military jet, to much media fanfare. He was accompanied by Montreal detectives, military personnel ... and one psychiatrist.

### *Extradition from Berlin*

May 2012 was, like most of my professional life up to that point, a steady and busy time. I had various responsibilities at the maximum-security forensic psychiatry hospital where I worked, the Institut Philippe-Pinel de Montréal. On May 29, 2012, I listened peripherally to the news. They discussed the discovery of Jun Lin's remains in Montreal and of the international manhunt for Magnotta. Two weeks later, on June 14th, my clinical director asked if I would be interested in accompanying Montreal detectives while they extradited Magnotta from Berlin. I gave it some thought and sought some initial advice on how to proceed. I then called the lead detective and accepted their request. The initial plan was for me to speak with Magnotta's jail psychiatrist, Dr. Thomas Barth, who was in Berlin. Due to the time difference and it being late in the week, we were not able to connect. Detectives told me that we would not likely proceed until the next week. I was therefore quite surprised when they tracked me down to a family cottage, four hours away in rural Calabogie, Ontario.

It was the early afternoon of Saturday, June 16th when I was told a Canadian Forces jet was picking us up in Montreal that evening. I had just enough time to drive home, grab my passport and a suit. Detectives picked me up so we could join the rest of the team at the airport. To say that I was feeling a bit out of my element is somewhat of an understatement. In reality, I had little idea what to expect and had to make up my 'mission plan' as it were, on the fly. Medical school, residency and fellowship training as a forensic psychiatrist hadn't prepared me for this type of role. I was, and still am, indebted for the advice, support and confidence of my clinical director, the director of professional services and the CEO of the hospital (Drs. Renée Fugère, Louis Bérard, and Jocelyn Aubut, respectively).

Not knowing what mental state Magnotta might be in and having no knowledge that he suffered from a serious mental illness, I tried to think of every kind of scenario and what questions I needed to ask when I arrived. I knew that I needed to inform Magnotta that any information I obtained I would document and keep as confidential medical information. My role was that of accompaniment, that is to monitor and provide any needed treatment strictly for the duration of the return flight. As such, I knew I would need to keep a record of this in private. I also knew that, given the unique role I had in meeting Magnotta so soon after his arrest, anything he told me and any observation I made of him would be highly valuable during his eventual trial. I knew that I would have to warn him that I might eventually be forced to divulge such information by court order. I also knew that my role would be to make sure that if he had any serious medical problem or had a significant suicide risk, I might have to insist that he be taken to a hospital for a formal medical or psychiatric evaluation upon his arrival in Montreal.

During the flight to Berlin, all of these possible scenarios (and more) raced about in my head. The detectives and military personnel on the aircraft were professional and quite accommodating. The detectives asked what I thought of the case. I had little to say given that I knew far less than they did. They wanted to know if I could tell them if any medication he was taking would prevent them from being able to question him on his return to Canadian soil. They made it clear that they felt a great deal of responsibility to the family of Jun Lin to try and obtain the whereabouts of the rest of his remains, namely his head. They eventually did ask Magnotta about this at length when he was returned to Canada. He was not forthcoming initially. Eventually, on July 1, 2012, they received an 'anonymous' tip detailing the exact whereabouts of these remains in a park in Montreal.

### *Run-down of Evidence*

Early on Monday, June 18th, the detectives provided me a run-down of some of the evidence accumulated to date so I might understand who I was dealing with that morning. At that meeting, little information was shared about Magnotta's history of mental health problems. A few hours later, I met Dr. Thomas Barth at the jail. He informed me that for about a week, he had been treating Magnotta with antipsychotic medication. Magnotta was described as quite unwell and psychotic.

Dr. Barth mentioned that Magnotta reported suffering from schizophrenia for many years. Schizophrenia is a serious psychotic illness that causes individuals to lose touch with reality. In Magnotta's case, he had delusions (fixed false beliefs) that he was being watched and filmed by a witch named 'Debbie'. He also believed he had been persecuted by a person called 'Manny', in addition to then-Canadian Prime Minister, Stephen Harper. Magnotta complained of auditory hallucinations (hearing voices that were not audible to others). Dr. Barth noted that Magnotta's emotional expression was typical of floridly psychotic individuals (he was frightened, suspicious, and withdrawn).

In the various media reports on Magnotta up to that point, I had heard that he might have a mental illness. As such, I was somewhat sceptical of the information provided by Dr. Barth. I was likely also biased in this way due to the seemingly organized and planned nature of Jun Lin's murder, the video's production, and Magnotta's escape to Europe. I knew that psychotic individuals are capable of planning and organized behaviour, but my forensic training had taught me to consider the possibility that he was faking 'mad', especially given the seriousness of his case and charges. My scepticism was on high alert when I met him, despite his presentation being just like Dr. Barth had said. I was surprised by how dramatically unwell Magnotta appeared. I thought that perhaps he was skilfully putting on a show. Nagging at the back of my mind, however, was the fact that he would have had to be an exceedingly good actor to pull off such a convincing presentation of psychosis. In retrospect, judging by his lack of success in the acting profession to date, this is unlikely. Dr. Barth also told me that he had experience working with forensic populations (that is, with people who might try and fake mental illness) and he was convinced of the genuineness of his illness. He confirmed that he had observed Magnotta consistently show signs of psychosis for a week, including symptoms rarely faked, so-called negative symptoms, such as a flattened emotional expression.

As planned, officials brought Magnotta to our aircraft at the Berlin airport. He was taken into Montreal police custody, read his rights, and informed of his arrest and charges. He was then shackled in a middle-aisle seat. We sat on the sweltering Berlin tarmac during a two-hour delay due to a last-minute jet engine malfunction, which needed to be repaired. Dr. Barth had given me a discharge summary and medications that I would dispense during the flight. As odd as it may seem, this too was a first. Psychiatrists (and most doctors, for that matter) are almost never the ones to give patients their oral medications. This is typically the role of nurses. I gave Magnotta antipsychotic medications at the prescribed times and recorded the details. He had very little to say during the flight and behaved himself. He asked politely to use the washroom and for a blanket when he was cold. When I offered to listen if he wanted to talk with me, he declined. In an odd, childlike tone of voice, he said, "I don't want to make any statements."

Near the end of the trip, the flight plan needed to be changed. German officials had announced they had released Magnotta into Canadian custody and this had tipped off the media. This, plus the two-hour delay prior to take-off had made the prospect of a media circus at the airport a real possibility. Due to security concerns, we landed in Mirabel, a smaller airport north of Montreal. There was considerable media presence, all the same. Due to Magnotta's relatively calm behaviour and lack of any suicidal or threatening behaviour, my role came to a close when he was escorted off the plane. I was driven home, with much to reflect upon.

I did not expect to have further involvement in the case at least not until the eventual trial. This all changed in July 2012, when Magnotta's Toronto-based attorney, Luc Leclair, called me. He wanted to meet me to discuss the possibility that I perform a forensic psychiatry evaluation of Magnotta. He wanted to know if his client could qualify for a Not Criminally Responsible (NCR) defence for his charges. I met with Leclair. He appeared to want to size me up and wanted to know a great deal about my role during the flight from Berlin. I told him that I needed to think carefully about whether I might be in a conflict of interest due to my previous role.

I contacted the Canadian organization that advises doctors about legal matters related to their practice. They confirmed what I suspected. Due to the fact that: 1) my initial role was simply to accompany Magnotta, 2) I was not contracted by police to provide any report to them, and 3) due to the confidentiality warning I had given Magnotta in Berlin, I could become involved as an expert if I wished to do so. I thought seriously about this request. Did I want to get involved in such a notorious, high-profile case? I knew that if I ended up testifying in court, I would face strong cross-examination about many things, including my different roles in the case. It would be a very stressful experience. Mentors and colleagues who had been involved in high-profile cases told me that many years of hard work are spent building a professional reputation. They taught that it could all be dashed in a heartbeat with one wrong move. Such a trial would provide ample opportunity for public humiliation. Conversely, I also knew that intellectual and professional challenges like this did not come around very often. I believed I had the training and the skills to do this type of complicated assessment. Little did I know the extent to which these would be tested over the course of this case. I certainly did not anticipate just how gruelling and time-consuming it would prove to be.

In retrospect, my decision to accept the mandate of defence expert was also due to my ongoing suspicion that Magnotta likely did not have a valid NCR defence. I did not believe it likely that my involvement as a defence expert would go very far. In my experience, at least half (if not more) of the defence-requested assessments I do result in me telling the attorney that their client does not have a mental disorder. At other times, even if they do have a mental disorder, they often still don't meet NCR criteria. In these cases, no formal report is written or submitted to the court. My involvement comes to an end and I receive compensation for the time I have spent on the case. If I was a betting man, I would have wagered against being very helpful to Leclair or his client in the summer of 2012.

### *New Role as Defence Expert*

By September 2012, I carved out time to begin interviewing Magnotta in my new role. I also began to receive hundreds of pages of medical records detailing his extensive history of schizophrenia. These dated back to his first psychotic episode and treatment in psychiatry, in 2001, at the age of eighteen. Many of the symptoms that I had observed at the Berlin jail were almost identical to those described by psychiatrists during those first years of his illness. During the fall of 2012, Magnotta became more and more dishevelled from one interview to the next. He remained psychotic until his symptoms began to stabilize in early 2013. The psychiatrist who was treating him at the jail had been increasing his antipsychotic medication to substantial doses and the illness seemed to be responding.

As I made my way through the evidence, I viewed a large quantity of video, including the very disturbing original source material for the "1 Lunatic 1 Ice Pick" video. With time, I began to formulate Magnotta's diagnoses. I concluded that he suffers from schizophrenia and was, more likely than not, quite ill in May 2012 and beyond. I also believe that he suffers from a combination of histrionic and borderline personality traits. These symptoms relate to longstanding problems with low self-esteem, a need for attention, fear of abandonment and a tendency to draw attention to himself by dressing flamboyantly. He often used dramatic expressions of emotions. He often overvalued the true nature of his relationships. He didn't recognize early enough when people where taking advantage of him. He would remain in violent or abusive relationships because he wanted to be loved and did not want to be alone.

I was convinced Magnotta genuinely suffers from psychosis and was psychotic at the time of Jun Lin's killing. Nevertheless, in order to be found NCR, Magnotta needed to prove that his mental disorder caused him to: 1) not appreciate the material consequences of what he was doing, or 2) that it was wrong to do it (in a moral sense). Most often, people found NCR in Canada suffer from a psychosis that made them lose touch with reality. This causes them to not be able to apply a rational understanding to what they did or why they were doing it. The Canadian criminal justice system recognises that it is not a just and fair outcome to punish individuals who lack moral culpability. In order for Magnotta to convince a jury that he met the NCR criteria, he would have to convince them that, because of his psychosis, he didn't know that killing Lin and doing all the awful things he did to his body was wrong. The jury would only have to be convinced of this 'on a balance of probabilities', equivalent to being fifty-one per cent certain or more. Despite this and given the state of the evidence, this was going to be a tough row to hoe. For the other experts and myself, assessing his eligibility for the NCR criteria was very complicated. From a diagnostic perspective alone, he was challenging. In addition to this, he reported memory difficulties related to the offenses (this is unfortunately a fairly common occurrence in murder cases). We also had to assess whether or not he was faking his symptoms.

I interviewed Magnotta throughout the fall of 2012. His pattern of thinking as well as his distress during our interviews resulted in this assessment being the most time-consuming one of my career to date. With the interviews totalling more than forty-four hours, it is quite unlikely that I will ever break this number in a single case in the future. The long interviews were largely due to Magnotta's alleged difficulty recalling a great deal of what happened to him in the past. He consistently reported difficulty remembering things related to his psychotic episodes and the emotionally traumatic moments of his life. This included Lin's killing and the days that followed. Magnotta, like some accused murderers I have assessed, showed many signs that he was horrified by the gruesome acts that he had committed to Lin. Having to recall them and talk about them was traumatic. I became convinced that he had some true amnesia, perhaps due to his psychosis. But he was also unwilling, or psychologically unable, to access his memories further to explain what had happened.

After a long and seemingly never-ending period of evaluation, my opinion about the NCR issue began to crystalize in early 2013. And it was keeping me up at night. I agonized for days as I gathered the points for and against my opinions for each of the charges. (The NCR criteria had to be assessed in relation to each one of Magnotta's charges.) Even after considering a multitude of alternative theories for his behaviour, the theory that his behaviour was irrational and driven by psychosis kept making more sense than the others ... but not by much. There was also the challenge of how to weigh various elements of his version of events that were unconfirmed, but plausible. I felt this information was genuine and not faked. For example, he reported that previous sex client 'Manny' was involved in the murder. I was convinced that this experience of his was in fact psychotic, even though this individual may have really existed at some point in Magnotta's past. Magnotta also said that he had made attempts to scare people away by threatening them online anonymously including, for example, the threatening letters and stories about his relationship to Karla Homolka. This was consistent with maladaptive and illogical behaviours some psychotic people adopt when they believe they are being persecuted. On the other hand, it also made it appear that on the surface, he was planning a cold-blooded killing.

This case occurred in a very fraught period of time in Canada's recent history, at least from the point of view of a forensic psychiatrist. Our profession had long benefitted from relative anonymity. This began to change in the early part of the 2000s when public opinion was riled up by infrequent, yet horrific, examples of individuals suffering from mental illness committing gruesome acts of violence. Guy Turcotte's first murder trial in Quebec had taken place only a few years before Magnotta's. A jury found Turcotte NCR for repeatedly stabbing his young children to death. The public was outraged and opinion quickly shifted to questioning the legitimacy of the NCR defence. Forensic psychiatry began to get a bad name. In Quebec, even general psychiatrists were accusing their forensic psychiatrist brethren of being, at best, incompetent. At worst, colleagues branded us 'hired guns'. The Conservative Harper government of the time played on the public's fears and prejudices. It introduced the Not Criminally Responsible Reform Act in July 2014. This legislation did not change the NCR defence itself, but created a 'high-risk offender' category. This was done against expert advice and despite the best evidence in the field, which showed that it was unnecessary and unlikely to make the public any safer. This environment was the turbulent background that contributed to many of my fears and anxieties while considering if I should take on a case as notorious as Magnotta's. My concerns ramped up considerably when my opinion about him was starting to form in early 2013. I had nightmares of being vilified by the press at trial for daring to say that Magnotta could be NCR. I ruminated at night about being dragged by lynch mobs to a public stockade to be tarred and feathered by angry colleagues, furious at me for dragging our profession even further down in the muck of public opinion.

I felt like I was in a pickle for other reasons too. As sometimes happens in NCR assessments, experts are not a hundred per cent convinced, or even eighty per cent convinced, that the NCR criteria apply to a person's offenses. In Magnotta's case I felt they did meet the legal threshold, of fifty-one per cent or greater. This was clearly not at a high level. I shared this with his lawyer. He asked me for a formal report and wanted me to testify at trial. I worried about how I would represent my opinion, at its true level of certainty. I also worried about the evidence against it, but this would have to wait for another day.

I submitted the report in February 2013. It was well over 120 pages, courtesy of the complicated nature of Magnotta's history, diagnoses and crimes. Anticipating that my opinion would be subject to intense cross-examination, the opinion sections of my report covered fifteen pages. I had never before felt the need to include a table of contents with my report. The Crown expert in the case, Dr. Gilles Chamberland, later commented in court that this case covered the gamut of the field of forensic psychiatry, all in one. This is one of the many things that all the experts in the case agreed on.

### *The Trial*

The long-anticipated trial finally began in September 2014. My involvement had taken a sabbatical since I submitted my report more than a year before, but the legal system had been hard at work. The international nature of the case led to the need for a complicated Rogatory Commission in Europe, which served to depose witnesses there. Jury selection in Canada required fully bilingual jurors, given much of the evidence would be provided by both French and English speaking witnesses. The Crown outlined their evidence over several weeks. The defence began the presentation of its evidence at the end of October. From that moment onward, psychiatric evidence was a primary focus of the trial. Dr. Gilles Chamberland, the Crown expert, Dr. Marie-Frédérique Allard and myself, the latter two being defence experts, were in court from the beginning of the defence's case until closing arguments.

Many of my colleagues can attest that trials are long and often monotonous affairs. They are punctuated by periods of boredom and brief moments of intense stress or even fear. Being under cross-examination often evokes the latter. Note-taking was an active and intense occupation during the trial. Sometimes it is possible to simply review transcripts of what is being said prior to attending to give testimony, but this is often impractical, especially in larger, complicated cases. Any new piece of evidence had to be considered for its possible affect on an expert opinion and testimony. Although many people, including general psychiatrists, believe that forensic psychiatrists make a fortune when in court, this is largely a myth. In this file, the other experts and I were remunerated as much, if not less, for our time in court than if we were seeing patients. Being away from our patient-care duties is also a hardship on colleagues who look after our patients.

For five long weeks, the jury was privy to testimony by numerous psychiatrists who had either treated or evaluated Magnotta in the past. Dr. Thomas Barth was flown in from Berlin to give evidence. As is often the case, the strategy regarding the order of witnesses changed frequently. This was particularly hard given the hours of preparation that I had put into preparing for my testimony. I wanted to be fresh, and yet in full command of all the details of the case, my report, and my opinion. Leclair and I debated about using a PowerPoint presentation to help make the issues easier to understand for the jury. A last minute decision was made to have Dr. Allard testify before me. By the time I did testify, I had put quite a bit of pressure on myself to try and distil my understanding of the case in a clear fashion to the jury. I also wanted to be true to the complicated nature of the case. I wanted to make it clear that although I was favouring NCR, there were many aspects of the case that gave me pause. I wanted to show the jury and the public that I had been thoughtful and reasonable in coming to my opinion. I wanted to be credible. I was not invested in a verdict, especially given that I had estimated, from the beginning of the trial, that the odds of an NCR verdict were slim to none. I still felt that my opinion about Magnotta's psychotic motives needed to be heard.

After a day or so of my direct testimony, Leclair surprised everyone following the trial, me included. He cut his questions short, before we even began to explain my opinion to the jury. The jury had already heard Dr. Allard explain much of what Magnotta had told us about his past. There was concern that they were going to be overloaded with repetitive information. I initially felt a bit like my legs were being cut out from under me. I would not be able to explain my reasoning to the jury and had to hope that their reading my report would suffice. I was also somewhat relieved. I was excited and ready for cross-examination to get on and over with. I have always enjoyed the strategic and intellectual challenge of cross-examination. I spent five days on the stand, most of it under cross-examination. (All three experts spent a similar amount of time on the stand during the trial.) I was ready to be done, and rclicvcd whcn it was.

My involvement at trial came to a close in early December 2013, when the last of the evidence was presented. Throughout my involvement in the case, I had no idea if Magnotta would testify or not. I didn't bother myself too much with this issue given that I knew, from my previous discussions with Magnotta, that he might not. He feared cross-examination and having to tell his version of the crime, the details of which still distressed him greatly. Whether or not he was to testify made no difference to my opinion. It did, however, profoundly alter the strength of the defence's argument, in the Crown's favour. Ultimately, for legal reasons, everything that Magnotta told me and any other expert, had to be considered by the jury as 'hearsay evidence'. This essentially meant that my opinion and that of Dr. Allard could not be given much, if any, weight in deciding the outcome by the jury. This led to the seemingly incongruous closing statement by Leclair. He essentially told the jury to ignore his experts' opinions and decide for themselves, based on the hundreds of medical files about Magnotta's previous treatment for schizophrenia that were in evidence.

The jury was sequestered. The publicity ban on things said during the trial in the jury's absence (for example when the jury was asked to leave during legal debates with the judge), was lifted. The media were then able to make public some of the more unsavoury aspects of the trial. The day after the jury was sequestered, a local paper pounced at the opportunity to publicize my remuneration for the trip to Berlin (they also overstated the amount). In July 2012, when I considered becoming a defence expert or not, I anticipated the Crown could try and discredit me by highlighting how much I was paid for Magnotta's extradition. After consulting several senior and well-respected colleagues, I had invoiced the Montreal Police for the fifty-four hours I dedicated to Magnotta's weekend extradition. I had considered a variety of factors, including the extraordinary nature of the role I was being asked to assume, and my lack of knowledge of Magnotta.

Shortly before I began my testimony, the Crown attorney, Louis Boutillier, addressed the judge, in the jury's absence. He expressed outrage at how much I had been paid. He also felt that I was in a conflict of interest because I had worked 'for the police' and then for the defence. At the time, I suspected that his impassioned speech was likely grandstanding for the media so they would write about it later when the publication ban was lifted. I also suspected that, for legal reasons of prejudice, there was little chance the judge would let him cross-examine me about the issue of my remuneration. The judge admonished Boutillier, stating that the invoice was not unreasonable, given consulting fees that legal professionals sometimes receive, especially in exceptional circumstances. In addition, during a pause in my cross-examination, the judge told the jury that I had not behaved inappropriately by working 'at the request of the police' and then as a defence expert and was not in a conflict of interest. I was thankful for his unknowing birthday gift, given to me on that particularly exhausting day of cross-examination. The newspaper article about my invoice was nonetheless displeasing, especially considering that I had worked for less than minimum wage on the NCR evaluation and report, considering the hours I had invested.

An additional aspect of my involvement in the case was not made public, even after the lifting of the publication ban. It occurred at about the same time that Boutillier shared his disgust with my fees. I received information from Magnotta's lawyer that I might be prosecuted for some rarely used criminal offence relating to a criminal breach of trust. This was also related to my different roles in the case. I suspected it was a trial tactic, serving either to scare me into withdrawing from the case before I testified, or to intimidate me so I would perform poorly on the stand. Despite my initial incredulity, I had to take this information seriously. After hours of time spent retaining and consulting with my own legal counsel, I was eventually reassured it was likely a bluff and that I had not done anything criminal. After ruminating about wearing an orange jumpsuit and the impact that criminal charges could have on my career (it could have been significant), I decided to proceed and not let such perceived posturing derail my eventual testimony. I believe it may have even motivated me to perform better under cross-examination. After the trial and out of curiosity, I spoke with other forensic psychiatrists in Canada who have been involved in high-profile contested cases. All expressed surprise, having never heard of such a tactic being used before.

After eight days of deliberation, the jury found Magnotta guilty of first-degree murder and all other charges. Society seemed to breathe a collective sigh of relief that this saga was over. Unsurprisingly, Magnotta initially decided to appeal the verdict. By February 2015, however, he changed his mind, stating he wanted to focus on rehabilitation in prison, with the hope of obtaining parole in about twenty years. Leclair wanted to be sure his client was making the decision to abandon his appeal with a clear mind. Given Magnotta's history of psychosis, he wanted to be sure that he wasn't making this decision due to delusional symptoms.

### *A Talented Actor? Or Not?*

In mid-February 2015, I met Magnotta for several hours at the Sainte-Anne-des-Plaines penitentiary, north of Montreal. We discussed the trial and his situation at the prison. He appeared relaxed and was unsurprised by the verdict. He had been warned, long in advance, that he would likely be found guilty. He explained why he did not want to appeal his conviction. It was borne out of a thoughtful consideration of his chances of succeeding an appeal. He also wanted to avoid being in the spotlight anymore and wanted to begin making some kind of reparations for what he had done, if only symbolically. He volunteered how he had wanted, for some time, to offer an apology to Jun Lin's family. He also wanted to offer them the chance to speak to him face to face. I promptly told Leclair that his client was clinically stable, taking his medications and was of sound mind in deciding to abandon his appeal.

Prior to Magnotta, I had not had the opportunity to talk to an accused I had evaluated who had been convicted, despite my opinion that they met the NCR criteria. When I learned that Magnotta no longer wanted to appeal the guilty verdict, the stakes for him to be transparent were arguably low. As I prepared to see him again after the trial, I relished the chance to explore if he had been faking or lying about anything to try and get an NCR verdict. It was a golden opportunity to test any lingering doubts about whether I, and other psychiatrists who met him, had been conned by a supremely talented actor or not. Although he seemed to be much less symptomatic from his psychosis, he still did not present evidence of being a manipulative, narcissistic, or antisocial individual. Perhaps, after forty-plus hours of face-to-face time with the man, I should have learned to trust my clinical skills and my forensic assessment. Still, I left that February 2015 encounter with the same degree of perplexity at how a person can do such horrendous things. I remained convinced that there was little credible evidence of him faking a mental illness. I remained convinced that he did not kill Jun Lin because he was a callous and cold-blooded killer seeking fame and notoriety.

It may not be very comforting to many people to hear, but I believe that there is an uncomfortable truth about humans and our behaviour. Very disturbing acts of violence are sometimes not easily explained at all, even by experts. It is well known in our field that it is often impossible to predict in advance who is likely to commit heinous acts of violence.

After reflecting upon this case and about things I have learned from meeting and evaluating accused murderers over the years, some observations about the human psyche have stuck with me. Murderers are often not the monsters they are made out to be in the media. They also happen to be quite likable when met one-on-one, regardless of their diagnoses and psychological challenges. I have no doubt that many will consider the Magnotta case closed and are comfortable with the version of events that the jury ultimately agreed with. As a forensic psychiatrist, I believe that the truth is more complex and perhaps stranger than we would like to believe.

***Louise Olivier** PhD is a South African psychologist, specialising in forensic psychology in the arena of criminal law, family law, third party claims and civil law. She also specialises in therapy with people that need some emotional support or guidance (individual and marital and sexual) as well as people that suffer from more serious psychological problems, for example mood disorders, dissociate identity disorder, sexual deviations, and anxiety disorders.*

*Dr. Olivier has published many articles and research reports pertaining to the needs and problems of the peoples of South Africa as well as on therapeutic interventions with children and adults. She lectures extensively nationally and internationally in hypnotherapeutic techniques, ethics, forensic work etc. Internationally, she has been invited to present workshops in Sweden, Israel, Australia, USSR, Germany, United Kingdom, USA, and Ireland. She was awarded the Laureate Award for 2009 from the University of Pretoria for her national and international contribution in Psychology and Forensic Psychology.*

# Dr. Louise Olivier

## A Battered Wife Kills
## The Revenge of the Unconscious Mind

DOMESTIC VIOLENCE formally defined in South Africa covers a broad spectrum of behaviour from inflicting physical harm with weapons and rape, to stalking, harassment, or even entering a residence without permission. Although a vast majority of such violence is directed towards women, domestic violence can also include threats of family murder and violence against men by their partners.

Although the United Nations has proclaimed that domestic violence is a universal problem, South Africa has a higher frequency than other western nations. Although this rate has dropped since the introduction of democratic reform in the mid-nineties, it remains alarmingly high with up to fifty per cent of women reporting some level of violence levelled at them in their lifetime. This necessitated the establishment of organisations in South Africa assisting women against abuse. Women often stay in relationships where they are abused for many reasons—for the sake of the children, because they believe that they can change the abuser or he can change in future, because they have no money or alternate place to stay, and the threat of further violence should they leave.

As a psychologist involved in forensic work and the project leader of a multi-disciplinary team doing research on family violence and family murder nationally, I found the case of Margaret Gouws an excellent example of the helplessness and catastrophic reactions of women to systematic abuse by a partner. I got involved with the case via the attorney and advocate of Margaret because they could not understand why a person with her personality style (fairly submissive, loving and non-violent) could suddenly commit homicide. Her medical practitioner who also testified knew her as a person who hated conflict and was peace-loving.

My initial opinion of Margaret Gouws was that I was surprised that she was a member of the South African Police because that was the most unlikely career choice for her, except for the discipline it entails. Understandably, she was more in the support system department. She was very sad about her husband's death and initially told me what a good man he was and how much she loved him. She was also shocked at her own behaviour because she was someone who adhered to rules and regulations her whole life (from childhood). I was able to establish a trusting relationship with her (which is normally difficult when doing forensic work due to the nature of the work) and she started providing me with much more detail than she had even provided her attorney with.

Five major factors united to direct and play out the story of Margaret and the tragedy that led to her escape from purgatory. These factors were 1) the South African social and legal system; 2) her unconscious mind; 3) the nature of woman abuse; 4) the community in which she lived at the time; and 5) her physical health. These factors should be explored before the story of Margaret can be told and understood from a human and forensic perspective.

### *The South African Social and Legal system*

Most of the cultural groups in South Africa historically have a patriarchal system in which the males are dominant and females should adhere to their wishes. Over the years this has changed, especially with the new constitution promulgated in the mid-nineties in South Africa where discrimination on the grounds of culture, race, gender, religion etc. was abolished. Margaret as a child grew up in the patriarchal system where women should be obedient to men regardless—so did her husband.

The legal system in South Africa is a system in which there is only the judge to make the legal decisions after the case has been heard, and no jury. At the time female judges were in the far minority. The appeal court also consists of three judges who hear the appeal.

### *The Nature of the Unconscious Mind*

The true nature of the unconscious mind was first investigated by an Austrian neurologist, born Sigismund Schlomo Freud but better known as Sigmund Freud. He was the first to realise the true power of the unconscious mind, as a psychoanalyst, and write of his theory. The dichotomy between the conscious and unconscious mind and how the unconscious mind can overrule the conscious mind is better understood today by professionals but still underestimated in the forensic arena. Modern neuroscience, however, is giving credence to how the human brain can override rational, conscious thought with more instinctual behaviour.

While there are many theories offered to explain human behaviour including more mechanical learning theories, I have found psychoanalytic theory to play an important role in criminal behaviour—and the following is such an example. In forensic cases hypnoanalysis as a diagnostic tool is sometimes utilised to access personalities in which the host personality (in cases of Dissociative Identity Disorder) vehemently denies being a killer (and is in fact not a killer) while one of the personalities may in fact be a serial killer. A case in question was the *State versus Edwards* in which the host personality was a kind and amiable person while one of his personalities was a psychopathic serial killer. The literature on Dissociative Identity Disorder clearly indicates trauma in childhood as one of the primary reasons for splintering of the personality and thus behaviour that is not part of the host personality. The psychoanalytic approach is also often used in conjunction with hypnoanalysis for diagnostic purposes, cognitive and behavioural approaches, and neuropsychological approaches based on neuroscience where applicable.

### *The Nature of Women Abuse*

Although women abuse is a well-known phenomenon and recognised since the early 1980s by behavioural scientists, the true nature of women abuse is still complex. The abused woman often will try and keep the abuse secret or protect the abuser and she often does not seek legal protection even if she has knowledge about the process.

### *The Community in which Margaret Lived*

In the early 2000s Margaret lived in a rural community in South Africa with staunch moral and religious values. Part of the religious value was that divorce was not acceptable (something that has become more acceptable with time), that the male is the head of the household, and the wife/woman should be respectful of this and one should not gossip about one's partner, even if what is said is the truth.

Typically of these communities in South Africa, secrets are not well kept and people know much more about each other than in the big cities. The community members however often have the perception that their secrets are safe. Margaret was a member of the South African Police Service and as such was well respected in her community at the time, but also expected to be an example to others.

### *Margaret's Physical Health*

Margaret had a high anxiety level and being an abused woman also experienced a lot of stress which led to two major health problems 1) she developed an ulcer of the stomach and had surgical intervention and 2) she then suffered from a 'Dumping Syndrome' due to the digestive problems. The syndrome describes the dumping of food directly into the small intestines too quickly which can cause symptoms like hyperglycemia (high blood sugar from the sugar in the food), nausea, rapid heartbeat, sweating, and light-headedness.

### *The Fairytale Part of Life*

Margaret grew up in the apartheid era in which, although she is white, she was still dominated by the males in the family and her male siblings, especially as it was a farming community. She however described her relationship with her parents to me as very good. The children were cherished by their parents and experienced a lot of fun and laughter in the home. Her father was a farmer and friends of the children were invited to visit the farm during holidays and weekends. Both parents were very protective of their children but female siblings had to be obedient. As a child growing up on a farm in the apartheid era she also witnessed some measure of suppression of the black farm workers.

Margaret had uneventful school years, but she was not very academically inclined so did not go to college or university after school but worked at a few companies until she joined the South African Police Service. While unmarried she stayed at home and enjoyed the company of her parents and siblings. At this stage, her life held a lot of promises and dreams.

## *The Fairytale Turns into a Horror Story*

Margaret met her husband (whom she later killed) while working for one of the companies before joining the South African Police Service. At that stage he was still married to someone else and had a son. He then got divorced from his wife and while his son stayed with his ex-wife, he started dating Margaret.

The marriage was celebrated in the whole town because it was a double wedding—Margaret's sister also got married on the same day, so they had a double wedding.

Margaret and her new husband started a family and shortly after the birth of their first child, the fairy tale ended. Her husband became addicted to gambling and the family experienced serious financial problems—to such an extent that their church had to provide food for them at times. This released a demon in her husband and he started physically and emotionally abusing her and their children. He was thus a 'family-only batterer', the most common form of batterer, making up about half of the group.

Tales of some of the abuse are the following: Once her husband tried to burn the house down with Margaret and the children in the house to get the insurance money; he frequently shoved her around and used vile language towards her; he would drink heavily and then hit her and the children (she taking the brunt of the abuse); in a violent rage he once threw a knife at her missing her by inches, in another incident he burnt all her clothes after hitting her with his fists. He would chase her and the children out of the house and lock the house and force her to wander the streets (she was too ashamed to ask help from friends and by that time both her parents were deceased). He also forced her to only speak when he gave her permission to do so. He often smashed the tables, chairs, and doors in the house in a drunken rage. He would also sit and drink with his son from his previous marriage and then abuse Margaret in front of his son. Her husband also forced Margaret to take out a loan of a considerable amount of money so that he could gamble and also to give him her engagement ring so that he could pawn it to get money to gamble.

Margaret's housekeeper in court testified how the husband would frequently abuse alcohol and then physically and emotionally abuse his wife, how he would grab his wife by her hair and drag her through the house, how he would knock her head against the wall and how Margaret would sometimes be locked out of their home.

### *The Efforts Made by Margaret to Escape the Horror*

While she was out on parole and I was evaluating her in my office, I asked Margaret if she had made any efforts to escape the abuse as I knew that the judge would find this an important fact to extrapolate on during the trial (to establish in his own mind why she simply did not take other steps, except homicide, to avoid the situation). My experience is that within the legal system in South Africa at that time there was not much insight into spouse abuse and its complexities.

The first time she decided to tell her husband that she wanted to divorce him was when he tried to burn the house down with her and the children inside, and she meekly promised to stay. As a member of the South African Police Service, she was aware that the most dangerous time for battered spouses was when they threatened or tried to leave the relationship.

She got the assistance of a social worker to arrange a sub-economic house for her and the children to leave her husband, but later returned to her husband because she and the children were living in poor circumstances but were too ashamed to confess this to anyone.

She often asked for guidance from the minister of her church and he would come to their home but simply pray and told her that she should trust that things would improve. She again moved into a flat without the children but then relented again and moved back home. The horror however was just escalating over time—to such an extent that she was almost daily abused and belittled by her husband.

In court, her medical practitioner testified that Margaret often told him how her husband would physically and emotionally abuse her, but she refused to give him permission to talk to her husband or to contact people who could safeguard her against her husband. In South Africa such reports are mandatory by health care providers if children are being abused but not adults.

### *Margaret's Unconscious Mind Decides to Take Revenge?*

In South African Criminal Procedures Act 51 and amended over time there is a defence of automatism (which is a non-pathological defence) that can be put forward in which the person is incapable of appreciating the wrongfulness of his or her act or is incapable of acting in accordance with an appreciation of the wrongfulness of the act. So the question that the forensic psychologist must be able to answer for the judge is the probability of the above ... or was her behaviour just a rational self-defence reflex or a cold blooded killing?

Margaret, as a member of the South African Police Service and having at least an average IQ (IQ = 100), would know that there is no reason to shoot someone when there are other people in the room (including other males) because self-defence cannot be a viable defence. She also did not have her pistol on her person but first fetched it from the room. So, as a psychologist doing forensic work, certain hypotheses had to be tested and investigated. A neuro-cognitive approach during the evaluation was utilised at first to determine 1) her memory and probable amnesia due to trauma memory; 2) if she was malingering; 3) if the abuse over years left neurocognitive sequelae; and 4) if there was an unconscious process that occurred which was not simply a self-defence reflex.

Freud's adapted theory on the death instinct as the cause of aggression indicates that negative energy is directed towards others to prevent self-destruction. This can be physically or emotionally. Aggressive behaviour cannot however be explained by one theory alone but by dissecting biological factors, frustration, and social influences. Aggression is an output that can be caused by intrinsic variables or external input. Different alternatives were considered by me and I chose the diagnostic style of looking towards the psychoanalytic theory, as the answers could not be found in the other theories. Margaret was not taught aggressive behaviour as a child, although she was frustrated by the advice of the minister this had happened before; the biological factors were the same as before; her personality was analysed and she did not have serious personality pathology or neuropsychological problems that would have caused the outburst of aggression.

I can only describe Margaret's behaviour as follows: Margaret's unconscious mind tried to assist her first by allowing physical symptoms to develop, informing people that she was under duress, as she was reluctant to communicate this to non-professionals. The physical problems were attended to but the origin of the problem was not addressed by the health care workers.

Her unconscious mind with her conscious mind then tried to assist her by giving her some support to leave the home a few times, but her ego strength was too poor to let her sustain this and she went back to her abuser rather than crying out for help and telling people what was really happening. As Margaret became more and more subservient to her abusive husband and was progressively more subjected to severe abuse, her unconscious mind developed a rage and plotted revenge.

### *The Events of the Day that Margaret Killed her Husband*

Margaret's stepson visited the home early in the day but they were told that they were not allowed to speak as her husband was watching the television and busy planning his gambling moves on the computer.

Margaret and her stepson then went to play pool at the nearby sports bar. There she had a tot of whiskey and some beer through a period of a few hours. They then returned home and found her husband in a foul mood.

He sent his son to buy more alcohol and Margaret served some food (the first food she had for the entire day and it was late afternoon by this time). After consuming the alcohol her husband wanted to use her car to drive to a casino. She refused and he then wanted to take her official car (police car) which she also refused because of the negative implications of this for her at work. She then phoned her minister to come and sooth her husband but he became even more enraged and started threatening her. The minister came but only prayed again and left, but after he left the house, her husband was in such a rage that he attacked her with his fists and kept on yelling at her that he would pulverize her face. This he did in front of her stepson and friends sitting in the sitting room.

### *The Unconscious Mind Takes Control*

Margaret then had the intention of going to her room, fetching her pyjamas and pillow and leaving the house to travel to the home of her sister and seek shelter. Her unconscious mind however had had enough and put the process in place for her to develop a Dissociative Fugue State. A Dissociative Fugue State was earlier also known as a Psychogenic Fugue. It is characterized by reversible amnesia for a period (lasting minutes or hours or days) which is caused by extreme stress or trauma. The amnesia is even for personality identity and for overt behaviour and in legal terms is often referred to as Automatism or Automatic Behaviour.

### *The Behaviour of Margaret while in a Dissociative Fugue State*

Facts that became apparent during the court case when reconstructing the few minutes before the death of the husband are the following: Margaret went to the main bedroom in the house but instead of fetching her pyjamas and pillow and leaving the house (which was her conscious intension) she simply, in a Dissociative Fugue State, went to the safe in the main bedroom, removed her service firearm—a Vector Z-88 9mm semi-automatic service pistol (which according to South African law she had to keep in the safe while not on duty), walked back to the sitting room and shot her husband point blank in front of the other people in the sitting room without displaying any emotion or saying anything. She then dropped the pistol and went to place herself in one of the chairs in the sitting room and looked withdrawn but did not react to the pandemonium that had broken loose around her.

After a while, she was observed to almost 'wake up' as one of the witnesses testified. She then looked around and started asking everyone why her husband was lying on the ground and was full of blood (apparently displaying amnesia for the period of the fugue state). She also wanted to know what the weapon (pistol) was doing on the floor not realizing that it was in fact her own service weapon.

### *The Aftermaths of the Killing Spree*

When realizing the facts of the matter, Margaret called her Commanding Officer, her medical practitioner and her minister, summoning them to her home.

Her medical practitioner stated that he saw that Margaret was in a dazed and confused state when he arrived at her home. He gave her an injection, and recommended that her sister take her to the hospital for observation as soon as the police allowed her to leave the house.

Her Commanding Officer testified that when he arrived at Margaret's home, he saw signs of physical abuse on Margaret (bruising on her face, arms and shoulders), he noticed a lot of empty beer cans in the room, and he noticed that Margaret seemed to be in extreme shock.

A friend who was present in the sitting room where the shooting took place testified that just before the shooting and just after it, it was as if Margaret did not even recognize her when looking at her.

A charge of homicide (murder) was then levelled against Margaret by the investigating officer of the South African Police Service and she was given bail in order for the case to be heard in the High Court in Pretoria.

It also became known that Margaret was a very good shot with a pistol and participated in events where the police competed in shooting competitions with elite sportsmen in target shooting.

### *The South African Law and Criminal Procedures*

The Criminal Procedure Act 51 of 1977 as amended by the Criminal Procedure Amendment Act 76 of 1997, the Criminal Procedure Second Amendment Act 85 of 1997, the Criminal Procedure Amendment Act 17 of 2001, and also the Criminal Procedure Second Amendment Act 62 of 2001 deal with the accused's capacity to understand proceedings (mental illness in relation to fitness or competence to stand trial and criminal responsibility).

If a South African Court at any stage of the criminal proceedings comes to the conclusion that the accused by reason of mental illness or mental defect may not be capable of understanding the proceedings, the court should refer the accused for observation and for a report of the findings of two persons under Section 8 (c) of Act 42 of 2001 (a psychiatrist or clinical psychologist). Margaret was not referred for observation as she was deemed to be able to understand and participate in the criminal proceedings and therefore fit to stand trial.

At the same time however the Criminal Procedure Act determines that a person who commits an act or makes an omission which constitutes an offence and who at the time of such commission or omission suffers from a mental illness or mental defect which makes him or her incapable of (a) appreciating the wrongfulness of his or her act or omission; or (b) of acting in accordance with an appreciation of the wrongfulness of his or her act or omission, shall not be criminally responsible for such act or omission. This is similar to many other common-law countries as it stems from the McNaughton rules from 1843 in England.

### *Court Procedure and Finding of the Judge of the High Court*

During the court procedure, I was the expert witness of the defence but the judge acknowledged that the perspectives given in my report were important in his view—not only with regard to Margaret's mental profile, but also regarding the information of her abuse, as the judge was able to confirm this from witnesses that testified in court. The judge however found the principle of a Dissociative Fugue State difficult to comprehend in view of the fact that it was found in my report that Margaret did not suffer from any serious personality disorder or mental illness and could stand trial. I testified that Margaret had experienced a Dissociate Fugue State during which she behaved in an automatic way without realising the consequences of her actions or having any memory of her actions after the fact. I testified that the Dissociative Fugue State was a result of years of abuse and suppression of anger and retaliation and absolute degradation regarding the person of Margaret.

The judge in the case of Margaret made the following finding: 1) that the state did not prove above reasonable doubt that it was homicide; 2) that Margaret was an abused woman and 3) that Margaret was negligent and should have foreseen the death of her husband due to her actions. The judge sentenced her to six years imprisonment but the sentence was suspended for three years.

### *Psychiatric, Physical, and Psychological Factors*

During the forensic evaluation I found the following factors contributed to Margaret developing a Dissociate Fugue State: 1) the fact that she suffered from Major Depression and felt helpless and extremely anxious when her husband physically and emotionally abused her; 2) That she had strong traits of a Dependent and Avoidant Personality Disorder thus experiencing difficulty in coping with conflict and to assert herself; 3) that she was found to be excessively sensitive and over-responsive to people; 4) that she felt threatened by the aggression directed towards her; 5) that she had tendencies to dissociate when in very difficult situations; and 6) her suffering from a 'Dumping Syndrome' expedited the Dissociate Fugue State due to the symptoms related to this syndrome.

### *Comments Regarding the Findings and Judgement of the Judge*

The following factors were against the finding of the judge that Margaret was negligent and could have foreseen the death of her husband due to her actions: 1) that during a Dissociative Fugue State the person does not have insight into her behaviour; 2) her levels of hopelessness and anxiety were high but she was found to be extremely conforming to the rules of society and tended to rather react to stress by directing the anger towards herself (developing physical symptoms) and not towards others; 3) that regardless of all her husband had done to her she had never in twenty-five years of being physically and emotionally abused by her husband, retaliated against her husband; and that 4) she was described by all as being a very responsible and trustworthy person.

### *Summary*

In my analysis this case is a classical case of the unconscious mind of a person taking control and causing the individual to act in an aggressive manner during a Dissociative Fugue State. The dissociation could have been expedited by the biological factors (such as the effects of drinking, not eating, suffering from the Dumping Syndrome etc.). This case has been a precedent to many other forensic cases in which aggression resulted while the person was in a Dissociative Fugue State, which I found different from cases I had done of a fugue state after an epileptic seizure or malingering automatisms.

Margaret Gouws, as a member of the South African Police, consciously knew the consequences of killing someone in front of witnesses, she had tolerated twenty-five years of physical and mental abuse without retaliation, she was an excellent shot and participated in shooting competitions so knew firearms well, she did not have an Antisocial Personality Disorder or Borderline Personality Disorder but conformed explicitly to rules of society, and did not like conflict.

In my experience the concept of a Dissociative Fugue State still causes difficulties in a forensic setting because: 1) legal personnel still find it difficult to understand the concept and to not view it as malingering or the accused falsely pleading amnesia in order to be found not guilty, and 2) it is made more difficult because of the apparent 'normal' appearance of the person as viewed by lay people while the person is in a dissociative fugue state.

This case has taught me to over the years make video recordings of a diagnostic hypnoanalysis session with the accused, with his/her permission, in order to demonstrate to the court the complexity of the dynamics of the Dissociate Fugue State or Dissociative Identity Disorder and during these sessions to ensure that the Orne safeguards are in place and no suggestions except necessary for the induction are given so that no leading questions can be surmised. During the evaluation I also use psychometric tests and the SCID interview to determine if the accused has any dissociative characteristics and to what extent.

The case has been used as one of the precedents for behaviour of battered women and legal opinion in such cases in South Africa. I was also invited by the State of Botswana (a border country of South Africa) and later by the defence to act as forensic psychologist in a fairly well-known case a few years ago where the accused was executed by hanging. At that time the death sentence was abolished in South Africa but still in place in Botswana. In this case there was some question of a Dissociate Fugue State or simply homicide but the accused was not an abused partner. So the possibility of a Dissociative Fugue State was considered from a legal perspective.

My opinion is that legal personnel in South Africa need to be trained in basic principles of psychological and psychiatric factors that may play a role in violent behaviour, the same as psychologists and psychiatrists are trained in basic legal issues.

***Stephen Porter** PhD is a Professor of Psychology at University of British Columbia, Okanagan and the Director of Centre for the Advancement of Psychological Science and Law (CAPSL). Prior to becoming an academic, he worked as a psychologist in a federal prison and at a forensic psychiatric hospital. He has published numerous scholarly articles on legal decision-making, lie detection, violent behaviour, psychopathic predators, and memory for crime. He has been consulted by police and prosecutors in serious crime investigations and provides training internationally in the areas of deception detection, interviewing, and psychopathy to law enforcement, mental health professionals, lawyers, and judges. He has been qualified as an expert witness in various Canadian courts. Recent awards include UBCO's Researcher of the Year (2013), UBCO's Educator of the Year (2015), and the Canadian Psychological Association Award for Distinguished Contributions to Education and Training in Psychology (2015).*

***Tianna Dilley** is a research assistant within the Porter Forensic Laboratory, researching secondary psychopathy, emotional facial expressions, false memories, and malingering. Currently, she is completing her honours thesis focusing on novel methods of detecting deception in high-stakes liars. Her research interests include psychopathy, deception detection, interrogation techniques, eyewitness memory, and criminal behaviour.*

# Dr. Stephen Porter and Tianna Dilley

## The Tina Eisnor Murder Case
## Treachery, Amnesia, and Dubious Retribution

In my entire career as a prison and forensic psychologist, never have I become involved in a case as compelling as that of the Tina Eisnor murder case.[1] With such a mosaic of legal, psychological, and philosophical issues, the Eisnor case stands alone in the annals of Canadian crime. My involvement in the matter was as an expert witness who testified about the defendant, Tina's estranged husband Wayne Eisnor, to the judge and jury in a packed courtroom where emotions were running high.[2]

### *June 30th, 2010 in New Germany: A Shattered Peace*

For the customers and employees of the Freshmart grocery store in New Germany, Nova Scotia, June 30th, 2010 seemed to be an ordinary summer day. However, the tranquility turned to horror when Wayne Eisnor confronted his estranged wife Tina at her vehicle in the Freshmart parking lot. Foreshadowing this encounter, Wayne had recorded his thoughts on sheets of paper later found at his home, musing at one point, "I told Tina that years ago if she ever done this to me she will not live."[3] After they privately conversed for several minutes in the parking lot, Wayne returned to his vehicle, retrieved a .22 revolver, and proceeded to shoot Tina twice in the head as she backed up in her vehicle. After fatally shooting his wife, Eisnor pointed the gun at his own temple and fired. As he lay on the ground critically injured, he was swiftly apprehended by the police and then escorted to hospital in Halifax where he remained in and out of consciousness for some weeks. Despite substantial injuries to the right hemisphere of his brain, Eisnor eventually regained consciousness but appeared to be disoriented, frequently asking to see Tina.

### *A Community in Disbelief and the Search for Justice*

Over the next few months at the East Coast Forensic Hospital in Dartmouth, Eisnor began to recuperate physically and regain his cognitive functioning. However, throughout his recovery he maintained that he had no memory whatsoever of killing Tina and was experiencing amnesia for several months preceding the shooting.[4] Eisnor insisted that he could not recall Tina ending their relationship nor any other motive he may have had for wanting her dead. He claimed that when he awoke in hospital, he believed that he had been in a car accident. These claims persisted for the three years leading up to his first-degree murder trial, during which Eisnor not only expressed an inability to recall Tina's shooting, but also denied being the perpetrator, testifying, "I did not shoot my wife" in response to a question from his defence counsel.[5] No doubt, this incredible claim and lack of contrition did little to boost sympathy for Eisnor in the minds of the jurors or judge. In fact, as soon as it became public knowledge, Eisnor's assertion of "I don't remember" was met with considerable scorn from the community. Even his own children Ashley Eisnor and Devan Illingworth expressed skepticism, and ultimately cut off contact with him.[6] Although Eisnor had long been disliked in his little town, he was now a much-hated man throughout the entire province.

The nature of the homicide and Eisnor's ensuing amnesia presented profound legal and psychological questions and made for a case publicly referred to by his defence counsel Roger Burrill as "very sad," but also "interesting" and "compelling."[7] Given that nobody would ever know the nature of the discussion between Wayne and Tina prior to he shooting, how could a level of culpability be determined? Was Eisnor guilty of first-degree murder, second-degree murder, or manslaughter? Or, should he even be tried in court for Tina's murder at all? If he could not remember anything about the shooting or recall any reasonable motive, how could he possibly defend himself in a meaningful way? Further, the nature of his brain damage seemed to have rendered Eisnor a changed man in terms of his cognitive functioning and even aspects of his basic character. This posed a broader question of whether we as a society should convict and punish someone who is a fundamentally different 'person' from the one who committed a crime, regardless of how horrific.

Could Wayne Eisnor defend himself against a charge of murder? The violent death of Tina Eisnor was no murder mystery. As Constable Terry Vinnedge would testify, the investigation was straightforward: "It wasn't a whodunit."[8] I became involved at the invitation of Eisnor's defence counsel, not to deal with the culpability of Tina's estranged husband, but rather to determine whether his claims were truthful. Did he really have no memory of the shooting (the *actus reus* component of a crime) or his motive (the *mens rea* component of a crime)? The Crown would contend that Eisnor's motive had been smoldering for weeks after Tina left him and became romantically involved with Peter Hirtle. If Eisnor could not remember such events, as his defence counsel would assert, perhaps the case was not as open-and-shut as it might appear. While I was consulted in the case to focus squarely on Wayne Eisnor's credibility, the defence counsel hoped to use my findings to speak to the fundamental issue of whether Eisnor should be put to trial at all.

*The Criminal Code of Canada* requires that a defendant meet specific criteria in order for the courts to be satisfied that he or she has the mental capacity to be sent to trial. If an individual does not meet these criteria, he or she will be found unfit to stand trial, meaning that he or she "is unable, on account of mental disorder, to conduct a defence at any stage of the proceedings before a verdict is rendered or to instruct counsel to do so."[9] Specifically, the mental disorder must render the defendant unable to "understand the nature or object of the proceedings, understand the possible consequences of the proceedings, or communicate with counsel."[10] In this case, if Wayne Eisnor did not meet any of these three criteria, he should not be considered fit to stand trial. Of particular concern was whether a defendant such as Eisnor, who claims to be unable to recall the *actus reus* or *mens rea*, can effectively communicate with counsel and meaningfully defend him or herself in court.

While Eisnor was recovering in the hospital, an initial neuropsychological report indicated that he should be found unfit to stand trial due to his high degree of cognitive impairment resulting from the traumatic brain injury. According to the assessment, Eisnor was unfit to stand trial because he was unable to retain memories over extended periods of time, implying that during a trial he would be unable to process or remember the charges, the evidence, or the details of the proceedings. As time went on, Eisnor's mental state gradually improved, and he regained the ability to form new memories that he could later recall. Because of his cognitive rehabilitation, Eisnor would now be able to remember ongoing details of a court trial and could be deemed fit to stand trial. However, in light of Eisnor's claim of profound retrograde amnesia, his defence counsel chose to argue aggressively that he could not defend himself and should be found unfit to stand trial. This was a high-risk legal strategy; never in Canada had a defendant been deemed unfit solely because of amnesia of the crime. Further, the Canadian court system relies on the rule of *stare decisis*, the doctrine specifying that legal decision-makers must rely on the findings of previous cases. But the overall details of the amnesia claim in this case, a first in Canada and perhaps any other jurisdiction, were so unusual that the counsel's argument appeared to hold considerable merit and, if successful, would represent a major legal milestone.

According to the original philosophy of fitness to stand trial,[11] a defendant's ability to remember and relate the incident under investigation should be a basic consideration in determining fitness.[12] An accused who cannot recall the offense may be unable to meaningfully assist in his or her own defence and, therefore, should not be considered fit.[13] In practice, however, amnesia has carried little weight in fitness determinations. In the 1968 case *Wilson v. United States*,[14] the judge concluded that although amnesia may be related to fitness, it is not necessarily a sufficient factor alone to negate an accused's fitness. This judge recommended that each report of amnesia should be evaluated on its own merits and its relation to fitness in any particular case. In *Morrow v. Maryland* (1982),[15] it was concluded that amnesia is relevant to fitness when the loss of memory would "obscure the search for truth" at trial. The reality, however, is that North American courts have a clear status quo to disregard amnesia claims, which we suspect may have less to do with their perceived lack of relevance to fitness than with a concern over the potential for malingering.[16] The Canadian judiciary has concluded that "—while the inability of a person to recall or testify about the immediate events surrounding a crime may be a factor to be weighed in determining whether the Crown has met its onus of establishing guilt beyond a reasonable doubt, amnesia has never been considered, by itself, to be a basis for declaring the accused unfit for trial or for relief from prosecution or conviction."[17] Although we think as psychologists rather than lawyers, we must agree with the contention of Eisnor's defence counsel that the details of his case might fundamentally challenge this legal canon. That is, if Eisnor's amnesia was genuine and he could not recall either his *mens rea* or *actus reus* components of the violent incident, it seems intuitive, even logical, that he could not defend himself in a meaningful way.

Some details of an earlier Ontario case, *R. v. Morrissey* (2003),[18] bore similarities to Eisnor's. After fatally shooting his ex-girlfriend Melissa Pajkowski, Peter Morrissey shot himself in the head with the same weapon. As a result of his attempted suicide, like Eisnor, Morrissey experienced extensive brain injury and had amnesia for the shootings. The defendant's counsel argued—unsuccessfully—that his amnesia rendered him unable to meaningfully defend himself and therefore he was unfit to stand trial. Although similar, a key difference between the amnesia phenomena claimed by both Morrissey and Eisnor was that Morrissey's memory loss was estimated to extend only to about forty-five minutes before the time of the shootings. Morrissey would have had the capacity to recall the victim ending their relationship weeks before, abducting her at gunpoint, and forcing her into a vehicle before the killing. Thus, Morrissey remembered his motive for killing Ms. Pajkowski. In contrast, Eisnor's claimed amnesia encompassed the entire period of the gestation of his *mens rea*.

### *Lying to Unearth the Truth: The Theatre of Forensic Psychology*

If Mr. Burrill's argument concerning amnesia and fitness were to proceed successfully, it would be necessary to convince the court that Eisnor's amnesia was genuine and not faked, as many believed it to be. Neuropsychologist Dr. Jeannette McGlone already had provided her opinion that Eisnor's brain injury and testing results were consistent with amnesia for up to several months before he sustained his injury. However, the inferences of neuropsychologists regarding the validity of amnesia symptoms are based mainly on patterns of patient brain damage. As professionals, they are not particularly well positioned to ascertain whether self-reported amnesia is genuine, especially in legal contexts where patients may be motivated to exaggerate or fake memory loss. Because of my specialized forensic background in both lie detection and memory for violent crime, Mr. Burrill contacted me and requested that I travel to Nova Scotia to conduct a forensic psychological assessment on his client. The main question: was Wayne Eisnor's amnesia genuine or was he lying through his teeth? To ensure the integrity of the findings, I provided no information to Eisnor's counsel, or Eisnor himself, that would have revealed any of the strategies, lines of questioning, or psychological tools that I would be using during our meeting. Throughout my communications with Mr. Burrill, he gave the impression of a lawyer of the highest integrity who agreed with this unbiased approach and genuinely wanted me to help establish the truth of Eisnor's credibility.

While I had much previous experience in assessing the sincerity of complainants, defendants, and prison inmates alike, I viewed my evaluation of Eisnor as extraordinary in terms of the confidence level I needed to achieve in determining the truth: I strived to be as close to a hundred per cent confident as possible. As such, I devised a virtual lie detection arsenal—with some well-established strategies in forensic psychology and others completely novel—that in my mind would be impossible for Eisnor to 'beat'. When assessing potential malingering, psychologists must go beyond simply asking the person whether he or she is being honest or relying on our gut instinct to decide (although incredibly I have seen such tactics used in some psychological reports); rather, we must use some level of deception ourselves in terms of what we disclose and do not disclose to the subject. As such, while psychologists must strive to maximize 'informed consent' with any client, this was a unique psychologist-client situation in which my deception had the potential to benefit both Eisnor and the triers of fact. In this case, I decided I had to use a greater magnitude of deception than I had with any other subject or client to date. With all due respect to Wayne Eisnor, his limited education and low-normal level of cognitive functioning made him an ideal subject for this approach. As I testified to the judge and jury, even a highly intelligent, sophisticated liar would be extremely susceptible to this type of unusually multifaceted assessment, and as a consequence, likely to reveal his or her deception.

To evaluate whether Eisnor was lying, I reviewed the entirety of his file, administered several psychological tests, and interviewed him using a variety of tactics over several hours. These tactics included novel lines of questioning which would have been unanticipated and highly diagnostic of deception, depending on his responses. Our interview contained a great deal of theatre, on my part at least. As I would testify to the judge and jury, Wayne Eisnor presented as a meek, polite, amiable individual, far from what one might expect in a wife killer and unlike the aggressive man described by his adult children and others who knew him before the shooting. After building rapport with Eisnor, I intentionally began to manipulate my tone of voice, facial expressions, and body language, often to communicate incredulity in relation to his account, and did so throughout the interview. On numerous occasions, I played cop as much as psychologist, ostensibly becoming exasperated with Eisnor, or telling him, sometimes using expletives, that aspects of his claim made no sense from a scientific point of view. In response to several of my challenges, Eisnor appeared to weep and said things like "then why don't I remember" or "please, please help me remember."

### *Putting Eisnor's Credibility to the Test*

As I would relate to the judge and jury, my psychological test battery included tests that have built-in 'lie-detection' scales. These are intended to reveal whether a patient is responding in a way that he or she believes a patient with genuine symptoms would answer rather than the way someone who is truly experiencing symptoms actually presents. For example, someone who is faking psychosis might agree that "I sometimes fly to the moon and eat peanut butter banana sandwiches with Elvis," when we know that even floridly psychotic patients rarely, if ever, would believe or say so. When a patient is faking memory loss, he or she may do poorly on a test of memory that appears to be quite difficult but actually is quite easy, even for patients suffering from dementia. With Eisnor, I used several such tests that focussed on whether he was intentionally faking memory impairment and/or generally trying to present himself in a particular way to seem credible. I introduced these memory tests by falsely telling him that most people who have real amnesia for shooting another person do poorly on such tests (untrue) but to please try his best. On a number of occasions, I misinformed Eisnor about his testing results, stating things like, "your results make no sense for someone experiencing amnesia for killing your wife." He always responded to such challenges with confusion and apology. The bottom line: his responses and the results of these tests consistently indicated that Eisnor was not attempting to fake or exaggerate his memory loss, or respond in a way to make himself look more credible.

One possibility was that Wayne Eisnor was a villainous character who would lie and manipulate others or the system to get himself out of any situation. Thus, as I testified to the judge and jury, I examined whether Eisnor had personality features that are associated with a high likelihood of lying in this legal context. In evaluating the truthfulness of a defendant's amnesia claim, a forensic psychologist must be especially concerned about the presence of Antisocial Personality Disorder (ASPD) or psychopathy. Psychopathic individuals are manipulative, callous, remorseless, impulsive, and irresponsible. Quite simply, they have a diminished or sheer lack of conscience. In addition to their penchant for aggression and violence, psychopaths are chronic deceivers, often lying for instrumental reasons such as to escape punishment but also engage in pathological lying or duping delight. While most readers will be aware of notorious Canadian psychopaths Clifford Olson and Paul Bernardo, most are undiagnosed. It is estimated that one per cent of the Canadian population (about 360,000 people) possess psychopathic traits. With Eisnor, I concluded that there was no evidence for ASPD and that he scored low on psychopathy. Interestingly, I estimated that his psychopathy score was considerably lower after his brain injury than it likely had been before the shootings. This is unusual because psychopathic traits, and personality traits in general, are highly reliable over the human lifespan.

Throughout the assessment interview, Eisnor struck me as a mild-mannered, polite individual who had low self-esteem relative to the general population and other inmates. When he was unable to remember the shootings or events within his amnesia period, Eisnor appeared distressed, apologetic, and confused about his lack of memory. He often held his head in his hands and questioned why he could not remember the shootings despite his substantial efforts. In my opinion, both Eisnor's test results and his observable behaviours and demeanour were consistent with an individual who is behaving with sincerity. Eisnor's submissive and timid personality was in stark contrast to the dominant, hostile, aggressive character described by people who knew him prior to his brain injury.

### Days in the Life

Another way of assessing whether Eisnor was telling the truth was to look at his self-reported pattern of autobiographical memories. I asked him about events throughout his life, including the events within the claimed amnesia period. Similar to the rationale for the psychological tests we described earlier, people who fake amnesia may report poorer memory for their life events in general. To examine whether Eisnor's memories before the reported amnesia period were worse than expected, I asked him about his memories for various periods spanning his entire life. In planning this approach, I had familiarized myself with Eisnor's personal history ranging from his childhood upbringing to the day of the murder. When prompted to recall his past, Eisnor showed an increasing chronological progression of remembering, similar to the expected memory recall of the average adult. He was able to remember specific events, such as his wedding, and provided several details about these occasions. To determine the validity of his amnesia symptoms, I subsequently examined Eisnor's personal recollections of events occurring during the amnesia period in question. Congruent with previous reports, he had no memory of the shooting nor some months prior. In fact, during his hospital stay, Eisnor read a news article that reported on a local shooting; he recalled pondering who would be involved in such an event, until he read his own name. He also could not remember his son's birthday, which occurred earlier in June, or his marital separation that happened a couple of months before the shootings.

Although Eisnor claimed he could not recall his personal memories for several months before the shootings, to know for certain, I had to challenge his memory further. How would he respond if asked to recall nonexistent, 'fake' events? My strategy was to ask a series of questions to which I already had the answers. I asked Eisnor about numerous real events known to have occurred in his life in the six months leading up to the shooting. Interspersed with these were a similar number of plausible false events that I had made up, but deceptively presented as true ("So ------ happened. What do you remember about that?"). Most of the questions I asked had an emotional component as I was interested in gauging his emotional reactions to provocative truths and fictions. If he responded with emotional arousal to the true events or a staunch denial to the false events, it would bring into question his amnesia claim. However, this did not happen. Eisnor seemed no more or less affected by the deceptive details than the true factual ones, responding that he simply could not remember any of the events. While I was satisfied that Eisnor was unable to remember personal events, I needed more evidence so I considered his recollection of public events.

### *Eisnor's Memory for Media*

Another completely novel strategy I devised for this case involved asking Eisnor unanticipated questions about high-profile media events. Knowing that Eisnor was an avid news follower, I examined his memory for thirteen randomly presented news stories occurring in the time (weeks, months, years) before, within, and after his alleged amnesia period. To do so, I Googled BBC, Time, CNN, and CBC News 'top news stories' for the corresponding time periods. With this exercise, faking amnesia would be extremely difficult because it is unlikely that someone would be able to comprehend my strategy, recall when each of the events had actually occurred, and then respond in a way that would be consistent with a period of true retrograde amnesia. As I testified to the judge and jury, the results showed that Eisnor was unable to recall any news stories within his claimed amnesia period, but immediately and clearly recalled half of the media events outside of his alleged amnesia period. Notably, he experienced poorer memory for the media events in the time after the shootings, likely as a result of his brain injury. Nonetheless, his pattern of responding was consistent with genuine amnesia for up to six months before the shootings.

Would Eisnor change his story when faced with false symptom suggestions? False symptom suggestion is a strategy with which the examiner provides false symptom information about a mental disorder, in this case amnesia, to the potential liar. The adoption of the suggested symptoms into the subject's presentation would be highly diagnostic of deceptive behaviour. As I later testified in court, I told Eisnor several details about amnesia that were untrue, and indicated that his amnesia story was highly unusual. For example, I told him things such as, "My own research clearly shows that people who have amnesia for killing another person almost always remember smells like gunpowder or blood or sounds associated with the incident when they can't see anything in their memory…and I've studied hundreds of such people with the same kind of brain damage as you, Wayne." I challenged the way in which he described his amnesia as being contradicted by scientific findings, and falsely informed him of the way his amnesia symptoms should really *look* if they were genuine. If he was lying, he might take the bait and change his clinical presentation.[19] However, Eisnor's symptom presentation did not change despite my suggestions; he merely became distressed and expressed that he had no idea why his amnesia was the way it was. Complementing this approach, my last line of deceptive questioning tested the possibility that Mr. Eisnor was faking amnesia because he thought that it would increase his likelihood of being placed in a hospital versus a prison, or being set free. As such, as I testified later, near the end of the interview I misinformed him that if found unfit to stand trial, he would likely spend thirty years or more in a hospital and then go to trial, likely resulting in him spending the rest of his life in prison. Although he appeared saddened by either outcome, his verbal response was "oh, okay" and he indicated that he would be "fine" and "okay" with either a hospital or penitentiary. Again, Eisnor's response patterns suggested that he was not attempting to mislead me.

Wayne Eisnor was telling the truth about his amnesia.

### *Expert Testimony and Jury's Verdict*

In August 2013, the widely respected Justice Glenn McDougall considered defence counsel's application to find Wayne Eisnor unfit to stand trial due to amnesia. In a brief written decision, he rejected the argument, citing the Morrissey case and following the status quo: "It is clear from my reading of Morrissey that this fact (amnesia), in and of itself is not sufficient to render the accused unfit to stand trial." A first-degree murder trial was set for the second week of September when a jury would decide if Eisnor was guilty of first-degree murder. Despite fitness no longer being on the table, three expert witnesses would be permitted to speak to the jury about Wayne Eisnor—neuropsychologist Dr. Jeannette McGlone, psychiatrist Dr. Aileen Brunet, and myself. Presumably, the jury could use our expert testimony to evaluate Eisnor's credibility and to contextualize his claims when he later took the stand to testify in his own defence. His counsel hoped that our expert opinions would provide evidence that Wayne Eisnor was not the calculated liar that the jury might assume him to be. Further, it would be considered part of the evidence in helping the jury decide upon one of four possible verdicts: not guilty, or guilty of first-degree murder, second-degree murder, or manslaughter.

In Nova Scotia, the horrendous killing of Tina Eisnor in broad daylight sent shock waves throughout the province and across the country. In light of the publicity, and the fact that everyone recognized that Eisnor was responsible for shooting his wife, finding an unbiased jury of Eisnor's peers in Nova Scotia would be a daunting affair. The initial list of potential jurors contained six hundred names[20] from which to select a set of thirteen (that is, twelve plus one alternate) citizens who did not acknowledge already having formed an opinion of Eisnor's guilt. But of course, we can never really be sure of what is going on in the minds of potential jurors. Was it possible that some of the jurors who were selected brought pre-existing judgements about Eisnor into the courtroom where they would ultimately be deciding his fate?

On Friday the 13th of September, I was qualified as a "forensic psychologist capable of providing opinion evidence in the area of memory and memory assessment" and testified in front of a packed courthouse in Bridgewater. Over several hours, I outlined the varied techniques I used to assess Wayne Eisnor, and concluded with certainty that Eisnor truly was experiencing amnesia for the shootings and several months preceding them. I also testified about the findings regarding Eisnor's current personality functioning, including that he no longer had an antisocial or aggressive disposition. It appeared to me that the judge and jury members seemed extremely engaged during this discussion. In the end, the Crown prosecutors and the judge were persuaded by the experts and concurred that Eisnor's amnesia was real. Yet, who knows what the jury believed?

On September 19th, the jury conveyed to the judge that they had come to a unanimous verdict. Justice Glenn MacDougall informed the tense courtroom to "try as best you can to maintain your composure. Try not to let your emotions get the better of you." Surrounded by sheriffs, Eisnor sat on the prisoner's bench on the side of the courtroom as his fate was sealed: guilty of first-degree murder. There was a quiet cheer, and Tina Eisnor's family and friends wept and hugged. In convicting Eisnor and sentencing him to life in prison, Justice MacDougall addressed Eisnor, stating, "It is beyond my comprehension how anyone could show such contempt for human life....There could be nothing more cruel or heartless." Eisnor was sent off to spend a minimum of twenty-five years in a federal prison before he would become eligible for parole. Recently, Eisnor's counsel appealed this conviction arguing he had wrongly been deemed fit to stand trial. This appeal was denied.

### *Concluding Thoughts*

Wayne Eisnor killed his wife Tina in a visible public area, leaving no doubt that he was responsible for her death. In deciding on a first-degree murder verdict, the jury concluded that it had been a planned and deliberate killing. As such, Eisnor received the maximum punishment available for criminal offenders in Canada. Public perception was that Wayne got what he deserved. The community celebrated the outcome and justice was served. Or was it?

For us, there are two lingering and troubling questions about justice in the case of Wayne Eisnor. First, we question how someone who truly cannot recall the *actus reus* or *mens rea* constituting his or her crime (an extremely rare set of circumstances) could be fit to stand trial and meaningfully defend him or herself. While it is not surprising that the judge followed the legal status quo (as confirmed in Morrissey), we think the legal system needs to reflect further on this scenario. Morally, was this the correct way to deal with a defendant who had no memory of the crime? Having said that, what would we do with someone like Eisnor if he were found unfit to stand trial? When we send someone who is found unfit to a psychiatric hospital, the goal is to try and 'fix' their mental issue such that they can be eventually released or put on trial. Sadly, there is no fixing Wayne Eisnor's amnesia for June 30th, 2010. Yet there seems to be something wrong when a bewildered individual sits in jail for life not understanding whether or why he committed a crime. Putting someone in this situation on trial and punishing him in prison seems absurd, even Kafka-esque.

A second troubling aspect of this case is that the Wayne Eisnor who was convicted of first-degree murder is not the 'old' Wayne Eisnor. It appears, ironically, that Eisnor's self-sustained brain injury had a therapeutic effect by somehow transforming him into a nicer, more gentle individual. In the field of psychology, there have been many documented cases of major personality changes due to brain injury, although not usually in the direction of naughty to nice. One well-documented case, with which most readers will be familiar, is that of Phineas Gage, who improbably survived an accident in which a large iron rod was driven completely through his head, destroying much of his brain's left frontal lobe. Phineas—who had once been a dependable, pleasant man—reportedly changed into an impulsive, irresponsible, aggressive individual in the remaining twelve years of his life.[22] In the case of Eisnor, we theorize that his personality shifted in the reverse direction. This begs the question: if a person's long-standing personality characteristics are suddenly and drastically altered, are they still considered the 'same person' as before? Should this 'new' person be subjected to punishment for criminal actions they perpetrated when they were the 'old' person?

Given these unanswered questions, it is unsurprising that neuroscience is playing an increasing role in legal decision-making throughout North America.[21] The most common scenario involves the defence counsel introducing abnormalities in the brain scan of a defendant as evidence for reduced culpability and as a potential mitigating factor in sentencing. However, the Eisnor case is unique because his brain damage occurred after his criminal action but before a jury was to decide his fate. The legal system needs to reflect on situations in which there are probable grounds to believe that an accused individual has experienced a sudden, biologically based, permanent shift in personality. Keep in mind that the courts already find individuals not criminally responsible for actions they have perpetrated while in an altered, psychotic state. Additionally when these individuals are found not criminally responsible, they must reside in a psychiatric hospital, and will only be released when they become a different, less dangerous person than the one who committed the offence. Similarly, we might ask whether Eisnor is a completely different and perhaps 'safer' person than he was before firing a bullet into his own skull. It's his own fault, yes? In theory, this is true, but punishing someone for an act committed by his truly former 'self' seems like questionable retribution.

Despite the complex and thought-provoking nature of the Wayne Eisnor case and the troubling questions regarding justice, we must not lose sight of the true victims of this tragedy: Tina, her family, and her friends. Although Wayne Eisnor cannot remember his crime, this in no way excuses his actions. Because of his violent and irrational choices, his children will live the remainder of their lives without their loving mother. The series of terrible choices made by Wayne Eisnor in the Freshmart parking lot led to a host of fascinating psychological and legal questions, but more importantly to the tragic loss of Tina Eisnor and its enduring impact on her loved ones.

NOTES 1. First person pronouns are in relation to the first author

2. The information provided in this chapter is available in the public record.

3. Beverley Ware South Shore Bureau, "Eisnor's 'musings' detailed," *Chronicle Herald* (Halifax, NS), Sept. 17, 2013. http://thechronicleherald.ca/novascotia/1154706-eisnor-s-musings-detailed

4. Beverley Ware South Shore Bureau, "Eisnor denies shooting his wife," *Chronicle Herald* (Halifax, NS), Sept. 16, 2013. http://thechronicleherald.ca/novascotia/1154451-eisnor-denies-shooting-his-wife

5. Ibid.

6. Beverley Ware South Shore Bureau, "Brain-injured accused can't recall day of wife's death," Chronicle Herald (Halifax, NS), Mar. 3, 2012. http://thechronicleherald.ca/novascotia/69534-brain-injured-accused-can-t-recall-day-wife-s-death

7. Ibid.

8. Beverley Ware South Shore Bureau, "Brain-injured accused can't recall day of wife's death," Chronicle Herald (Halifax, NS), Mar. 3, 2012. http://thechronicleherald.ca/novascotia/69534-brain-injured-accused-can-t-recall-day-wife-s-death

9. Criminal Code, RSC 1985, c C-34 s 2.

10. Ibid.

11. *Dusky v. United States* (1960). 362 US; Mathew Hale, The history of the pleas of the Crown. (London: E.R. Nutt & R. Gosling, 1736).

12. Roesch, Ronald, James RP Ogloff, and Stephen L. Golding. "Competency to stand trial: Legal and clinical issues." Applied and Preventive Psychology 2, no. 1 (1994): 43-51.

13. Porter, Stephen, Angela R. Birt, John C. Yuille, and Hugues F. Hervé. "Memory for murder: A psychological perspective on dissociative amnesia in legal contexts." *International Journal of Law and Psychiatry* 24, no. 1 (2001): 23-42.

14. *Wilson v. United States* (1968). 391 F. 2d 460.

15. *Morrow v. Maryland* (1982). 443 A. 2d. 108 (Md. Ct. App.).

16. for example, Porter et al. (2001)

17. *R. v. Morrissey*, (2007). ONCA 770

18. *R. v. Morrissey*, (2003). CanLII 8150

19. Symptom suggestion proved to be a key factor in establishing that Kenneth Bianchi was lying about his amnesia in the Hillside Strangler serial murder case. Bianchi claimed to have Multiple Personality Disorder (MPD) and amnesia for the murders for which he was charged. His ruse was revealed upon his adoption of false symptoms of MPD provided by psychiatrist Dr. Martin Orne. Bianchi confessed about lying and then agreed to plead guilty.

20. Beverley Ware South Shore Bureau, "Eisnor jury pool whittled down," *Chronicle Herald* (Halifax, NS), Sept. 3, 2013. http://thechronicleherald.ca/novascotia/1151828-eisnor-jury-pool-whittled-down

21. Hughes, Virginia. "Science in court: head case." Nature 464, no. 7287 (2010): 340-342.

22. Harlow, John M. "Recovery from the passage of an iron bar through the head." Publications of the Massachusetts Medical Society 2, no. 3 (1868): 327-246.

***Donald Dutton** PhD is Professor of Psychology at the University of British Columbia. He co-founded, in 1979, a court-mandated treatment program for men convicted of wife assault and used the men as research subjects for studies on domestic violence. He has published over a hundred papers and five books, including* The Domestic Assault of Women *(1995),* The Batterer: A Psychological Profile *(1995),* The Abusive Personality *(2006),* Rethinking Domestic Violence *(2006) and* The Psychology of Genocide *(2007)). He serves as an expert witness in civil trials involving intimate abuse and in criminal trials involving family violence. Dutton has provided numerous workshops to professionals based on his work, including talks at The Université Paris-Sorbonne, the U.S. Army at Walter Reed Hospital, Navaho Nation in Winslow, Arizona, the joint ABA-APA Taskforce on Domestic Violence in Washington, D.C. the US Department of Defense and the Department of Psychiatry at Rockefeller University, the World Bank and the International Monetary Fund.*

# Dr. Donald Dutton

## The Carnation Killers
## *Folie à deux*

On Christmas Eve 2007 in Carnation, Washington, a small town northeast of Seattle, Joe McEnroe and his live-in girlfriend, Michele Anderson sat down for dinner with Michele's parents, Wayne and Judy Anderson. Joe and Michele hadn't travelled far for the Christmas meal as they lived in a trailer a short distance from the parents' home, on the parents' property. Before enjoying their dinner, the family, including Joe, awaited the arrival of Michele's brother Scott, Scott's wife Erica, and their two children, Olivia and Nathan. While they were waiting for the rest of the family to arrive, Michele drew a gun and shot at Wayne but her gun jammed. Wayne, who was large man, charged at Michele and at that point, Joe drew his gun and shot Wayne. Then, apologizing to Judy, he shot her in the chest. Both were killed. Michele and Joe dragged Wayne and Judy's bodies into a shed and re-commenced their wait for Michele's brother and family. When Scott and his family arrived, Michele shot her brother Scott once. Then her gun jammed again so Joe shot Scott and Erica. To finish off the destruction, Joe shot the two children.

Joe and Michele left the four bodies where they lay and drove in circles for twenty-four hours in a state of confusion; driving south in an attempt to flee to Canada, instead of heading north to the border. Finally, they were stopped by the police near the crime scene and appeared flustered when asked routine questions. When taken into custody and interviewed by the police, they both admitted to the killings. Rationalizing the killing of the children, they said, "there would be no one left to care for them." Eventually both Joe and Michele were charged with Aggravated Homicide which can carry a death sentence in Washington State. Both Michele and Joe faced the Death Penalty and were to be tried separately.

In March of 2008, about three months after the killings, I was contacted by Katy Ross and Bill Prestia, public defenders in Seattle who were representing Joe. I am a forensic psychologist who has appeared in many homicide cases, many of which involved a potential death sentence for the perpetrators. The most high profile of these was the O.J. Simpson case, where I was an expert for the prosecution.

I saw a newspaper photo of Joe and he looked Satanic—shoulder-length dark hair and a strange look in his eye. I expected the worst. I began the first of fifteen interviews with Joe in March of 2008 and these would continue until 2015 when he was finally tried for murder in Seattle. The interviews all took place in the King County Jail in downtown Seattle. I came to know the place well; the numerous locked doors and the routine of getting to a locked interview room and then having Joe brought in with wrist and ankle cuffs by two burly guards.

### *Encountering Joe*

My first encounter with Joe defied whatever expectations I had formed based on the newspaper photo and description of the crime. He was excessively timid and had a speech impediment—he could not pronounce the letter 'r'. Joe was also medicated during much of his pre-trial incarceration and was on strong anti-depressants. He experienced unrelenting guilt over the killings, and found it difficult, even after some time had passed, to describe the killing of the children, Olivia and Nathan Anderson.

The first interviews focussed on his upbringing; he was raised by his mother in California and he had never known his father. His mother had a penchant for men, she would even bring them home from the streets—men who were described by Joe as having a sign reading 'will work for food'—and have loud sex with them in the tiny bachelor apartment she shared with Joe and his two siblings. Only a blanket separated the children from the loud sex.

Joe was basically put in charge of caring for and raising his siblings, since his mother was either out working or out looking for men. Joe's unkempt appearance at school led to an investigation, when he was fourteen, by Santa Clara County, California Child Protective Services. The investigation report read, in part, "the family appears quite dysfunctional…no parent to provide. Child left alone unattended by mother.... Home was unclean and unsafe." In this home environment, Joe began to withdraw and retreat into himself; first to television, then to the Internet.

Over the next several years, his mother brought home a series of disturbed and sometimes abusive boyfriends, many of whom were ex-cons. The typical pattern was they would live at her place, not work, drink and/or use whatever drugs they could find, and counsel Joe on the meaning of life. The relationship would break up and Joe's mother would go in search of a replacement. Joe was in a constant pattern of being "the man of the house," being abandoned when the new man-hunting search began, then being replaced by a new boyfriend.

According to Joe, when these new boyfriends came into the family, Joe was shaped into a protective role; he never knew how much threat each of them presented for his mother. The family moved around the country—from California and Washington, to Arizona—all at the whims of his mother's search for a man. Joe would try in the midst of all this to go to school but was repeatedly harassed and bullied for his cheap clothes and speech impediment. He never disclosed this to his mother—she wasn't interested.

Joe had no memories of ever being soothed or supported by his mother. Instead, he developed a psychological response to serve that necessary function; his personality split into entities—quasi-hallucinatory experiences that became chronic and vivid and visited him during times of stress. These were 'entities,' that is, distinct personas who looked like Joe but were of both sexes and had names. Their names included Crowe, Melissa, Void, and God and each had distinct personalities—Melissa was playful and wise, for example, and knew Joe from a previous life.

Joe worked at odd jobs outside of school to help support the family—he had to pay all the utility bills on his five-dollars-an-hour pay. At age twenty-one, Joe saw a chance to leave because his mother had finally found a semi-respectable mate. Joe's emancipation took him to North Carolina where he got a job stocking shelves in a Target store. He had no close friends; he had a couple of roommates but hardly knew them. He would go online and on two occasions met women who seemed interested in him. In both cases, he took time off work and flew out to other cities to meet them. Each time they rejected him, and as he described it to me, this left him depressed and suicidal. All his time away from work was spent online. His only friends were his entities who visited him during times of extreme stress and served a soothing function—calming him and, on more than one occasion, preventing him from committing suicide. Joe called them his 'spirit guides' but didn't tell anyone about them for fear of being thought to be crazy.

Joe's third try at finding a girlfriend online was with a woman named Michele Anderson. They seemed to like the same type of action flick movies, played the same computer games, and both had spirit guides. This shared spirit guide experience was a strong draw for Joe because he could now share his secret entities with someone who would not ridicule him. Joe flew to Seattle from North Carolina to meet Michele and he couldn't help noticing that she was quite a bit heavier than in her pictures. He inadvertently let this slip to her and she never let him forget it.

Michele had a dominating personality and she had tirades against the people in the world who she felt were disrespecting her; mainly people at work but also her family. Joe noticed that Michele took every conflict as a slight and every slight as someone 'dissing' her. She would then ruminate on it. In fact, she took to keeping 'hit lists' of people she wanted to kill, as she put it, "to make the world a better place." Joe simply placated her and tried to avoid confrontations, but she would blow up over minor conflicts like his speech impediment or his failing to clean the refrigerator. Her tirades would last for hours. Each minor conflict was a sign to Michele that she was being dissed again.

### *Psychological Assessment Tests*

I gave Joe some psychological assessment tests; the Millon Clinical Multiaxial Inventory (MCMI), the Structured Interview of Reported Symptoms (SIRS), and the Diagnostic Interview for Borderlines (DIB). The MCMI is a broad-spectrum self-report scale that provides a clinical profile consistent with current categories of the *Diagnostic and Statistical Manual of the Mental Disorders, Version 5 (DSM-5).* The SIRS is an elaborate screen for 'malingering' which means the production of factitious psychological problems to avoid sanctions. SIRS assesses this empirically by adding scores on scales that measure a tendency to report symptoms that are rarely found together, symptoms that are absurd, or to endorse everyday problems as symptoms. An overall score indicates the likelihood of malingering.

The DIB is a scale specifically designed to assess Borderline Personality Disorder, a serious disorder beginning in adolescence affecting cognition, affect, and behaviour, and having central features of impulsivity and suicidality upon relationship dissolution. Joe had shown signs of these features, for example dropping everything to fly off to the promising new relationships and becoming suicidal when they didn't work out, but the true proof would be in his test results. It's a high bar to register as a borderline on the DIB and when it is combined with the SIRS to rule out malingering, the results are convincing, especially when they are corroborated by the respondent's life history information. For Joe, all the ducks lined up in a row. He had borderline personality disorder. In his relationship with Michele, this made him especially malleable; she would simply have to threaten to leave him and he would give in to whatever she wanted.

There was more to Joe's psychopathology than borderline personality though; his 'spirit guides' were beyond the transitory psychotic states of the borderline personality; they were hallucinatory experiences that he reported having had since he was eleven years old. He did not actually see or hear these spirit guides, instead he sensed them. They did not blot out the visual field. When I asked him if he would be able to see me or if a spirit guide was between us, he responded in the affirmative but said I would be blurred "like bad TV reception."

I would obviously not see the vision and would just find Joe to be preoccupied. Joe's primary guide was Crow, who resembled Joe but painted his face "sort of an Indian deal" and who was wise and aloof—Joe's mentor. Crow talked to Joe and assured him everything was going to be all right. Crow had advised Joe to move to North Carolina, had talked him out of suicide, and had advised him to leave before the killings started in Carnation, Washington, but as Joe regretted, "I didn't listen to him, I couldn't leave her."

At the thought of being separated from Michele by prison, in his police interview Joe wailed, "She's all I have!" His other spirit guides also resembled Joe physically but some were female and one, called 'No Name' was, as he put it, "my self-loathing and guilt." When Joe killed Judy Anderson, No Name split off and Joe said, "I felt something break in me."

### *Telepathic Communication with the 'Entities"*

Joe believed the entities existed outside of him. He felt their presence and sensed the content of their conversations. To Joe, this communication was telepathic. Joe also reported beliefs in "bindings and wardings"—spiritual protective zones that he could put around people to protect them. He also believed that mirrors did not actually reflect reality but were a "little bit off and that he could hear electricity and what people were thinking"—flashes of thought, as he put it. Joe also had memories of prior lives in which he was tortured. On the SIRS, Joe never reported any inconsistent symptoms, he wasn't making up the spirit guides. Three other persons knew about them—his mother, Michele, and a friend of Michele's.

Joe was reporting chronic strange dissociative experiences but he did not assume an alternative perspective for these experiences, as would a Multiple Personality (aka Dissociative Identity Disorder). He always saw the world from the perspective of Joe but what a strange world it was. The experiences of spirit guides were quasi-hallucinatory; they met all the criteria of a hallucination, that is, were vivid and clear 'perception-like' experiences without an external stimulus that had the impact of normal perception, and were not under voluntary control. Except one. His spirit guides were not experienced through a sensory modality such as hearing or vision, as would be a 'hallucination,' but were, instead, experienced telepathically.

Schizotypal Personality Disorder is listed in the DSM-5 as schizophrenia spectrum disorder (a type of psychotic disorder) and is described as a "pervasive pattern of social and interpersonal deficits that is marked by acute discomfort with, and capacity for close relationships, as well as by cognitive and perceptual distortions and eccentricities of behaviour, beginning in early adulthood." Amongst the criteria for diagnosis are that the person had 'odd beliefs,' such as beliefs in clairvoyance or telepathy that are inconsistent with subcultural norms; unusual perceptual experiences; odd thinking or speech; and an eccentric appearance. Joe, I argued in court, had all of these and two others; social isolation and social anxiety. Both schizotypal and borderline PD have a few things in common; they are severe disorders, and both indicative of structural flaws in the ego. They run deep and, in Joe's case, made him particularly susceptible to influence in an intimate relationship.

### *A Turn of Bad Luck*

Joe had the great bad luck to meet Michele Anderson. She was the first woman who had appeared to take him seriously—although there was evidence that Joe didn't understand that she saw his value to her as being his capability of being manipulated. From my early interviews with Joe, it seemed to me that Michele had a Paranoid Personality Disorder; according to Joe she was constantly monitoring the neighbours at one place where they lived in suburban Seattle in case they walked across the lawn. She forced Joe to adopt a routine of hiding on the floor of the car until she drove it out of the garage so he could surprise anyone who thought she was alone and might attack her.

In spite of all this paranoia, Michele had never been a crime victim. Michele began to spin to Joe a liturgy of complaints about her family; for example how she had been abused by her sadistic father, how her mother had tried to kill her, and how her brother Scott owed her money for a car and would not pay her back. Her brother's wife Erica had apparently put him up to this. Joe believed these stories—after all, the abuse would explain Michele's strange personality. Michele's step-sister never confirmed the abuse stories, instead she mentioned Michele's strange personality as having early roots. As time went on, the stories Michele told Joe became more extreme and she began to develop some new elements; her unhappiness was caused by not getting even with people who had wronged her and this prevented her from moving to another spiritual plane. According to her, this had to change.

When Joe and Michele moved to a trailer on her parents' property, they were completely isolated and the stories deepened and worsened. Now they included the thought that Michele's family had to die. Each one of the adults had 'dissed' Michele in some grievous way, and the children were contaminated by exposure to the adults. I could not diagnose Michele since I had never personally interviewed her and had only third-party reports of her personality, which nevertheless seemed consistent from the several sources contacted (all people who knew her). My provisional assessment, however, was that she had a

Paranoid Personality Disorder and that Joe was incapable of leaving her and resisting the adoption of her paranoid delusions. Joe could see that she was extreme in some respects, but he played along to avoid conflict with her. He didn't make the connection of her extreme views to her family myth, however he believed she had been abused and the abuse had caused her strangeness. More likely the strangeness caused her distorted memories of abuse. Her step-sister, who had grown up with the family, disconfirmed that physical or sexual abuse had happened.

The court case against Joe and Michele was delayed over several pre-trial skirmishes—were they to be tried separately or together; should the judge recuse himself, was it a Death Penalty case? Some of these questions had to make their way to the Washington State Supreme Court for decisions. Time passed. It was decided to try them separately, that it was a Death Penalty case, and that Joe's trial would go first. By 2014, Joe's trial was slated to begin.

### *Michele's Psychological Report*

At that time, we were finally provided a psychological report on Michele Anderson by Dr. Mark Cunningham who had assessed Michele for her defense team at her Competency Hearing (whether she was competent to stand trial) during the wait for trial. This had been done in 2008 but the report was not released to Joe's defense team by the prosecution until 2014. The report not only confirmed the provisional diagnosis of Michele's paranoia but took it a step further—out of the realm of a Personality Disorder and into the realm of a Delusional Disorder, which is defined as fixed beliefs that are not amenable to change in the light of conflicting evidence. Delusional Disorder, therefore, includes bizarre delusions, clearly implausible and not understandable to same-culture peers and not derived from ordinary life experiences; that is, loss of control over mind. Common themes include: being persecuted, referential (strangers are talking about me), somatic (something is wrong with my body), religious, grandiose (I am destined to be a great historical leader). This is an encapsulated psychosis, more confined to a specific set of beliefs than schizophrenia, and outside of this delusion, functioning is not impaired.

In Michele's case the delusions came to include not only her family and co-workers, but eventually her defense counsel, whom she fired more than once. These delusions were not just misunderstandings but were gross misrepresentations of the history of various interactions. She had the persecutory type of Delusional Disorder; that is, she believed she was being spied on, cheated, followed, poisoned, maligned, harassed, and obstructed. Individuals with this disorder may resort to violence against those they believe are hurting them but have apparent normalcy when delusional beliefs are not being acted upon.

Dr. Cunningham's findings strengthened the argument that Joe was a victim of a shared psychotic disorder called 'Folie à deux', meaning, in French, 'a madness shared by two', first described in medical literature in 1877. There was no question that Michele was the dominant party in the relationship or that her negative beliefs about her family originated with her. Joe was a passive sidekick who was incapable of dissenting or leaving and who suffered from ongoing verbal and emotional abuse. Michele played perfectly on his existential guilt and his self loathing. He resisted the idea of killing the family, but Michele convinced him he would just have to show up as protection and to help her clean the mess—she was going to do the killing with or without Joe's help, but if he was really a man he would help protect her. Joe adopted Michele's dogma about her family much in the same way a cult member buys into a social reality of the cult. Joe still was a true believer when I first interviewed him; it was not until counsel had showed him some family pictures of Michele in which all were clearly happy and smiling that he began to doubt the dogma.

Joe never claimed that he was not the shooter and originally the plan was to enter the finding of shared psychotic disorder as a 'Not Guilty by Reason of Insanity' plea at the guilt phase of the trial. For some unknown reason, the judge ruled against that and we were forced to present it as 'Diminished Capacity' at the penalty phase. In the United States, a Diminished Capacity plea differs in important ways from Not Guilty by Reason of Insanity. Reason of Insanity is an affirmative defence to crimes. That is, a successful plea of insanity will, in most states, result in a verdict of 'Not Guilty' and commission the defendant to a mental institution. 'Diminished Capacity', on the other hand, merely results in the defendant being convicted of a lesser offense in the guilt phase of the trial or, in the penalty phase as not being fully morally responsible for his crime. The jury split on the Death Penalty and Joe's life was spared. I'd like to think that my arguments about his defective personality and the abusive relationship with Michele made some difference. He now faces life in prison without parole. The last time I interviewed Joe he was philosophical about this—prison, he offered, was better than living with Michele.

### *Unique Aspects of the Case*

There were several unique aspects to the Joe McEnroe case. The type of intimate terrorism that was shown in his relationship with Michele is usually associated with male perpetrators, but the research evidence clearly indicates that either sex can be a perpetrator. The view that only women are victims is a political myth. Also, when abuse is chronic and extreme, one usually finds personality disorders or some combination of personality disorders in the perpetrator, or perpetrator and victim. The way they played out in this case was complementary—Michele externalized blame for everything, Joe internalized blame. She blamed him, he took it on. This feature, more than gender per se, is the key aspect of abusive relationships. It is also noteworthy how Joe's upbringing shaped him. He was never nurtured and as a result developed 'entities' to serve this purpose. He was always alone and the isolation led to his strange personality—one formed to avoid pervasive social anxiety that may have stemmed from being ridiculed at school and having no secure base to return to, formed through an imagination honed in cyberspace and culminating with imaginary friends that became lifelong friends. Joe was no match for Michele and was a great candidate for slavish conformity to her delusions. Psychosis, under some conditions, can be contagious.

The public tends to overestimate the frequency with which insanity defences are used in court, in part because such cases are often high-profile ones and a media effect occurs. A study in the U.S. found 'Not Guilty by Reason of Insanity' to be used in only one per cent of American jury trials and that a plea succeeds in only one-quarter of one per cent (.25 per cent) of trials. Results in Canada are nearly identical; a similar study in Canada found a point two per cent (.2 per cent) success rate for insanity defences in Canada. When the defence succeeds, is usually fits the stereotype the public holds of insanity; that is that the perpetrator has had previous psychiatric supervision for psychosis and had a psychosis operating at the time of the offence. The recidivism rate for insanity offenders is actually less than for the general prison population. In Joe's case, of course, recidivism is a moot point; he will spend the rest of his life in jail.

***Barry Cooper*** *PhD is a Registered Psychologist in Kelowna, B.C., practicing in clinical and clinical-forensic contexts. A former Senior Psychologist for the Correctional Service of Canada and a former Psychologist for the Forensic Psychiatric Services Commission, he is a founding Partner and Vice President of Research and Development for The Forensic Alliance. He is also the Director of the Interprofessional Clinic at the University of British Columbia-Okanagan and an Adjunct Professor in the Department of Psychology at Simon Fraser University. Additionally, Dr. Cooper is in private practice which involves assessment and consultation services. His interests include investigative interviewing, memory, credibility assessment, special needs, and risk assessment. He has provided training to various groups including mental health and criminal justice professionals. Dr. Cooper has also provided evidence at Review Board hearings and has served as an expert witness in court for both the prosecution and defence.*

***Jacqueline M. Kanipayor*** *is a PhD Clinical Psychology student at the University of British Columbia-Okanagan. Ms. Kanipayor has worked primarily with Borderline Personality Disorder and substance use populations. Her research interests include assessment and treatment of Borderline Personality Disorder, cross-cultural variations in psychopathy, quality of life in mental health, development and modifications of psychologically based interventions, and quantitative/qualitative methods in clinical research.*

# Dr. Barry Cooper and Jacqueline M. Kanipayor

## Not Criminally Responsible; Or Not

APPROXIMATELY A DECADE AGO, on a small remote island in rural Canada, Terrance Tupan was arrested and charged with a series of crimes involving the murder as well as the post-mortem dismemberment and sexual mutilation of his father, Samuel Tupan. The depth of these violent acts echoed in the collective shock of this small community. One year after the murder, the court heard evidence that the accused, Mr. Tupan, had been suffering from a psychotic illness driven by delusional thinking and command hallucinations, which were argued to have influenced his behaviour at the time of his offences. There was no dispute that Mr. Tupan had killed, mutilated, and dismembered his father; however, his mental state at the time of the offences had come into question. After a lengthy criminal trial, Mr. Tupan was found Not Criminally Responsible on Account of Mental Disorder (NCRMD) and was transferred to a high-security mental health facility for assessment and treatment as a forensic inpatient. I, the first author of the present chapter, was one of the individuals who assessed Mr. Tupan following his NCRMD verdict and placement in hospital. I was asked specifically to assess his personality including whether or not he was psychopathic; I was also asked to determine whether or not Mr. Tupan was malingering—had he been *faking* his psychosis?

The present chapter provides an overview of my assessment of Mr. Tupan and related issues. Although many chapters in the present volume concern actual cases with intimate details unchanged, the present case was altered to preserve the anonymity of the patient in question including the patient's real name. As well, other aspects of his case were scrubbed. The general flavour of the case, however, remains. This chapter presents issues concerning the finding of NRCMD followed by overviews of the constructs of psychopathy and malingering—factors of which are often considered in forensic assessments by psychologists and psychiatrists. Thereafter, my assessment of Mr. Tupan is explored in detail although aspects of his case are interwoven throughout.

### *Not Criminally Responsible on Account of Mental Disorder*

Media responses to high-profile NCRMD cases often echo the assorted opinions of the public at large around issues concerning criminal responsibility. Indeed, few concerns at the intersection of mental health and the criminal justice system have provoked as much public interest and controversy as the legal verdict of NCRMD. According to *The Criminal Code of Canada* (1985), "... no person is criminally responsible for an act committed or an omission made while suffering from a mental disorder that rendered the person incapable of appreciating the nature and quality of the act or omission or of knowing that it was wrong." An NCRMD finding is a legal—not a mental health—determination, although mental health professionals are involved in the assessment process and offer recommendations to the court. An accused may be diagnosed with a serious mental disorder and still be held criminally responsible for an offence committed. Indeed, jails and prisons are teeming with inmates suffering from mental disorders such as those with depressed moods and high levels of anxiety. However, if a mental disorder such as schizophrenia is determined to interfere with a person's ability to judge right from wrong or to appreciate the potential consequences of his or her actions at the time of the offence, a judge or jury may render a verdict of NCRMD. This is not to say that the person has been acquitted nor found guilty of committing a criminal act; rather, the absence of criminal intent (*mens rea* or guilty mind) or a conscious ability to control one's behaviours (*actus reus*) exempts the person of criminal responsibility. In the case of Mr. Tupan, it was argued that his violent behaviours were driven by delusional thinking ("my father is evil and is causing harm to society ... I must protect society") and voices in his head commanding him to carry out violent acts ("kill your father or you will be killed"). Therefore, the court ruled that Mr. Tupan's psychotic illness rendered him incapable of appreciating the consequences of his actions. But was he?

Common misbeliefs surround NCRMD verdicts such as a) the belief that most of these cases reflect serious offences involving violence, b) the verdict is given too frequently, c) people faking a mental disorder can successfully avoid criminal punishment, and d) NCRMD verdicts result often in brief hospitalization followed by immediate release back into the community with a high risk of reoffending shortly thereafter (Baillie, 2015). Findings from the National Trajectory Project—the first longitudinal study to provide an accurate portrait of people found NCRMD across three Canadian provinces—indicate that, contrary to the misbelief that NCRMD-accused people perpetrate mostly violent crimes, serious violent crimes such as homicide and sexual offences represent only 8.1 per cent of all NCRMD index offences (Crocker, Seto, Nicholls, & Côté, 2013). Minor assaults, property offences, and other nonviolent criminal violations accounted for nearly fifty per cent of all NCRMD offences (Crocker et al., 2015). It has also been shown that NCRMD verdicts are relatively rare events and individuals spend typically more time hospitalized versus in prison if found criminally responsible. Further, whereas release from prison is statutorily determined in Canada for most offenders, release from a forensic mental health facility is dictated largely by the patient's risk of re-offending. Forensic patients are detained typically in hospital until they are determined to no longer pose a high risk for re-offence.

Following a verdict of NCRMD in Canada, a disposition hearing is held to determine what will happen to the accused. Typically, courts defer this responsibility to provincial Review Boards. Review Boards are independent tribunals established under the *Criminal Code of Canada*. These Boards are commissioned to render and annually revise dispositions of individuals found unfit to stand trial or NCRMD. Review Boards are responsible for protecting the safety of the public while also safeguarding the rights and mental health needs of the individual in question. One of three dispositions can be rendered on a case-by-case basis: a person found NCRMD may be detained in a hospital, conditionally discharged, or discharged absolutely, where the individual is determined not to be a significant threat to public safety. In Mr. Tupan's case, his initial Review Board disposition resulted in his detention in a secure hospital for continued assessment and treatment.

According to his forensic file, Mr. Tupan was oriented to person, place, and time upon his intake into the hospital. He presented as guarded, "possibly paranoid," angry, entitled, and irritable; his intake interview with a mental health professional had to be prematurely terminated due to his belligerence. Further reports from staff on his living unit indicated that Mr. Tupan was impulsive, lacked signs suggestive of anxiety, exhibited a full range of affect, and was noted to smile to himself, often inappropriately. The latter observations suggested to some at the hospital that he was psychotic, symptoms of which he denied at the time ("I'm not crazy … I made a stupid decision"). At the time, Mr. Tupan also refused oral medication and resisted the administration of antipsychotic injections ("I'm allergic to medications"), which resulted in him being placed in seclusion. After spending a day in a seclusion room, Mr. Tupan claimed he was "considerably depressed … because of the system." He was placed on antidepressant medication and, after a day, he suggested that he no longer experienced symptoms of a depressed mood. His treatment team questioned his uncharacteristically quick improvement. A few days later, Mr. Tupan produced a bright painting, which he suitably titled, "Cured."

Staff reports on Mr. Tupan's psychotic symptoms were mixed. Nurses on his living unit produced numerous chart notes without any direct observations of possible symptoms of psychosis. For example, his thought processes were reportedly rational and there was no evidence that he may have been responding to internal stimuli, which might have suggested the presence of auditory hallucinations—voices. Furthermore, Mr. Tupan had denied experiencing any psychotic symptoms during his first week in hospital. However, he informed his treating psychiatrist that he "suddenly" started hearing a voice "telling me to do drugs" and to intimidate other patients. Soon after, he was diagnosed with schizophrenia, a diagnosis consistent with the one he received prior to his trial by another mental health professional. Although Mr. Tupan denied that he was mentally ill, he agreed to take his medication so that he would "never kill again." That said, he was of the belief that his father "deserved to die … it was God's will."

Not long after his mental health placement in a high security hospital, all of Mr. Tupan's reported symptoms of psychosis abated and he claimed to be "cured." However, his behaviours proved problematic as evidenced by the bullying and intimidation of other patients.

Moreover, many of the staff at the facility had mixed opinions of Mr. Tupan, some of whom questioned whether he was actually mentally ill. Other staff were impressed at his drive, determination, charisma, and 'charm'. The mixed opinions of Mr. Tupan arguably led to a referral to conduct a psychological assessment. In particular, I, the first author, was asked by Mr. Tupan's treating psychiatrist to assess Mr. Tupan's personality—with attention towards possible psychopathy—with a focus on possible malingering. Issues concerning psychopathy and malingering are discussed in turn below.

### *Psychopathy*

Most people think they know what it means to be a psychopath. However, few personality constructs have evoked as much controversy and misunderstanding as psychopathy. Indeed, psychopathy has amassed a number of characterizations including the giftedly charming-yet-deceptive con artist, the persistent criminal offender, the notorious serial killer and, more recently, the intimidating and manipulative yet charismatic corporate employee. Despite mixed opinions on what exactly psychopathy is, there does exist a clearer consensus on what it is not. Psychopathic individuals are not all violent, in fact some psychopaths carry no history of violence or criminal behaviours. Psychopathy does not equal psychosis—psychopathic individuals are generally rational, well adjusted to their surroundings, and free of delusions. Psychopathy and Antisocial Personality Disorder are not one and the same—antisocial personality is measured by a history of chronic antisocial and criminal behaviours whereas psychopaths are distinguished largely by distinct personality traits such as shallow affect, callousness, and lack of empathy and remorse. Indeed, psychopathy has come to be defined by a constellation of personality traits *and* behaviours. Interpersonally, psychopaths are superficial, grandiose, and deceitful. Affectively, they lack remorse, empathy, and acceptance of responsibility. Their behaviours reflect impulsivity, irresponsibility, and a lack of goal setting. Further, psychopaths tend to exhibit a history of poor social control as well as adolescent antisocial behaviour, and adult antisocial behaviour.

Our contemporary understanding of psychopathy can be traced back to the works of Hervey Cleckley. In *The Mask of Sanity* (1941),

Cleckley offered the first comprehensive description of the personality and social peculiarities characterizing the psychopathic personality. Modern methods used to assess psychopathy emerged largely from Cleckley's work, including the approach used to assess psychopathy for the purposes of Mr. Tupan's assessment. As opposed to typical psychological tests in which the subject of the assessment is provided with the questions, usually in the form of self-report, the most effective way to assess psychopathy in clinical-forensic contexts is to employ a semi-structured interview and file-based approach. Because psychopaths are prone to deception and manipulation, we must ensure that we have information independent of their self-report in which to challenge or corroborate the information they provide.

The construct of psychopathy has brought into question the issue of criminal responsibility; should psychopathic individuals be held responsible for their crimes or should they be excused of criminal responsibility via an NCRMD verdict? On one hand, the question centres on whether psychopathic individuals possess a fundamental capacity for moral reasoning; do they know the difference between right and wrong? Most researchers and practitioners would argue a resounding, yes—they know, but they just don't care. Indeed, their ability to reason about moral issues has been shown to be similar to the moral reasoning of nonpsychopathic individuals. On the other hand, there is some debate whether psychopathic individuals possess the conscious ability to behave within the limits of societal norms. We know that psychopathic offenders enter the criminal justice system at a young age and engage in more crimes including planned, goal-directed violence compared to nonpsychopathic offenders. However, brain-imaging studies suggest that abnormalities exist which may negatively affect psychopathic individuals' abilities to control their impulses and make rational decisions. Nevertheless, at present, the presence of psychopathy is not an 'NCRMD-able' defence in Canada. Rather, the presence of psychopathy in a forensic patient claiming mental illness often raises the issue of malingering. Indeed, the nature of Mr. Tupan's offences and some of his behaviour in hospital led some to believe that he was psychopathic and had likely faked a mental illness in order to avoid possible life imprisonment. But was he?

### Malingering

According to the *Diagnostic and Statistical Manual of Mental Disorders Fifth Edition* (DSM-5; American Psychiatric Association [APA], 2013), North America's current 'bible' of mental illness, two conditions can be characterized by a conscious production of symptoms: factitious disorder and malingering. These concepts are often referred to interchangeably but can be distinguished by the type of incentive sought. Factitious disorder is defined in the DSM-5 as the deliberate exaggeration, faking, and/or creation of physical or psychological symptoms in order to obtain *primary gains* or *internal incentives*—such as sympathy and emotional attention from assuming the 'patient role'. In contrast, malingering behaviours are driven consciously by "external incentives such as avoiding military duty, avoiding work, obtaining financial compensation, evading criminal prosecution, or obtaining drugs." Thus, malingering is distinguished by a clear drive to achieve a *secondary* gain or *external incentive*. In the latter case, one does not need to fake an illness entirely to be suspected of malingering. Indeed, a person may have a mental illness but exaggerate the symptoms, perhaps with the intention of appearing more ill.

Cases of malingering are often thought to be more common in criminal forensic settings compared to other medico-legal contexts. However, malingering occurs more frequently across civil proceedings for personal injury (twenty-nine per cent) and disability (thirty per cent) claims, whereas criminal evaluations account for only nineteen per cent of malingering cases (Mittenberg, Patton, Canyock, & Condit, 2002). In the criminal justice setting, malingering may motivate an accused to enter a plea of NCRMD, with faking a psychotic disorder being most likely to yield success from the perspective of the accused. Indeed, a person may malinger a mental illness in the hopes of avoiding going to prison—they may rest on the belief that a forensic psychiatric hospital would be a more comfortable place to reside. Research has shown that almost twenty-one per cent of defendants have been found or suspected of engaging in malingering in assessments of criminal responsibility (McDermott, 2012). What about Mr. Tupan? He was found NCRMD by the court based on a pre-trial mental health opinion that he was psychotic at the time of his offences. However, as indicated above, one of the referral questions for

Mr. Tupan's psychological assessment concerned addressing whether or not he was malingering the symptoms of a mental illness. Thus, even though he was found NCRMD, there were subsequent questions about the validity of his claimed symptoms. The goal of such post-trial assessments is not to usurp the role or circumvent the finding of the court. Rather, the goal is to assist with further assessment and treatment of the patient. These assessments are not easy to conduct. In fact, they are of the most challenging types of assessments to complete. I was, however, up to the challenge.

### *Assessing Mr. Tupan—A Multi-trait-Multi-method Approach*

Few psychological syndromes are as easy to define, but difficult to detect reliably as malingering. In criminal justice settings, clinicians should use a multi-trait-multi-method assessment strategy to reliably confirm or disconfirm cases of malingering. In fact, all forensic assessments, according to best practice guidelines, should involve this type of approach. It does not matter whether the referral question is risk for re-offence, diagnosis, neuropsychological in nature, or malingering. Clinicians must gather and piece together data from multiple sources on any given trait, behaviour, or symptom. In Mr. Tupan's case, as indicated earlier, I was asked to assess his personality—including the possible presence of psychopathy—and to examine whether or not he was malingering a major mental illness such as schizophrenia. Our standard assessment procedure in clinical-forensic contexts, regardless of the referral question(s), involve a review of file/collateral information, clinical interviewing, psychological testing, and consultations with relevant staff. Gathering information from each of these areas is particularly important in the assessment of psychopathy and malingering. Data from each area concerning Mr. Tupan is reviewed below, including my interviews with him and the results of psychological testing *(note: some of this information is also reviewed above).*

Research and practice suggest that the available file/collateral information from family, friends, medical or insurance records, and police reports should be reviewed carefully before the initial clinical interview. Such information assists the evaluator in developing appropriate interview questions and navigating the interview accordingly. According to Mr. Tupan's file, there was no history of major mental illness in his family such as the presence of a psychotic illness. It is noted that Mr. Tupan was abused physically, emotionally and sexually by his father, who was described as a "heavy … hard drug user." Not surprisingly, the abuse, particularly the sexual abuse, had a traumatizing effect on Mr. Tupan, who reportedly felt ashamed and angry as a result. According to Mr. Tupan's forensic file, he struggled to make friends in elementary school and produced average grades. Reportedly, he enjoyed high school, particularly art class where he "came out of [my] shell…my teachers were amazed by my talents." Some of Mr. Tupan's file information suggests he attended 'the most prestigious art school'; other file information indicates he was primarily self-taught—"school is a waste of time … everything I learned, I taught myself." According to Mr. Tupan's forensic file, he had been employed his entire life, working in different areas, although collateral information suggests that he likely overstated his employment pursuits. However, he was not working at the time of his offences because he started to "hear voices," which negatively impacted his ability to concentrate. Mr. Tupan reported his passion to be in his art and had planned to pursue painting as his primary occupational focus had he not been detained.

In terms of intimate relationships, Mr. Tupan's forensic file indicated that he had reported having a number of long-term heterosexual relationships, which all ended due to his boredom; "it started to get old." His characterizations of his intimate partners were superficial and impersonal, resulting in questions about the extent of his commitment to them. It is noted that one of his relationships ended due to his heavy consumption of alcohol, the level of which he denied. Mr. Tupan's abuse of alcohol was, however, confirmed by collateral information from known associates. According to his file, Mr. Tupan had denied using any other substances, however, collateral information suggested he was a frequent user of marijuana and an occasional user of cocaine and methamphetamine. It is noted on his file that he was arrested on a number of occasions for erratic driving and driving under the influence of an intoxicant. These contacts with law enforcement represented the entirety of his criminal history prior to his offences.

Mr. Tupan's forensic file suggested that he did not experience any mental health challenges as a child or adolescent. He reported that he first experienced an auditory hallucination as young adult, that is, in the months leading up to his offences. Around this period of time, he had been reportedly experiencing problems in his relationship and at work and was also considerably "stressed out," as he put it. Some evidence suggests he may have been paranoid about the intentions of others and also held "delusional beliefs" around this period of time. For instance, it was noted that he felt that he was "extraordinarily special … and chosen for a righteous mission." However, there was no collateral evidence to corroborate Mr. Tupan's claimed mental health deterioration in the short period of time preceding his offences. Rather, information suggests that some of his behaviour could be explained by his bravado, grandiosity and/or use of illicit substances.

Due to the need for brevity, the above examples of Mr. Tupan's file and collateral information represent highlights of the information I reviewed for the purpose of his assessment. After a thorough file review of relevant available information, it is recommended that a clinical interview be conducted wherein mostly open-ended questions are asked so the patient is provided the opportunity to report his or her history and symptoms in their own words. For the most part, when interviewing, it is recommended that clinicians keep to themselves any suspicions of malingering to avoid arousing defensive and guarded responses from the subject of the assessment. Of course, at later stages in the interview process, it may be wise to alert the patient to certain hypotheses in order to assess the situation more thoroughly and provide the patient the opportunity to explain apparent inconsistencies, etc. It is also recommended that, for most of the interview, the interviewer should be careful not to ask leading questions that might hint at 'correct' responses. Interviewers must watch closely for signs of possible malingering such as reports of rare and improbable symptoms that are endorsed infrequently even by severely mentally ill patients (Rogers, 2008). That said, the interviewer might consider deliberately asking about improbable symptoms to test whether patients will endorse them. Interviewers must also watch for any inconsistencies in the patient's presentation, for example internal: conflicting statements; external: discrepancies between reported symptoms and actual symptoms observed such as when a patient alleges experiencing active auditory and visual hallucinations but shows no signs of being distracted (Resnick & Knoll, 2005).

The aforementioned interview strategies were utilized throughout Mr. Tupan's assessment. In fact, I interviewed Mr. Tupan on six occasions for about five hours in total, the length of time necessitated by the complex referral question and the multi-method-multi-trait approach employed. I recall vividly my first clinical interview with Mr. Tupan, an interview that transpired mid-morning. He presented in a suit and tie, rare for forensic inpatients, and his grooming and hygiene were impeccable, also an oddity considering the context. Mr. Tupan wanted to give me one of his recently completed paintings as a present, the one he labelled "Cured." After I informed him that, ethically, I could not accept a gift in this context, he insisted that I receive his art work as "a gift to the entire psychology department," noting that much insight could be gleaned about his psyche from observing his art. Mr. Tupan asked that subsequent interviews transpire in the mornings so he could spend his afternoons outside with his peers. "I want to enjoy the outdoors … it helps with my healing," is the way he put it. Although there were suspicions at the time, it was only after all of the interviews were completed that it was discovered that Mr. Tupan had been trafficking methamphetamine in the afternoons. In the afternoon interviews, he was concerned with completing the session by a certain time, often looking at his large, bright and flashy watch as that time approached. Again, it was only after all the interviews were completed that it was confirmed that the time in question was the time in which trafficking was found to have occurred on the grounds at the hospital.

Across all interviews, Mr. Tupan appeared to have exerted significant effort towards making a positive impression, the gift at the first interview being a choice example. Further, on many occasions, he voiced concern about my impression of him, for example, "how am I doing so far, boss?" He also denied minor difficulties and faults that most individuals typically acknowledge and generally presented with the appearance of controlled demeanour. Mr. Tupan often engaged in what has been termed 'verbal hedging' throughout the interviews; that is, he frequently repeated the interview questions before answering. This was not construed as a sign of misunderstanding the question but as a way for him to have more time to consider his apparent carefully crafted responses. For the most part, Mr. Tupan was selectively disclosive with his answers and often provided vague responses lacking substance. However, at other times, he spontaneously initiated dialogue and elaborated on topics such as his past and planned future accomplishments or his abuse history. In terms of the former, Mr. Tupan spoke at length about his natural propensity for the arts and his plan to achieve high status and wealth. Although within the realm of possibilities, given the state of his legal affairs and his then accomplishments, his overly optimistic statements and inflated views of his skills were viewed as remarkable.

With regard to the latter, Mr. Tupan frequently and spontaneously broached the topic of his history of childhood abuse by the hand and other body parts of this father as well as via household items that were used as weapons. He vividly and at length spoke of repeated beatings he received by his father such as being struck with kitchen utensils and telephones. He also recalled the emotional and sexual abuse he experienced, including anal penetration by objects and by his father's penis. Not surprisingly, Mr. Tupan perceived the sexual abuse to be particularly "traumatizing." Despite the nature of the abuse he experienced, he denied experiencing stress-related symptoms, which was inconsistent with his previous claims as per his forensic file ("the past is the past"). For example he denied experiencing any intrusive or involuntary distressing thoughts or images and, when discussing the abuse, he frequently yawned and, occasionally, exhibited a micro-expression of happiness.

For the most part, Mr. Tupan's emotional expression over the course of the assessment was shallow and did not alter, irrespective of the topic broached. He was not emotionally flat, however, as is often the case in individuals with psychotic illnesses or with patients heavily medicated. Indeed, after discussing what could be perceived as objectively affectively negative topics such as the murder of his father or the experience of anal rape, he was observed to smile and laugh at ease. In addition to not presenting with stress-related symptoms, there were no observations from the clinical interviews that Mr. Tupan was experiencing active symptoms of a psychotic disorder. For example, there was no evidence that he was responding to internal stimuli such as 'voices' and his thought processes appeared organized, goal-directed and rational. Interview information, however, is only one source of data. What about other data gathered for Mr. Tupan's assessment?

Another important piece of the puzzle in forensic psychological assessments concerns the issue of psychological testing. There are general psychological tests that assist in narrowing hypotheses about personality and mental health such as one used for the purpose of the present assessment. The results of this self-report test indicated that, in contrast to what is commonly produced by individuals attempting to malinger a mental illness, Mr. Tupan did not try to depict himself in a negative or pathological manner. Rather, the test results suggested that he attempted to portray himself as relatively free of common shortcomings to which most individuals admit, which was consistent with his statements in the clinical interviews. The overall pattern of results suggested that hypotheses generated about Mr. Tupan's mental health should be viewed with caution as he may not have answered the test in a wholeheartedly sincere manner. Mr. Tupan did not produce a clinical profile on the self-report test that would suggest the presence of a serious mental illness. The only subscale elevation of note concerned grandiosity, which was consistent with file information and clinical impressions gleaned from the interviews.

Grandiosity is a symptom of narcissism and psychopathy. As indicated above, one of the referral questions concerned whether or not Mr. Tupan was psychopathic and, to this end, he was assessed for psychopathy using a clinical rating scale that incorporates interview and file information. Consistent with the other testing results and clinical impressions from the interviews, Mr. Tupan met criteria for grandiosity. For example, he was described as such by his parents in addition to staff and patients on his living unit and, across interviews, he presented with an elevated view of himself and his abilities, saying, "I have always been considered special." Interpersonally, Mr. Tupan came across as glib via his unsophisticated use of psychological jargon and as superficially charming as evidenced by his slickness and cheap attempts at positive impression management. He said to me, for example, "you are the best psychologist I have ever met." There was also evidence of manipulativeness and pathological lying. In terms of the former, Mr. Tupan reportedly 'shammed' his way through a number of intervention programs motivated by his desire to appear concerned about his rehabilitation as opposed to making positive changes to address his mental health and behaviour. For example, he parroted back information he 'learned' in group treatment. With regard to the latter, Mr. Tupan frequently lied throughout the interviews and, when challenged with file information at direct odds with his self-report, he did not present as uncomfortable. Rather, he would alter his account again, with a subsequent statement suggesting credibility—"trust me ... I am being honest."

Core features of psychopathy represent an affective deficit that is thought to 'drive' the pathological personality disorder. That is, the scientific literature suggests that because psychopaths cannot experience secondary emotions such as love or guilt, they are prone to prey on others without the capacity to feel remorse for their actions or empathy for their victims. In this regard, there was ample evidence that Mr. Tupan lacked remorse and guilt for killing and dismembering his father, saying "I was sick when it happened ... I am cured now ... he deserved it ... the world is a better place." Any regret over his actions related to the effects of his behaviour on his current circumstances, for example, "I am the one inside here ... eating this shitty food day after day." As well, there was ample evidence indicating Mr. Tupan is an affectively shallow individual. For example, staff on his living unit commented on his limited range of affect beyond primary emotions such as happiness and anger; which was consistent with interview impressions. Indeed, he equated love with affection, anxiety with impatience, and he could not recall an event in his life that led him to experience guilt. There was also some indication of callousness as evidenced by the gratuitous manner in which he killed, dismembered, and sexually mutilated his father, irrespective of real or perceived psychosis. Moreover, Mr. Tupan described his behaviour in a detached, casual manner, as if he was describing what he viewed on television the previous evening. He did not understand his surviving family's grief over the death of his father; rather, he produced a superficial appreciation of his family's suffering—"he deserved it ... I heard voices ... and had countless delusions on top of paranoia."

There are a number of other characteristics of psychopathy possessed by Mr. Tupan, notably a failure to take responsibility for his actions and lack of realistic long term goals. However, he did not meet criteria for certain other primarily behavioural features (for example, criminal versatility), which was partially attributed to his relative young age at the time of assessment. Overall, Mr. Tupan did not meet the diagnostic criteria for psychopathy; however, his scores on the items measuring the interpersonal and affective qualities of the disorder were elevated. In fact, he could not have scored higher on these domains. As discussed above, some of Mr. Tupan's interpersonal psychopathic characteristics included a penchant for deception and manipulation. As malingering is a special type of deception—lying about mental illness—motivated by a manipulative attempt to achieve some secondary gain such as avoiding prison, was Mr. Tupan able to fool a psychological test specifically aimed at detecting malingering?

Mr. Tupan was administered the gold standard in the assessment of potential malingered psychosis in clinical forensic contexts in the form of a structured clinical interview. The results of this measure were interesting. In terms of Mr. Tupan's answers to the questions on the test, the results were mixed—some of his answers were suggestive of potentially malingering psychosis. For example, he endorsed symptoms that are rarely experienced by truly mentally ill individuals. However, other quantitative results suggested Mr. Tupan was genuine in his response to the test and, therefore, he was not likely malingering. It is these types of messy results that often cause evaluators concern. Although quantitative results such as the content of individuals' answers to tests are important, it is often the quality of the results of psychological tests that are just as or perhaps even more important considerations. That is, how a person answers questions on a test can provide insight into the inner workings of their psyche. In this regard, Mr. Tupan was observed to be frequently smiling when answering questions on this test, which was possibly suggestive of duping delight—the pleasure one feels when deceiving others. Further, questions that, on the face of it, appeared more clearly related to obvious questions of malingering led to increased mental effort or cognitive load on the part of Mr. Tupan. That is, he paused more and appeared to be relatively deeper in thought when answering certain questions, which suggested that some questions were answered in a socially desirable manner as opposed to a forthright manner. These qualitative results suggested to me that malingering remained a distinct possibility. The possibility of malingering was particularly salient when viewed in conjunction with the other data collected for the purposes of assessing Mr. Tupan. For example, it became clear that Mr. Tupan did not meet criteria for any known diagnostic category of mental illness.

In short, a multi-method-multi-trait assessment approach

resulted in serious questions about the validity of Mr. Tupan's mental health challenges as they related to his claims of psychosis. Let's review the data. According to file information, there was no evidence that Mr. Tupan was mentally ill as a child or adolescent. Reportedly, he experienced symptoms of psychosis as a young adult for a period of time before acting on delusions and hallucinations, which culminated in the death of his father. He was found NCRMD and, in hospital, his symptoms of psychosis quickly abated. Staff observations were mixed, with some suggesting he may have malingered a mental illness to avoid prison. The results of psychological testing were also variable and clinical interviewing revealed multiple attempts at impression management.

Is Mr. Tupan psychopathic? No. However, he has certain features of the disorder that, coupled with his history of abuse by his father, could partially explain his motivations that led to the murder of his father. Mr. Tupan did not appear to be experiencing, or to have experienced, significant symptoms of any known major mental illness. Rather, the data suggested he had likely manufactured a psychotic mental illness or exaggerated the symptoms of such for secondary gain. In our view, he fooled the system. He was found NCRMD on the partial basis of having a psychotic disorder, the symptoms of which reportedly impacted his ability to appreciate his actions that led to the death of this father. Although it is not our place to challenge the findings of the court, it is our duty as evaluators to provide a comprehensive assessment addressing the referral questions with information from a variety of sources based on best practice suggestions from the scientific literature.

Not surprisingly, Mr. Tupan did not fancy the results of his psychological assessment, the impact on his case of which is unknown at the present time. He also wanted his "Cured" painting, which he had insisted initially be hung in the psychology department library, returned to him.

## References

American Psychiatric Association. (2013). *Diagnostic and statistical manual of mental disorders* (5th ed.). Washington, DC: Author.

Baillie, P. (2015). A valuable (and ongoing) study, the national trajectory project addresses many myths about the verdict of not criminally responsible on account of mental disorder. *The Canadian Journal of Psychiatry*, 60, 93-95.

Cleckley, H. M. (1941). *The mask of sanity*. St. Louis, MO: C. V. Mosby.
Criminal Code, R.S.C. 1985, c.46, s.231(6).

Crocker, A. G., Nicholls, T. L., Seto, M. C., Côté, G., Charette, Y., & Caulet, M. (2015). The National trajectory project of individuals found not criminally responsible on account of mental disorder in Canada. Part I: Context and methods. *The Canadian Journal of Psychiatry*, 60, 98-105.

Crocker, A.G., Seto, M.C., Nicholls, T.L. & Cote. G. (2013). *Description and processing of individuals found Not Criminally Responsible on Account of Mental Disorder accused of "serious violent offences."* Final report submitted to the Research and Statistics Division, Department of Justice, Canada.

McDermott, B. E. (2012). Psychological testing and the assessment of malingering. *Psychiatric Clinics of North America*, 35, 855-876. doi: http://dx.doi.org/10.1016/j.psc.2012.08.006

Mittenberg, W., Patton, C., Canyock, E. M., & Condit, D. C. (2002). Base rates of malingering and symptom exaggeration. *Journal of Clinical and Experimental Neuropsychology*, 24, 1094-102.

Resnick, P. J., & Knoll, J. L. (2005). Faking it: How to detect malingered psychosis. *Current Psychiatry*, 4, 13-25.

Rogers, R. (2008). Detection strategies for malingering and defensiveness. In R. Rogers (Ed.), *Clinical assessment of malingering and deception*, (3rd ed., pp. 14-38). New York, NY: Guilford.

***Marc Nesca*** *PhD R. Psych. is a forensic psychologist and head of the Criminal Justice program at Athabasca University. He has been qualified as an expert in forensic mental health at all levels of Court in Alberta, and his opinions have been accepted in criminal court cases across western Canada and in the Northwest Territories. Dr. Nesca has also consulted on homicide investigations in both Edmonton and Calgary, and he has contributed educational seminars on forensic topics to both the Edmonton and Calgary Police Services. His research findings have been published in national and international journals, and he recently co authored the book* Forensic Interviewing in Criminal Court Matters: A Guide for Clinicians, *published by Charles C. Thomas.*

# Dr. Marc Nesca

## Catathymic Murder and Necrophilia

IN THE LATE EVENING OF JUNE 11, 2009, Cst. Kimberley Deal[1] heard a knock at the front door of an RCMP station in a remote community in northern Canada. Looking through a frosted glass window on the door, Cst. Deal noticed a young man crouched on the ground. She asked the man to stand, show his hands, and back away from the door. John Squire stood slowly, raised his hands, and stepped backwards, as ordered. Blood was now visible on his hands and clothes. As he stepped backwards, without prompting, he stated "I killed my girlfriend." Cst. Deal asked him to repeat himself, and he replied "I cut her throat. She's back at the apartment."

John's words were oddly emotionless and he seemed unaware of, or at least unconcerned about, the blood on his hands and clothes. The unusual circumstances of this apparent confession left Cst. Deal wondering whether John was mentally ill. As a precaution, John was placed in a holding cell and officers were dispatched to the address he provided. Emergency Medical Services (EMS) were also called as a matter of routine in a potential homicide case.

Police officers and EMS arrived at John's apartment shortly before midnight. The door was locked and there was no response to repeated knocking. Eventually, the decision was made to forcibly enter the apartment and an officer literally kicked the door in. On entering the apartment, police found a trail of bloody footprints in the hallway, between the washroom and the bedroom. The apartment was clean, but spartan. Signs of a struggle were obvious in the bathroom.

The victim was located in the bedroom, bent over the bed, face down. Her arms were stretched out beside her head, revealing a birth defect that had left her with one hand largely absent. Her leggings had been pulled down, exposing her genitals, and her legs were splayed. She was shirtless but wearing a bra. A bottle of personal lubricant was on the bed beside her. Blood staining was visible on her arms and head, and to a lesser extent on her buttocks and between her thighs. Relatively little blood was on the bed under her body or on the floor under her knees.

A much larger pool of blood lay about a foot away from the body, and portions of the adjacent wall and a white dresser were covered in arterial spray. A bloody folding knife, along with the victim's underwear and top, were inches from the pool of blood. Two pairs of men's blue jeans were slightly off to the side.

The victim had defensive wounds on her hands and arms. A large and very deep wound to her neck was also apparent once the body was moved. There was also evidence of post-mortem sexual activity. She was barely nineteen years old.

### *The Offender*

Although the perpetrator's identity was not in question, police in this case conducted a wide-ranging investigation that ultimately came to include information provided by the victim's friends and family. John's friends and family, as well as several of his co-workers and neighbours, were also interviewed by police. The portrait that emerged from these interviews was that of a well-behaved young man who had enjoyed a good childhood. Although painfully shy at times, John apparently got along well with others and he enjoyed reasonable success at school. His work history was also quite positive, with his co-workers unanimously describing him as reliable and hardworking but quiet. Without exception, everyone interviewed described John as non-aggressive.

Although John had briefly experimented with drugs during adolescence, from a forensic perspective his use of intoxicants was insignificant. All of his family members also confirmed that John had no history of trouble with the law and that he had not suffered abuse or trauma during childhood. Everyone, including the victim's parents also agreed that he was deeply in love with his girlfriend, though everyone also noted that he could be jealous at times. John's brother provided a bit more insight into this jealousy by noting that John struggled to accept that his girlfriend had been sexually active before they met.

Some minor jealousy notwithstanding then, the overall profile that emerged from these third-party interviews can reasonably be described as unremarkable—a term that is used in forensic settings to identify an area of inquiry that fails to identify anything unusual. In other words, everyone seemed to agree that John was a 'normal' young man: He wasn't a drug addict, he was law abiding and hardworking, he had no history of violence, he came from a good family, and he was a good partner to his girlfriend. How then does one explain the brutality and deviance that characterized this crime? This is not a rhetorical question as legal decisions often hinge on an understanding of an offender and his or her crime. At minimum, an explanation was required to determine whether John was to be held responsible for his actions or whether this crime was the product of a mental illness that absolved him of criminal responsibility.

### *The Assessment*

My involvement in this case began with an email from a lawyer I had never met. The email included a polite introduction, brief mention of familiarity with my work, and a relatively lengthy description of an 'unusual' case involving a young man without criminal past. The initial email concluded by asking if I would consider performing an 'NCR assessment'. The NCR acronym refers to a defence that is commonly referred to as 'Not Guilty by Reason of Insanity' among the general public.

For an NCR finding to properly apply, it is not enough for an accused to be mentally ill. The crime and the illness must be directly linked in a manner that altered the perpetrator's experience of reality. Consider the example of a person who suffers from Capgras Syndrome, a replication phenomenon that leaves sufferer's believing that people around them have been replaced by evil duplicates. If this individual kills her husband believing him to be a dangerous alien life form, she would likely qualify for an NCR defence because her mental illness directly caused the crime and because she had no idea that she was killing a person. On the other hand, if she killed a random stranger during an episode of road rage, her mental illness would be irrelevant, as it did not directly influence the behaviour in question. Much as very young children are absolved of criminal responsibility because they are deemed to be unable to understand the true nature of their actions, alleged offenders with a mental illness that robs them of their ability to accurately gauge reality are deemed NCR and given treatment rather than incarcerated. A successful NCR defence in this case would, therefore, place John in a forensic hospital for treatment rather than in a correctional facility.

After formally accepting the referral, I requested the entire disclosure package (all the legal documents relied on by the prosecution). Although some lawyers, and some of my colleagues, find this sort of request excessive, in all but the simplest cases I begin by reviewing all available documents. I follow this process for two reasons: 1) I am uncomfortable relying on case summaries prepared by others when a person's life hangs in the balance, and 2) a thorough review of the file provides a fund of information that allows me to both generate an interview specifically tailored to the case, and to check the accuracy of the information provided by the patient. The latter is critically important as patients in forensic settings have very strong motivation to lie or distort facts. This procedure is also consistent with standards of practice in forensic mental health that require forensic opinions to consider multiple sources of information. In this case, my opinion was based on documentary evidence that included information from police and civilian sources, extensive interview contact with the patient, and formal testing. Both my interview and the test battery that I relied on were significantly shaped by information that I gleaned from reviewing the disclosure package.

My review of the documents in this case revealed two observations that struck me as unusual and potentially relevant to my assessment. First, John had attempted a military career that had failed within weeks. This failure occurred not as result of John's inability to satisfy the physical or intellectual demands of military services but rather because he could not tolerate the yelling. It simply overwhelmed him. Second, a longtime friend and former roommate of John's reported that he had once eaten the same three meals every day for more than two years and that he would refuse to eat whenever that specific meal was unavailable. Although these observations are subject to multiple interpretations, within the context of other information about John's past, I recall thinking they suggested an extremely anxious and rigid young man who sought to combat his anxiety by structuring his environment (always eating the same thing) and avoiding excessive stimulation (constant yelling). As a rule, anxious patients will seek to minimize uncertainty and stress in their lives, often leading to a highly structured lifestyle. Whether this anxiety was part of a more severe mental illness such as schizophrenia could not be determined without examining John.

I met with John on five separate occasions, over the span of two weeks, for a total of about twelve hours. During that time, I interviewed him and tested him with instruments designed to assess various mental illnesses, malingering (faking mental illness), and sexual deviance. My interviews revealed a polite but insecure and relatively immature young man who cooperated fully with every aspect of the assessment. Although clearly unhappy with his situation, John was not mentally ill in any formal diagnostic sense. He did, however, present a complex psychological portrait that included dependency traits that tended to manifest mostly as submissive and clingy behaviour in his relationships, intense anger that he seemed largely unaware of, and very negative attitudes about women.

His mother, whom he literally idealized as the embodiment of perfection, was the only woman completely exempt from John's negative views about women. This created a powerful conflict for him in that he hated women but craved their affection and attention. John sought to resolve this conflict by seeking virginal partners whom he could paint with the fantasy brush of purity and thus elevate (almost) to the level of his mother or by seeking physically flawed partners who he believed were unattractive to anyone else. Both of these criteria (saintly and flawed) revealed a deep sense of inadequacy, with an accompanying desire to avoid comparisons to other men: Virgin saints literally had nothing to compare him to and physically flawed partners would, in his mind, be grateful just to have a sexual partner. In either case, he was spared the pain of possible comparison to other men, and the judgements that such comparisons imply.

John also discovered pornography at a relatively early age. Although not uncommon in our time of Internet pornography, John quickly became dependent on sex as a means of managing his emotions. While most of us experience sex, particularly with a genuinely loved partner, as emotionally soothing, some people become reliant on sexual activity as a general stress-management strategy. This dysfunctional use of sex is most commonly seen among sexual offenders, where it can be a risk factor for recidivism. In this case, John's problematic sexual behaviour was compounded by an equally rapid move toward extremely deviant sexual themes. He masturbated frequently, for example, to child pornography, found cannibalism sexually arousing, and had a history of sexual involvement with dogs. Mostly, however, John enjoyed videos about necrophilia. Note that all of these themes share the absence of possible comparison judgements and therefore allowed John to satisfy his sexual urges—and, by extension, his emotional needs—without disruption by feelings of inadequacy.

I also asked John about the two observations that I had made while reviewing the disclosure documents provided to me. John explained that he left the military because the yelling made him feel anxious and "like people were thinking I was stupid." He also added

> I couldn't take orders from a woman. I can't have a woman in a position of authority over me. Women must be subordinate....The male is the dominant. I don't like women being taller than me, stronger than me. I always have to be better than them.

Although I questioned him at length about his views on women, John could not identify the source of his feelings beyond indicating that he had "always been like that, since I was a kid." However, as I was scanning my notes in preparation to move to another topic, he spontaneously added "My mother is a Saint. My mother is exactly like I expect women to be." This unprompted statement identified a link between his misogyny and his mother. His earlier statement dating his dislike for women to childhood also suggests a point of origin that lies in his family of origin. Clearly, if John disliked women since his childhood, his feelings could not be attributed to negative experiences with girlfriends. Yet, his parents were apparently quite devoted to each other and, by all accounts, they enjoyed a reasonably good relationship and did not teach sexist values to their children. Unfortunately, John proved either unable or unwilling to explain himself further, leaving me to speculate on the psychological origins of this complicated love-hate dynamic.

My inquiries into the food matter proved even less fruitful, providing little beyond simple confirmation that this odd behaviour reflected an attempt to reduce uncertainty in his life. More specifically, when asked about the information provided by his roommate, John admitted that he had eaten the same three meals for "two to three years" and he explained his actions as simply motivated by the desire to produce a predictable routine that would reduce the number of decisions he needed to make on any given day: "Every single day, same work, same food, same sleep. It was simple." Although he may have simply been successful in concealing it from me, I could not find any indication that this peculiar behaviour was related to paranoid concerns about poisoning.

The battery of tests administered to John confirmed that he was not mentally ill in a conventional sense. In more formal terms, testing confirmed my clinical observations regarding the absence of acute mental illness and personality disorder. In other words, John was not burdened by a mental illness that caused him to be unstable or that altered his experience of reality, and his personality development had not been distorted in a manner that conformed to one of our diagnostic categories. Testing also ruled out the possibility that he was a Psychopath. Surprisingly, given the extremely violent crime he had committed, John's test results also indicated that he was generally *less* aggressive than the average person in the community.

John's test results did, however, reveal two noteworthy findings. The first involved *dissociative tendencies*. Dissociation is a relatively common phenomenon that includes experiences ranging from daydreaming to severe mental illnesses that completely undermine a person's contact with reality. The automatism defence in criminal court, for example, involves a severe dissociative episode that literally reduces one to the state of an automaton. More commonly, dissociation can be seen to operate when one drives to a location and on arrival has little memory of having navigated the route. In this relatively common experience, decisions are made, traffic laws are obeyed, and a destination is reached without full conscious awareness of the activities. Dissociation, therefore, occurs when the normally integrated functions of memory, behaviour, emotions, and perception are fragmented so that one or more of these functions splits off and operates independently.

As I noted earlier, in extreme cases such as automatism, dissociation can have a severe effect. The mental illness spectrum of dissociative illnesses, however, also includes less severe conditions that essentially distort but do not completely alter reality. *Depersonalization*, for instance, creates the experience of watching oneself perform various activities, much like one watches a character in a movie. John's test results indicated that his dissociative tendencies were more intense than those of the average person but still less intense than what is seen in severe dissociative disorders. In essence, his test results suggested a heightened vulnerability to dissociation rather than a formal disorder.

After reviewing these test results, I asked John questions about dissociation. Questions of this sort are posed indirectly to avoid biasing the patient's answers. In response he reported a history of dissociative episodes triggered by stress, especially the stress of being criticized. In his own words

> When someone criticizes me, its like a switch. Its like I'm watching myself get yelled at. I just kind of shut down, zone out .... It's not anything I can help, it just happens. It feels like someone else is getting yelled at instead of me.

The other test finding of note objectively confirmed what John had disclosed about his sex life: namely, that his sexual behaviours and fantasies were extremely deviant. Thus, his test results revealed strong sexual arousal to children, sadism, and rape. John also enjoyed hypoxyphilia (oxygen deprivation during sex, usually by choking), necrophilia, coprophilia (sexual arousal to feces), urophilia (sexual arousal to urine), and zoophilia (sexual arousal to animals). Some of these preferences were simply fantasies, others he had actively experienced. Regardless of whether they were fantasy or reality, John's sexual deviance was unusually deep and broad, a condition referred to as *polymorphous sexual deviance* or, in older Freudian terms, *polymorphous perversity*. Essentially, this condition refers to the ability to find sexual satisfaction in most situations and with an unusually wide range of objects and organisms—both human and non-human. A variety of theoretical explanations exist for polymorphous perversity, but most of these are quite old and, to some degree, unsatisfactory. The condition is largely ignored by contemporary researchers who prefer to simply note that sexual deviancies sometimes occur in bunches.

John's description of his offence was remorseless and self-centered. Not in the psychopathic sense of indifference to humanity in general but rather in an emotionally vacant description of events that focussed almost exclusively on his experience. He also repeatedly referred to his girlfriend in the present tense, as if she was still alive. The events leading to this crime began several days earlier, when the victim disclosed to John that she had been more sexually active in the past than he had been led to believe. This disclosure shattered John's fantasy of a not-quite-as-good-as-my-mother but ultimately acceptable partner and exposed him to the danger of sexual comparison judgements. It also placed him in a profoundly conflicted situation: He cared for the victim but had now come to recognize her as "just another whore."

John struggled with this conflict for days. He developed vague flu-like symptoms and vomited several times as his stress escalated. Eventually, he began to buckle under the weight of his emotions and his thoughts became infused with the misogynous view of women as manipulative.

> I couldn't eat, sleep, I couldn't do anything anymore...I thought she was the one...then I learned she was different...she was lying to me. She never really loved me. I tried to fight it but it was always in the back of my head. It just got harder and harder to fight whatever it was that I was feeling.

A few days before the offence, John attempted suicide by hanging. His attempt to kill himself was aborted by thoughts of his brother weeping at his funeral. This concern for his brother reveals an ability to form emotional bonds that distinguishes John from the cold psychopath who is unable to truly care for others. Oddly, throughout these struggles John experienced very little conscious anger. Instead, he felt mostly fear and confusion: Fear of being alone and confused feelings about his girlfriend.

On the day of the offence, John arrived home from work exhausted and stressed. He also had a knife in his pocket. When I asked him why he was carrying a knife, John could not explain himself beyond saying that it was a work knife that was usually in his car and that he felt he should bring it inside. His girlfriend arrived shortly after he did and John immediately asked to speak with her. He began by telling her that he loved her and by describing how he was struggling with her sexual history. She apparently responded with some variant of "get over it." They then briefly argued until she left the apartment to cool off. While she was gone, John was flooded by feelings of betrayal and he alternated between viewing his girlfriend as either his 'true love' or as 'a whore'. He also wondered whether she had gone to meet a former lover.

When she returned, John began to apologize repeatedly. She apparently remained dismissive and cold, until announcing that she intended to shower. As she headed to the bathroom, John placed his hand on her shoulder in an effort to calm her and continue their talk. John described this touch as gentle and indicated that she responded by coldly shrugging his hand off without looking at him. According to John, this act of rejection was the immediate trigger for the violence that followed. Before the victim had opportunity to speak or take another step, John stabbed her in the neck. He stabbed her several more times and then dragged her into the bedroom, where he cut her throat until she was dead.

John's initial attack on the victim triggered a depersonalization episode that caused him to experience these events as a detached spectator. He described seeing his hands performing the violence as if they belonged to someone else and that the sounds of the victims were muted, as if the volume had been turned down. John also recalled feeling calm while he watched these events unfold.

> Everything looked zoomed out. Like if you look in binoculars the wrong way. I couldn't hear anything. There was no sound. I couldn't feel anything in my hands.... It was all very peaceful, very quiet.

Eventually, the sounds of the victim began to gradually penetrate John's consciousness and he became fully aware of the situation. At that point, the victim was badly injured but still alive. Instead of stopping, John killed her. He explained that he wanted to silence the victim as he found the sounds she was making intolerable. He then stood, surveyed the situation, and calmly dragged the victim to the bed, where he positioned her as she was found and performed various sex acts on the body. He then drove to the police station and confessed to the crime.

Instead of panic or guilt, John experienced relief in the immediate aftermath of this crime

> ...like it took a big weight off my shoulders...like an angel said 'everything is going to be alright now. It's over'...I felt like I was floating under water, weightless. Everything was gone. It felt really peaceful.

It is common practice to end an interview by asking the patient whether anything important has been missed or whether he or she has anything to add. When I did this with John, he replied with a question that perfectly captured the essence of the legal system's concerns in cases like these.

> I've been a model citizen my whole life. All of sudden I am up on first degree murder charges?

### *Analysis*

John had indeed been a model citizen all of his life. So how was it that he came to commit this heinous crime? Although this complex case poses many questions, ultimately I needed to answer only three. The first question was the most directly relevant to legal proceedings: Was John mentally ill in a manner that had robbed him of his ability to fully understand what had happened? In other words, was he criminally responsible for his behaviour or was this crime the tragic consequence of a mental illness that absolved him of criminal responsibility? While doctors do not directly make this judgement, the information we provide has direct bearing on the final opinion of the Court. The remaining questions that I faced were relevant to legal proceedings but more clinical in nature. That is, I needed to explain the eruption of lethal violence in an otherwise non-violent man and the sexually deviant acts that followed.

The question of criminal responsibility was the easiest to answer. Recall that for an individual to be absolved of criminal responsibility he or she must suffer from a mental illness that leads directly to the crime. More specifically, for the Court to render an NCR finding, the crime in question must be the product of a mental illness that either 1) prevented the accused from truly understanding what he or she had done—in legal terms, appreciating the "nature and quality of the act," or 2) prevented him or her from knowing that the act in question was wrong. To return to our earlier example, the woman who kills her husband believing he is a dangerous alien would likely be found NCR for this crime because she didn't appreciate she was killing a human being ("nature and quality of the act"). One could also argue that this woman had no reason to believe that killing a dangerous extraterrestrial would be wrong.

In his case, John had no history of diagnosable mental illness and I found no evidence to suggest he had suffered a psychotic break during the crime. To be sure, he was falling apart in the days leading to this crime and he experienced an episode of depersonalization during the crime that left him feeling like a detached observer. However, developing physical symptoms and feeling overwhelmed by negative emotions are not sufficient to trigger an NCR finding. Remember, the line in the sand for a successful NCR defence is a mental illness that prevents one from understanding "the nature and quality of the act."

Although John's experience of these events was altered by depersonalization, he remained fully aware that his girlfriend was being harmed, and the final act of killing occurred after his mind had cleared and he was fully engaged with reality. Additionally, the episode of depersonalization was *triggered* by the violence, a finding that is not uncommon in extremely violent crimes. This crime, therefore, began and ended with a mind that was unclouded by a reality altering mental illness. Finally, John's confession to police reveals adequate appreciation of the nature and quality of his actions because, logically, if he did not appreciate that a crime had occurred he would have no need to confess to police. The statement "I killed my girlfriend" also indicates full awareness of the nature of the events in question. For these reasons, I argued that an NCR defence was not viable in this case.

My next task was to understand how a previously law-abiding man could commit such a violent and deviant crime. There was no prior history of domestic violence, no one had described John as controlling or domineering in his behaviour, and most saw him as quite loving toward the victim. There was also no indication that disinhibiting intoxicants such as alcohol had been a factor in this crime. In short, this did not appear to be the typical domestic violence case involving power and control dynamics, and John's negative feelings toward women did not appear to colour his interactions with the victim. Nor were the details of this crime consistent with what is usually seen in a case of a drunken or drug-fuelled assault.

As a first step in this analysis, I created a list of John's personality traits and the main features of his violent act. The former is relatively long, but, most relevant to this analysis, includes a fragile psyche leading to dissociative tendencies, a pervasive sense of inadequacy that left him fearing comparison judgements with other males, misogyny, and polymorphous perversity. The violence he had committed was peculiar in that 1) it was preceded by days of debilitating psychological tension that produced physical symptoms of nausea but was oddly free of conscious anger, 2) it culminated with necrophilia, and 3) it produced a powerful sense of relief.

The absence of pre-offence (conscious) anger and the presence of post-offence relief provided the clues that led me to a relatively rare form of violent behaviour: Catathymic Violence. Catathymia was first identified in the early 1900s by a psychiatrist who noticed that some of his patients developed a 'rutlike fixation' that undermined their ability for logical, reality-based thought and that threatened their personality integration. In more practical terms, these early patients appeared to become so fixated on an idea that their thinking became illogical and they began to fall apart. This coming apart is difficult to explain in a handful of non-technical terms, but it occurs at the very core of the psyche and results in some (or even complete) loss of control over thoughts, emotions, and behaviour.

Imagine trying to fill a very fragile but cracked vase with water. Gradually, the vase will lose its ability to contain the liquid and the contents will begin to seep out until it finally shatters. That, in a very general sense, is what occurs when a personality begins to lose its structural integrity; except instead of water, previously censored impulses, thoughts, and behaviours begin to leak out. Unrestrained sexual behaviour, substance abuse, and delinquency are common examples of what results when a personality begins to disintegrate. Vague physical malaise, such as flu-like symptoms, also commonly accompanies reduced personality integration. Stress is the most common cause of personality disintegration and everyone in modern society has experienced this to some degree. In forensic settings, stress is a risk factor for recidivism among sexual offenders as it reduces their ability to contain sexual impulses by undermining their personality integration.

Shortly after the original papers on catathymia were published, other practitioners began to notice a link to seemingly unprovoked violent outbursts, creating a bridge to the forensic arena. By the 1960s, a substantial body of work was available, including a number of case studies linking catathymia to acts of extreme violence committed by otherwise nonviolent and noncriminal people. Although a complex phenomenon, the essential core of catathymia is a conflict that overwhelms a person until he or she settles on violence as the only option for preventing complete personality disintegration. Note that this decision is not necessarily conscious so that the violence may be experienced as sudden by both the perpetrator and the victim. Feelings of inadequacy, dependency and a vulnerability to dissociation are commonly associated with catathymia in the professional literature, and loved ones are frequently the victims of catathymic aggression. Violence in these cases tends to erupt when the victim somehow threatens the perpetrator's adequacy, and the goal of the aggression is always to remove the threat.

In his case, John's core personality traits created a perfect storm for a catathymic homicide: his dependency combined with his misogyny to leave him alternating between loving and hating the victim and his brittle personality began to crumble under the stress of this conflict. Eventually John developed the physical malaise that is associated with catathymic violence and, though he experienced no conscious urge to harm the victim, it seems reasonable to suggest that he was unconsciously preparing for violence when he placed a knife in his pocket. The final trigger for the explosion of violence was the victim's dismissal of John's conciliator touch, an act that directly hit on his feelings of inadequacy ("felt like nothing I do is good enough for her"). The powerful sense of relief that John experienced after this crime is an almost universal feature of catathymia and reflects the removal of the terrifying threat of complete personality disintegration—essentially psychological death. Not in the sense of the objective reality most of us share, but in John's subjective world, he ultimately acted in self-defence.

The textbook interpretation of the necrophilia that followed this murder is of a final act of domination over the victim. I am not inclined to reach this conclusion. John never sought to dominate the victim and most people who knew the couple described him as rather quiet and somewhat submissive in the relationship. Instead, it is my sense that John was seeking one final safe union with a person he cared for. That this desire for intimacy was expressed sexually is not surprising given the massive sexual deviance that John harboured.

John's polymorphous perversity and his misogyny ultimately proved impossible for me to fully understand, as he was unable to shed light on the origins of these characteristics. As I noted earlier,

John was not raised in a family that openly promoted or modeled sexist beliefs, he was not exposed to domestic violence, and his greatest romantic trauma had been a cheating girlfriend in high school. None of this helps explain the harshly negative attitudes he held toward women or his unrealistic idealization of his mother. I could interpret John's feelings for his mother, and all other women, by reference to a number of theoretical explanations that exist for these observations. In the end, though, it would all be purely speculative and, I feel, disrespectful to John's parents as all theoretical explanations make reference to inadequate parenting of some sort.

Although contemporary forensic thinking favours behavioural explanations that explain sexual deviance as the product of prior learning, I do not believe these relatively simple models can adequately explain the perversity in this case. Many people become deeply involved with pornography and even sample deviant sexual themes without developing the range and depth of deviance that characterizes this case. At the risk of sounding excessively dramatic, in all my years of practice, I have never seen a more sexually deviant man than John. The sheer depth and breadth of his sexual deviance, the absence of sexual trauma or deviant learning experiences, his ability to find sexual pleasure in almost anything, and his feeble personality structure all lead me to view this case as best explained by Freud's idea of a fixation that left John psychologically stuck in a developmental stage where sexuality is emerging and as yet unfocussed. According to Freud, this developmental stage occurs in middle childhood and is a time of poorly formed sexual drives that are later shaped by learning and social expectations. In some regards then, this can be viewed as time of primitive sexual behaviour. Existing biases against Freudian thinking notwithstanding, I believe psychoanalytic concepts best explain John's sexual deviance.

Forensic psychologists are expected to provide objective, dispassionate services to the legal system. I take this responsibility seriously and make a point of never following a case after my involvement is complete. I do not, therefore, know what has become of John other than his lawyer abandoned the NCR defence after I submitted my report. In the end, I am not sure my findings would have mattered much beyond ruling out an insanity defence. The legal system, and this not a criticism, simply cannot deal with complex clinical issues like catathymia and polymorphous perversity. All that really matters is that a young woman was killed by a young man who was legally responsible for his actions. The remaining details of this case are dealt with at sentencing hearings. Sadly, the findings of this assessment are also unlikely to be of much importance to treatment providers as our correctional system favours the behavioural explanations I mentioned earlier. I imagine that, as I write this, John is being cycled through several behavioural programs. He will be asked to sit in a classroom, take notes as a prison guard or 'program staff' lectures from notes prepared by someone else and he will be given homework to do. All in the service of educating him about effective problem-solving or recognizing the red flags for sexual re-offence. None of these absurdly simplistic interventions will even scratch the surface of John's problems.

NOTE 1. Dates and names have been changed, and appropriate consent to publish was obtained.

# PART THREE

# Insights and Glimpses of the Future

*To think the world therefore a general Bedlam, or place of madmen, and oneself a physician, is the most necessary point of present wisdom: an important imagination, and the way to happiness.* —Thomas Traherne

***Jeffrey Waldman*** *MD FRCPC has demonstrated a keen interest in the interface between Mental Health and the Law since his residency training program. He incorporated two years of his residency training in Forensic Services in the Department of Psychiatry at the Health Sciences Centre. As a resident, he won the Fellowship Award of the Canadian Academy of Psychiatry and the Law in 2002. Upon completion of his residency in 2003, he immediately joined Forensic Services and has gone on to qualify as a subspecialist in Forensic Psychiatry in September of 2013. In March 2013, Dr. Waldman became the Medical Director of Forensic Services for Manitoba. Dr. Waldman also provides didactic teaching on topics in Forensic Psychiatry for residents doing their training at the University of Manitoba, as well as providing clinical supervision to medical students and residents at the PsycHealth Centre of the Health Sciences. Dr. Waldman is an Assistant Professor in the Department of Psychiatry in the Faculty of Medicine at the University of Manitoba.*

# Dr. Jeffrey Waldman

## Vince Li

JOHN KREPSY. That was the name of the 'bogeyman' when I was growing up. He was the character in the stories told around campfires. He signified the evil that kept me from touching my bedroom floor with my foot for fear of what might be under the bed. When I was a child, John Krepsy was a fictional character that personified evil in my mind. For my children, like countless other children and adults across Canada, the nonfictional character that embodies evil for this generation is Vince Li.

This past year, my son took a class called, 'Canada in the Contemporary World' which touched on mental illness and the meaning of the legal finding of 'Not Criminally Responsible'. The class learned about mental illness in the context of media reports regarding a possible change in Vince Li's Disposition Order, which would allow him to roam freely in the community. As a part of that class, my son participated in an on-line blog with his classmates discussing the prospect of increased liberties for Vince Li that would allow him to move around in Winnipeg, Manitoba freely. The level of the fear that Vince instilled in my son's peers was profound and somehow difficult to understand. While we were ignorant about severe mental illness when I was young, mental illness is now openly discussed. There are educational campaigns. There have been statements from various levels of government about care and respect for those suffering from severe and persistent mental illness. Even 'Hockey Talks'. But an ongoing lack of understanding of severe mental illness, and learning about mental illness from the media reports of cases like Vince Li, continues to feed the fear of the person, rather than the illness.

In the past decade, Winnipeg has been known as 'The Murder Capital of Canada'. There is no shortage of brutality that occurs in the context of homelessness, poverty, substance abuse, and domestic violence, often fuelled by alcohol. There never seems to be a shortage of violent crime triggering assessments of criminal responsibility by our program. But in the time that I have been doing this work, nothing has terrorized this province like the image of the evacuated Greyhound bus and the subsequent eyewitness accounts of Vince Li calmly but viciously stabbing, decapitating, and cannibalizing Tim McLean. The seemingly arbitrary and public nature of the attack contributed to the terror, with every Canadian devastated for the innocent victim, his family, and his friends. The images of Mr. Li also contributed to the nation's horror: his lack of affect, his lack of response, and his apparent lack of emotion. We now know these were all symptoms of a severe episode of psychosis. These factors all contributed to the nation's horror at what had occurred, and triggered a nation's desire for justice. Those images, and the feeling that we all have for the victim, have combined with a lack of understanding of mental illness, stigma and fear, to leave even educated people expressing fear of Mr. Li being allowed to freely roam the Winnipeg streets.

### *Distorted Reality*

The Honourable Shelly Glover was Minister of Canadian Heritage and Official Languages when she was quoted as saying; "Just the mere fact that this brutal act happened indicates … that he is a risk to cause grave harm to the public" and that "because of the brutal nature of what he did, we ought to fear there is the potential for him to reoffend." It has been pointed out by cynics that Ms. Glover may have been using the Review Board decision regarding Mr. Li to advance the Harper Conservative Party's political views. In any case, many people share her fear. I socialize with university-educated professionals. They attend fundraising events for mental illness. They read the newspaper and news magazines, and are, for the most part, socially responsible and caring people. I consider my friends intelligent humanitarians, but I consistently hear them express sentiments similar to those of Ms. Glover. It is these conversations with my peers that demonstrate the impact Mr. Li has had upon this country and the fear that is maintained by the majority of Canadians of those who suffer from severe mental illness.

At the time Mr. Li was arrested, I was working as a Consultant in Forensic Psychiatry. I was providing psychiatric care to inmates at a Provincial correctional institution, Headingley Correctional Centre, as well as providing care and completing out-of-custody court-ordered assessments in the Outpatient Department of Forensic Services. I was not involved with the initial court-ordered assessment of Mr. Li, which was completed by Dr. Stanley Yaren. There was a subsequent report provided by an Ontario psychiatrist, Dr. Jonathon Rootenberg, at the request of Mr. Li's lawyer, Mr. Alan Libman. Both Drs. Yaren and Rootenberg agreed that Mr. Li was suffering from the effects of a severe mental disorder that affected his ability to appreciate the nature and quality of his actions and to know what he was doing was wrong. Mr. Li's reality was distorted by the effects of an illness that led him to believe he was carrying out God's will.

I have never been psychotic and, as such, I can never really know what it must be like. But after talking to thousands of patients who have experienced psychosis, I think the best way for someone to understand what it must be like is by watching horror movies. A common premise in horror movies is that the main character begins to notice things around them that suggest something odd is occurring. Then it progresses to noticing that others are involved in those events. When the protagonist tries to talk about it, no one believes them and no one sees it the way they do. Those events become more and more clear as we see the 'truth' through their eyes. The phenomenon becomes clearer through messages, coincidences, visions of spirits, evidence of possession by demons, or influence of alien beings; ending in an often-violent climax where the protagonist saves themself and defeats the evil force. And no matter how bizarre the premise, we can accept that the protagonist has resorted to violence in those circumstances. It was the only reasonable thing to do.

To someone who is psychotic, their experiences are their reality. They are responding in a way that makes sense based on what they believe is going on around them, no matter how bizarre or unrealistic it may seem to others—and the potential for that violent episode exists depending on the content of the psychotic person's experiences and beliefs. For Mr. Li, his symptoms had persisted for three years before they reached the intensity where he resorted to violence. He was living with the belief that he was the 'Chinese Jesus' and that his mission on earth was being gradually communicated to him by God.

On July 8, 2008, Vince Li left Edmonton, Alberta in response to God's voice instructing him that he was to return to Winnipeg. Prior to his departure on the bus from Edmonton, he bought a knife from a Canadian Tire store, based on God's voice warning him that he may have to protect himself from evil forces on his journey. While on the Greyhound bus, Mr. Li began to get messages from what he believed to be God telling him that the man in the seat next to him was evil and that this man would tear Vince's intestines out of his body if Vince didn't kill him. As he was attacking the victim, Mr. Li heard what he believed was God's voice telling him that if he did not remove this person's various body parts, the evil being would reanimate and kill him. This resulted in the dismemberment of his victim's body after his death, his victim being twenty-two-year-old carnival worker, Tim McLean.

Based on the evidence provided by both expert psychiatrists, Mr. Li was found 'Not Criminally Responsible on account of a Mental Disorder (NCR).' The experts testified that Mr. Li's reality was so strongly influenced by his symptoms that he had no appreciation of the reality of what was occurring when he killed Tim McLean. So although he did cause the death of Tim McLean, there was no conscious intent to do so and he had no appreciation of the consequences of what he was doing.

After being found Not Criminally Responsible on Account of a Mental Disorder (NCR) Mr. Li remained on the fifteen-bed Forensic Assessment unit at the Health Sciences Centre for approximately one year. This was a long stay compared to the ten days he'd spent in hospital after his first episode of psychosis. He was then transferred to the eighteen-bed Forensic Unit at Selkirk Mental Health Centre in Manitoba. By this time, Mr. Li had essentially made a full recovery from his episode of psychosis.

Manitoba does not have minimum or maximum secure facility designation. The Forensic Unit at Selkirk Mental Health Centre is essentially a long-stay rehabilitation unit in a provincially run facility that had been the site of Manitoba's Asylum for many years and continues to maintain its focus on inpatient psychiatric treatment. There is no outpatient program attached to the Selkirk Mental Health Centre. In 2014, after Mr. Li had spent six years in hospital, psychiatrist Dr. Stephen Kremer was considering providing his opinion to the Criminal Code Review Board that Mr. Li no longer posed a risk to the public and that he could be safely managed in the community. The Forensic Services Program in Winnipeg offered to provide a second opinion in the form of a comprehensive multidisciplinary assessment. Mr. Li was transferred to the Forensic Unit at the PsycHealth Centre of the Health Sciences Centre in Winnipeg, which is a teaching hospital program.

I had been the Medical Director of Forensic Services for approximately one year, and had become the only Forensic psychiatrist on the inpatient unit which acts as an Assessment Unit, an Acute Care Unit and also performs transition planning. As such, Mr. Li was admitted under my care.

My first introduction to Vince Li was shocking, considering the fear associated with his name and the image I had in my mind from six years of Mr. Li entering court while he was still very ill. Vince was unlike most of our patients in Forensic Services. He did not have a substance abuse disorder. He did not have a personality disorder. He was well educated. Up until the time of his index offence, Vince had worked consistently throughout his adult life and had maintained a long-term marital relationship—a relationship that had ended in the context of his illness. Vince was warm and engaging. The cold stare he'd had around the time of his offence was replaced by a warm smile. He has a way of making people feel relaxed and comfortable just being around him. He has taken advantage of all the opportunities provided to him, working with his treatment team to fully understand his illness and his need for medication. He has demonstrated a clear commitment to his recovery and ensuring that he never becomes ill again. He continues to demonstrate profound remorse for what occurred when he was ill, and has used this to motivate himself towards achieving a full recovery. He quickly went from being one of the most notorious and dangerous offenders in our program to being extremely well liked and posing essentially no risk to the public. But let's not get too far ahead of ourselves …

### *Early Life*

Vince Weiguang Li was born on April 30, 1968 in Dandong City in Northeastern China. His father was a janitorial custodian and his mother was a math teacher. He has an older brother and a younger sister, both of whom have post-secondary educations. His early family life was unremarkable. There is no history of physical or sexual abuse, substance misuse or chronic illness, however he does have one maternal uncle with a history of mental illness.

Vince was born one month prematurely and his family described him as 'very fragile' and sickly until his early teens. His ex-wife explained that Vince was spoiled because of his family's perception that he was fragile. According to Vince, the 'spoiling' consisted of getting one egg per day in a time when there was not enough food in China to go around. His parents were told that Vince's lung disease would get better if he had the nutrients of an egg. As such, he received this extra egg every day for a year. His brother and sister were very jealous of this special treatment; Vince indicated that this resulted in some sibling conflict. Vince was an intelligent young man who did very well in high school. As a result of his academic achievements, he had the opportunity to go on to study engineering in central China. He graduated with a four-year engineering degree in Applied Electronics and Computer Engineering from the University Of Wuhan Institute Of Technology in 1992.

After obtaining his Engineering Degree, Vince found a job in his chosen field. He began working in a factory, designing and building computer hardware. It was at this job that he met his wife who was working as an electronics assembly assistant at the same factory. Vince and his wife dated for three years prior to getting married. He worked on the factory's hardware development for two years, and when that contract was completed, he was rehired by the same factory to develop their Internet network. He completed that contract two years later and once that job was completed, he obtained another contract providing similar services to another factory. Around this time, Vince and his wife had been planning to come to Canada for a better life that they'd hoped freedom in Canada would afford them.

### *Emigration Challenges*

Vince and his wife emigrated to Canada in 2001. They had initially intended to move to Toronto, but after some online research, Vince realized that the cost of living in Winnipeg compared to Toronto would allow them a better standard of living while he looked for employment. As is common with many educated immigrants in Canada, he had difficulty finding employment to match his training. His first job was working in the kitchen area in a McDonald's restaurant (his English was not good enough at the time to serve customers). He worked at McDonald's full time, his wife obtained a job in a Thai Restaurant and both attended English as a Second Language classes. After working at McDonald's for a year and a half, Vince quit to pursue a Computer Programming Diploma from CDI College with the hope that he could find work in his chosen field. He completed his Computer Programming Diploma in 2002 but even with this additional training plus his prior work experience in China and his University education, he continued to only find lower-level labour jobs. After he received his diploma, Vince accepted a job for six months through a job placement agency setting up a new Sears department store. After that job was completed, he found another labour job working in shipping and receiving with a Chinese food warehousing company in Winnipeg. He stayed there for a year and a half.

While Vince was working at the food warehousing company, he saved enough money to buy the couple's first car. While stopping at Tim Horton's on his car-shopping day, a woman approached him asking questions about his background and what he was doing. Vince explained that he and his wife had emigrated from China, that they were both working, and that he was looking to buy a car. The woman told him that if he went to a certain church in the city, the people there would help him get a car. Excited with the prospect of getting some help, he went to the church. No one gave him a car, but both he and his wife got jobs there.

Vince hadn't been involved previously with this church, but after meeting kindly people who were interested in supporting them, Vince and his wife decided to start attending services. In retrospect, Vince identifies that his thinking began to change around this time. His thinking, as he put it, became more sped up. He had lots of interests. He had more energy, and decided that he was going to run a marathon. He worked from two o'clock in the afternoon until eleven o'clock at night and got into the habit of running through Assiniboine Park for two to three hours every night after work. He became fascinated with Canada's harsh weather and the original settlers and for some reason that he finds difficult to explain, he was inspired to spontaneously move to Thompson, Manitoba against his wife's wishes. He remained there for four months and found a job working the midnight shift at a Walmart, stocking shelves. It was while Vince was on his own in Thompson that he first began to hear a voice from the sun telling him that he was the Son of God, and that he was the 'Chinese Jesus'. Whenever he made decisions at that time, he would walk outside and stare at the sun to wait for instructions about what to do.

What he did next was take a Greyhound bus to Toronto. He had been in Canada for four years and had no friends, no family, and no support system. His wife did not understand that he was experiencing emerging symptoms of psychosis and the two of them became disconnected. Vince knew that a childhood friend from his home town in China had moved to Toronto, so at the direction of the voice he was attributing to God, Vince went to Toronto to connect with this childhood friend. When Vince got to Toronto he did not know how to find his friend. He was experiencing intense symptoms and was completely immersed in a distorted reality that was dictated by his psychotic symptoms. He had spent all of his money by this time and turned again to the voices for direction. The voice told him to go to the airport as someone there would help him return to Winnipeg. After spending hours asking strangers for money at the airport without success, he was directed by the voice to simply walk back to Winnipeg. After two hours of walking down Highway 427, he was picked up by an ambulance and taken to hospital. Vince's memory of his time in hospital is vague. He recalls receiving one injection, sleeping for two days and then escaping from the hospital. Documentation from the hospital paints a different picture.

Vince was hospitalized at the William Osler Health Centre at Etobicoke Hospital Campus from September 3, 2005 to September 13, 2005. He had been brought to hospital by police officers involuntarily after he was found walking on Highway 427 in Toronto. Vince maintains that he was aggressive with staff upon admission to hospital due to the fact that he was receiving information via hallucinations instructing him that staff were somehow intending to harm his wife. Vince was described as "dishevelled, confused and unable to talk." They also describe him as

> ... vague, seemed to be hallucinating, staring into space. He was talking occasionally and asking staff not to hurt him. He was unable to give any history. He has not slept or eaten well for the last three days.

Based on his presentation that day in Etobicoke, he was diagnosed with 'Schizophrenia-Catatonic State.' Despite the description of the severity of Vince's symptoms, he was hospitalized for a relatively brief ten-day admission. During that brief stay he was treated with multiple medications initially to address psychotic agitation including intramuscular Olanzapine, intramuscular Clopixol Acuphase, as well as oral Risperdal at a dosage of 2 mg, three times a day. After a few days in hospital, an antidepressant agent, Celexa, was added at a dosage of 20 mg per day. The day before discharge, he was started on Epival (a mood stabilizer) at 500 mg twice a day.

Vince reports that he did not understand why he was in hospital. He believed he was being punished and he had no understanding of any of the five different medications that he had been started on during his brief ten-day admission. According to documentation, Vince requested discharge and as such was discharged against medical advice. According to Vince, he had no contact with mental health professionals after being discharged from hospital and took no medications from the time he left hospital in September of 2005 until that tragic day on July 30, 2008.

After leaving the hospital in Toronto, he was able to get his wife to help him return home to Winnipeg. As far as she understood, he had gotten into trouble and had been hospitalized because he had done something wrong. During the previous six months, he had been going wherever he wanted and was spending all of their money and did not consult or listen to her. He was talking about things that did not make any sense to her, and so when Vince returned to Winnipeg she made arrangements to return to China the next day to secure a divorce. Neither Vince nor his wife understood that he had become ill, neither knew that he required treatment, and even if they had understood what was happening, neither knew how to access help.

According to Vince, he continued to experience auditory hallucinations after leaving Toronto. The voices continued to influence his behaviour and his perception of reality for the next three years. Vince was of the opinion that he was hearing God's voice from the sun and he was compelled to do what it told him to do. Although he was socially isolated and now divorced, he remained surrounded by co-workers and acquaintances from the church that he regularly attended. But, he was completely alone with his hallucinations and the distorted view of the world created by symptoms of psychosis. Vince's life had become a nightmare, with risk and messages at every turn. He had been carrying a knife with him for months prior to the offence in response to hallucinations and delusional beliefs.

How does a hardworking, educated immigrant from China with no history of violence become one of the most notorious killers in Canada? A number of factors had to come together for this to occur. The most obvious reason is the severity of symptoms that Vince was suffering at the time, as a result of his persistent and protracted untreated episode of psychosis. Even with these symptoms, the level of violence that occurred is still uncommon. Despite the frequency with which psychosis occurs, most of the patients in our program engage in violence in the context of psychosis because of difficulties that co-occur with psychosis; these can include substance abuse, a history of trauma, and often personality traits including maladaptive coping strategies and emotional problems that predate the emergence of the psychotic illness. However, Vince does not have a personality disorder or, as far as we were able to determine, a history of trauma. Vince does not have a history of substance abuse nor was he intoxicated at the time of the offence. The most significant factor that contributed to the tragedy, aside from the severity of his symptoms, appeared to be his isolation and lack of supports.

Vince had had a previous episode of psychosis, for which he had been hospitalized. That first contact with mental health professionals resulted in a quick release from hospital without treatment providers having any opportunity to educate Vince about his illness. Nor was Vince connected with any mental health services upon his release. Vince's wife, at the time, did not have any understanding of what was happening to her husband. As such, she divorced him in the context of an emerging severe mental illness that went untreated for almost three years. It appears that he was symptomatic through this entire time, though he continued to work and stayed involved with his church. He did not, however, have any supports to assist him in accessing necessary treatment. It is hard to imagine that none of the people with whom Vince was working, and none of the men or women in Vince's church, understood what was happening to him well enough to help him access treatment. It is possible the image of this isolated immigrant slowly becoming immersed in psychosis triggered too much fear regarding Vince in those around him, and that this fear further isolated him.

After the killing of Tim McLean and subsequent comprehensive psychiatric assessment and medical workup, Vince began treatment with the antipsychotic, Olanzapine. His symptoms gradually subsided during his time in hospital. He has consistently taken his antipsychotic medication since September 2008 and he had shown gradual improvement to the point where he has not been experiencing any symptoms of psychosis since 2009. A review of Vince's history is not consistent with any medical illness other than a psychotic disorder.

The death of Tim McLean was a tragic event. Tim McLean was an innocent bystander with whom every Canadian could relate. His death devastated his mother, every person on that bus, as well as the first responders. This tragedy has had a profound impact on the general public locally, nationally and even internationally. There were countless victims as a result of Tim McLean's death. I would count Vince Li as one of those victims, along with his wife. There were countless lives destroyed by a very serious illness that resulted in Vince's episode of psychosis. Unfortunately, it appears Vince, his ex-wife and those that knew Vince did not understand what was happening to him nor did they appreciate the dangers of a prolonged, untreated psychosis. If they did understand what was happening, they did not understand how to help him access treatment.

Prior to my work on the Forensic Assessment ward, I worked on a Psychiatric Intensive Care unit for seven years. That unit treats those who have severe symptoms of a psychiatric illness that is thought to put them at risk for violence. Because of the scarcity of psychiatric hospital beds, there is incredible pressure to move patients through as quickly as possible. There are, however, limited community resources available for patients on discharge from hospital. I have seen many patients who could have had an equally tragic outcome as did Vince Li. There are countless people, along with their families, who have to suffer the consequences of psychosis in isolation without being able to understand what is happening.

### *Response to the Tragedy*

Vince has now been provided with support, effective education and treatment. He is doing very well from a mental health perspective. Our country would benefit from a system where those who suffer from psychosis could access appropriate treatment and support prior to, or instead of, being found NCR for a tragic event. The most frightening aspect to the horrible Greyhound bus event is that the response to this tragedy has gone towards developing legislation that punishes those who get sick rather than creating a system that educates the public about severe mental illness and facilitates access to treatment. The Harper Conservative government's response was to create a 'High Risk Accused' designation for those found NCR for a 'brutal' crime and a process for prolonged detention of someone who has shown to have had no criminal intent. Instead, the Canadian government could now choose to focus their efforts on providing education, ensuring easier access to effective treatment, and focusing on decreasing the fear and stigma of severe and persistent mental illness. It could be argued that the real injustice is that we learned nothing from this tragedy, and have done nothing to ensure that it is any less likely to happen in the future.

***Lawrence Ellerby** PhD has provided clinical services to violent and sexual offenders since 1987. He is the Clinical Director of Forensic Psychological Services, Ellerby, Kolton, Rothman and Associates, a practice specializing in assessing and treating high risk/high need offenders. Lawrence is a consultant to the Canadian Center for Child Protection and the RCMP Crisis Negotiation Team, a trainer for the Canadian Police College, the Chair of the Sex Offender Management Sub-Group of INTERPOL'S Specialist Group on Crimes Against Children and a past President of the Association for the Treatment of Sexual Abusers. Lawrence is a Lecturer for the Department of Psychiatry at the University of Manitoba, has published articles and book chapters related to working with high risk offenders and has given invited addresses in Canada, the United States and Europe. He is a past recipient of the Canadian Criminal Justice Association's National Crime Prevention Award.*

# Dr. Lawrence Ellerby

## Taming the Lion
## A True Story of Community Risk Management

So what do you do when a sexually sadistic, mentally disordered homicide offender is released to your community? You manage the risk. I conduct psychological risk assessments and provide treatment to men who commit violent and sexual crimes. I have been doing this for over twenty-five years. I have provided clinical services to men incarcerated in federal correctional institutions and provincial corrections centres, those detained in provincial mental health facilities, plus individuals released to or sentenced to community dispositions. Most of my treatment work has been in the community, where the rubber hits the road and risk management is a live issue. In the community, an offender can experience stressors that may escalate risk including negative peer pressure, or easy access to alcohol, drugs, pornography, and weapons.

My experience is that when high-risk offenders are provided a comprehensive and integrated risk management 'treatment' plan that includes support, supervision and monitoring, risk can be successfully managed, even with dangerous offenders. This approach to offender risk management is often overlooked and under-emphasized. A treatment plan for the high-risk offender is complex. It is long term.

Some will argue that it is too expensive and not where we should be allocating precious tax dollars. The reality, though, is treatment is more cost effective and has a better outcome in enhancing community safety than most public policies we have in place that claim to be tough on crime. Another reality is that most offenders are released back to the community. Would you prefer they have treatment or not?

Most of the forensic clients I see are designated high risk and high need. In spite of this, I can tell far more success stories of long-term positive treatment outcome than stories of failures and sensational incidents of re-offending. There is a capacity to alter the life course of individuals designated high-risk and help them remain safe in the community. This challenges the public's perceptions about this population and highlights the contributions we shrinks can make in this difficult and complex social problem.

To illustrate this, I want to share the story of Darren William Smith. Darren consented to me writing this chapter and we reviewed it together prior to publication. He agreed to me telling his story because he wants people to know he is committed to never hurting anyone again and that it is possible to move from deviance to rehabilitation. His story is true, but his name has been changed for his privacy and confidentiality.

### *The Crime*

On a summer day in the early 90s, the body of a seventeen-year-old female was found on the outskirts of a rural municipality in Manitoba. A Crime Stoppers tip identified Darren William Smith as a suspect, the caller noting that he had boasted about being responsible for this murder. Darren was arrested and charged with Second Degree Murder. He remained in custody until his trial and was ultimately convicted of Manslaughter, receiving a nine-year sentence. His mental health and intellectual functioning were considered mitigating factors in sentencing. Details about his psychological functioning, offence motivation and history of violent pre-occupation and behaviour were not known. Had this information been available to the court, a Manslaughter conviction would not have been considered.

According to the police investigation Darren picked up a teenage girl who was hitchhiking in Winnipeg, Manitoba at two o'clock in the morning. It is believed that when he drove away from her desired direction, she began to resist and a physical confrontation occurred between the two. Darren drove out of the city to the outskirts, slowed the vehicle and his victim jumped out in an attempt to escape. He then struck her with the vehicle, exited the car and proceeded to strangle her; first with his arm, then using a belt and finally with his hands. Following the murder he removed her coat, shirt and bra, pulled down her pants and ripped her panties in order to look at and access her body. There was evidence, and later an admission, of post mortem aggression and sexual contact. Darren spent considerable time with the body, leaving and then returning to the crime scene. He disposed of articles of her clothing, some of which he later led police to. Other pieces were never located. Police believed the unfound items were hidden to be retained as his souvenirs and/or trophies.

During the investigation, a search of his hotel room revealed that he had produced a number of child-like drawings depicting women being physically assaulted, sexually assaulted, and murdered in variety of ways including choking, stabbing, shooting, and drowning.

In describing their interactions with him during the investigation, police described Darren as "a master at the art of manipulation." In an effort to secure his release from custody, he threatened suicide if he was not released, implicated another person as responsible for the murder, and attempted to have support people advocate on his behalf. Police noted that he had a very strong desire to return to the crime scene. During police interviews he disclosed having killed other women and spoke of disposing their bodies in a specific forest. He offered to guide them to this location. Police drove him to locate the other bodies on a couple of occasions. The trips required travelling the route Darren had taken his victim to commit the murder. As they travelled, he was described as having a "glazed over" look in his eyes; police believed he was replaying his offence in his mind. No other bodies were discovered.

### *The Man*

In my years of working with hundreds of men who have engaged in perpetual violence, sexual crimes, sadistic offences, and murders, I have learned that the vast majority of these 'evil' acts are not committed by evil people. There have only been a handful of occasions when I actually felt I was in the presence of evil; confronted with a personality who was beyond what, I believe, we know how to address and manage from a mental health perspective. In the majority of cases, when I meet the man I have been asked to assess or treat I am struck by how this 'monster' looks entirely normal; in front of me stands an individual who is broken, fragile, and in many ways vulnerable. The curtain has been drawn and the Wizard of Oz is not really a wizard at all.

As an astute client once related in a group therapy session, "hurt people hurt people." This in no way suggests that a person's history of neglect, abuse and trauma diminishes or excuses their culpability for criminal behaviour. What it does do, however, is provide a context for how they arrived at this behaviour. It outlines the origins of their disenfranchisement, hostile perceptions towards others, rage, and attempts to escape reality through alcohol, drugs, pornography and/or immersion into a distorted and destructive violent and/or deviant sexual fantasy world. It helps us to understand how and why they learned the coping strategies they did and brings humanity to the person in spite of the inhumanity of the acts they committed.

Darren William Smith was born in 1968. He entered the world with the cards stacked against him. He was born with an intellectual disability resulting in cognitive impairments that would impact his intellectual capacity, ability to process information and learn, impair his ability to think abstractly and problem solve, and inhibit his ability to regulate his impulsivity and emotions. His mind was prone to think concretely and be black and white in its perceptions. He is also disposed to fixate. His ability to read social cues is impaired as are his other social skills. Darren was also born with a severe speech impediment. This made him difficult to understand and presented a further obstacle to interacting with others, forming relationships and gaining a sense of acceptance, connection, belonging, and self-worth.

With these challenges came further disruption. He was born to parents who themselves were limited in their capacity to raise a family of five children, two with special needs. Darren's father was cognitively limited and, like Darren, also had a speech impediment. He was an alcoholic who was abusive towards his family and physically aggressive towards his wife and Darren. His anger was particularly focussed on Darren, likely due to a negative identification with his son. Darren's mother was ineffectual. She did not have the skills or ability to nurture—she didn't know how to properly parent her special-needs children and was limited in her capacity to protect her children from her husband's abusive behaviour. When Darren was ten years old his mother abandoned him. She left her husband and the family home taking his siblings with her and leaving Darren behind. Life was not kind to Darren. He was left in an environment of neglect, an absence of caring and love, and raised by a father who continued to drink and who subjected him to verbal, emotional, physical, and possible sexual abuse.

Not surprisingly, Darren struggled in school both academically and socially. His elementary and early grade-school experiences were marked by failure, rejection, and ridicule. He struggled in all subject areas and required modified programs and extra support. He had some assistance from teachers, but this was not enough to outweigh his abusive home environment and social rejection at school. His poor social skills, speech impediment, awkward gait, and poor hygiene made him a target for being ostracized. Darren did not fit in with any peer group and was rejected, teased, and bullied by both male and female students. He built walls of self-protection against the constant barrage of mistreatment he endured at home and in school. He learned to see people as a threat, didn't trust anyone, and developed a negative and hostile attitude towards people, particularly females. He had a few friends in his early school years, one girl in particular who also had an intellectual disability and was bullied. He became protective of her and became enraged when she was teased, acting aggressively towards children who taunted her. This friendship was short-lived as her family relocated, resulting in another loss.

Darren began acting out in a variety of ways that resulted in him receiving some in-home support through respite workers who looked after him when his father was out working. Darren was eventually placed into a specialized group home at age sixteen. Life continued to be challenging. Although he had some meaningful relationships with support staff and showed a strong desire for connection, he was on a destructive life course and immersed in revenge and sex-based violent fantasies. He was also escalating in his aggressive behaviour.

Darren became preoccupied with the idea of obtaining a driver's licence and a vehicle, which he saw as a symbol of competence, maturity and independence and as a means of having more mobility to meet women. Although he harboured mistrust, fear and anger towards females, at the same time he desired attention, acceptance, nurturing, belonging, connection … and sex.

At age eighteen, Darren was discharged from the group home as child welfare ended their involvement with him as he transitioned to being an 'adult.' A retired child welfare worker who knew Darren but did not work directly with him allowed Darren to move in with him for just over a year, which offered some buffer, however Darren then attempted independent living. He was joined in his second apartment by his father, who needed a place to stay. Darren was found to be in violation of the lease by having another person living in the apartment and was evicted; however his father remained. After living in his car for almost two weeks, Darren moved into a hotel.

In the years leading up to the murder, Darren lived a pathetic existence. He was alone and isolated with no substantial relationships. He lived in a seedy hotel room. He had limited skills for independent living. The condition of his home was deplorable. His diet was abysmal; he ate mostly frozen food, canned food or partially cooked or overdone food. He was on welfare, had a limited budget, but managed his finances well enough to purchase and maintain a vehicle. His car was his prized possession. He took pride in owning it and being able to do minor repairs. His vehicle was his freedom and later became a tool for realizing his deviant fantasies.

The last straw for Darren appeared to come at age twenty-three when his grandmother tragically passed away. Although he did not have regular contact with her, he experienced her as a kind and caring woman. She became a symbol of having received some affection in his life and he cherished her and those memories. All the important females in his life had left him.

### *The Escalation*

As with most individuals who commit violent and sexual offences, there was a progression of feelings, negative and distorted thoughts, and destructive styles of coping that escalated over time and culminated in a series of increasingly aggressive acts leading up to Darren committing murder.

Darren's progression to violence began with spending time in his head, ruminating about the abuse he had endured and fantasizing about revenge and becoming the one with the power, control, and dominance. His aggression began with fighting those who bullied his female friend and evolved to acting out his anger by hurting animals. At age fifteen, he began to rebel by frequently lying, stealing, avoiding home, and staying out all night. He also commenced what would be a life-long pattern of aggression against inanimate objects—throwing, breaking, punching, and kicking things in close vicinity. Also at fifteen, he began sexually acting out at school by grabbing at peer-aged female students' breasts and genital areas. The education system was of course alarmed by his behaviour and child welfare was brought in to assist and manage this difficult young man. The focus however was predominantly on setting limits and establishing external controls with little attention to addressing 'why' he was behaving so badly. One-on-one supervision was put in place to thwart his constant attempts to sexually act out at school and his behaviour shifted to making obscene calls to his teachers. This ultimately resulted in being expelled from school.

In his mid-teens, Darren's sexual fantasies began to incorporate themes of violence, escalating to include thoughts of killing women. These fantasies offered a means of venting his rage and fulfilled his desire to strike back and make others suffer as he had. He also believed the only way he could associate and have sexual contact with a female would be to use aggression and force compliance. Darren began to believe that killing a woman would prevent rejection and ridicule and would offer him unobstructed sexual access and a means to fulfill his fantasies. He offered that he did not want to experience further rejection as it just hurt too much.

During the time these fantasies were forming, Darren attempted to suffocate a female support worker. He snuck into her room in the middle of the night and held a pillow over her face. She awoke and pushed him away. This act was identified as being triggered by her setting limits and enforcing rules. However, in considering his fantasy content of homicide and necrophilia, it is more likely he was attempting to create an opportunity to have sex. This act of aggression was handled internally within the care agency with little apparent consequence and was never reported to police. Despite Darren's very unsettling behaviour, there was no information to indicate that child welfare, criminal justice, or mental health interventions were put in place to address these concerns.

As Darren's fantasy life became more entrenched, his sexual and aggressive acting out escalated. In his early teens he developed a predatory pattern of seeking out animals, particularly cats, and harming them. Between ages fourteen and twenty-four, he identified having tortured and killed approximately forty animals, killing them in a variety of ways, including strangling with a belt. At age twenty-one, Darren was charged and convicted for cruelty against animals. He had been observed calmly picking up a cat, taking it to the school yard and throwing it to the ground several times and kicking it. A psychiatric assessment completed for court indicated that Darren was very impulsive and used aggression against inanimate objects and animals as a means of venting his anger. No evidence of mood disorder or psychosis was identified and he was diagnosed as suffering from an impulse control disorder with antisocial personality traits. Darren admitted to the offence and was aware his actions were wrong. He identified with being 'mad', although he offered varied explanations about why he was mad. In addition, he was described by the psychiatrist as having no remorse. Darren was sentenced to one year of supervised probation. He did not receive any psychological intervention.

Darren disclosed thinking about and planning the commission of a sexually motivated homicide for approximately one year prior to his offence. He identified a plan to trick a vulnerable woman into his vehicle, noting that a vulnerable female would be easier to entice into the car. She would also be less likely to be missed, enhancing his ability to remain undetected. He also described a plan to take his victim to a pre-determined isolated site to act out his fantasy. Later in my work with Darren he revealed having moved beyond fantasies and that he had planned actual 'practice runs'. He described cruising the streets at night offering rides to women who were walking alone or standing at bus stops and also identified approaching sex-trade workers. He related having been thwarted by various situational factors that prevented him from being successful in luring a woman into his car or keeping them in his vehicle until the time of his offence.

With all this additional information, it was clear that Darren's level of psychopathology was high, his offence was pre-mediated and he was quite cunning and dangerous. Although Darren lives with intellectual and mental health challenges, as he likes to assert, he isn't stupid.

### *The Road to the Community*

After he was sentenced, Darren was incarcerated at Stony Mountain Institution (SMI) where he served most of his sentence. He was housed on a specialized range for mentally disordered offenders and over the course of his incarceration, attended various life skill and correctional programs. He was referred to the Regional Psychiatric Centre (RPC) in Saskatoon, a forensic psychiatric facility operated by Correctional Service of Canada (CSC). There he participated in an intensive treatment program for individuals with intellectual disabilities who had committed sexual crimes. Darren attended programming at RPC on three occasions over the course of his sentence; in the mid-90s for two years; a few years later for a year, at which time he was discharged for his lack of progress and for becoming preoccupied with violent and sexual thoughts about a pregnant nurse and beginning to stalk her; and a year after that for six months for intensive programming prior his release.

Some limited gains were noted as a result of Darren's participation in correctional programs, however he continued to present with significant issues and remained preoccupied and aroused by violent and sexually violent thoughts. He was repeatedly assessed as high risk. He was detained by the National Parole Board of Canada, meaning he was required to serve his entire sentence with no eligibility for an early release as he was deemed likely to cause serious harm or death to another person should he be released prior to the end of his sentence. There was a sense of fear and hopelessness surrounding the management of his case. The CSC team working with him did their best to address his issues; however most mental health and correctional professionals who worked with Darren were convinced it was inevitable he would sexually harm and/or kill another woman. The comment most frequently offered in his case was, "it was not a matter of if he will re-offend in a violent manner, but when."

In 1996, the Chief Psychologist at SMI requested I provide individual psychotherapy for Darren. She believed the best opportunity for risk management, in this case, was to have Darren develop a long-term working relationship with a psychologist with whom he could continue to work after his eventual release to the community, offering a continuum and continuity of care. I began working with Darren and met with him at SMI on an ongoing basis up until his return to RPC in 2000.

Darren was a very resistant and challenging client. He could be demanding, easily angered and was extremely concrete, egocentric, immature, and stubborn. When he discussed his past acts of violence against animals and females or reflected on a scene depicting violence against a woman he had seen on television he would become very excited, smiling, rocking, and laughing. He acknowledged becoming aroused to sexualized violence and continued to perseverate on these types of thoughts and fantasies. Prison cell searches at various times discovered he was continuing to produce drawings of violence, sexual aggression, and murder. One search resulted in a strange discovery of miniature cut-out figures of people. Darren reported creating these for a game, in which he tortured the figures; hanging them, lighting them on fire, stabbing them, tearing them apart.

The central goals of treatment in this case were to help move Darren to a place where he would be prepared and have some investment in managing his risk, see the benefits for himself and others of not hurting anyone else, and develop some basic skills to manage his emotions and deviant sexual interests. The first, and probably most critical and challenging task was to develop a therapeutic rapport with him. A young institutional psychologist asked me what the point of providing therapy to Darren was, given the extremely poor prognosis. My response was that if Darren can form an attachment that will facilitate him reaching out and seeking support when he has violent or sexually violent thoughts in the community versus acting on them, treatment would be a success. This was the goal for me: to connect with someone who did not trust, was antisocial, deceptive and manipulative, and who had a very limited history of any type of attachment. Over time, a relationship evolved. I would be greeted as I entered the therapy room to him writing out 'you are crazy' or 'my best bug' on the white board. Perhaps not typical terms of endearment, but signs of connection nevertheless! All these years later, he still regularly reminds me that I am his 'best bug' and proclaims, 'don't you forget it.' Amongst the intense and difficult therapeutic discussion was lighthearted teasing that went back and forth as part of the relationship development. Darren *loved* liver. I *hated* liver. I challenged him that if he was able to remain offence free and in the community I would take him to a restaurant and we would eat liver together on his fortieth birthday. This became a running joke between us.

As the working relationship developed, we were able to explore the origins of his violent and deviant sexual interests and identify the historical, emotional, cognitive, behavioural, and situational factors that led up to his offence. Knowing what contributed to his offenses enabled us to work on developing knowledge, skills, and strategies to manage these risk factors. Much time was spent giving simple messages and teaching him that violent thoughts and fantasies are not okay; that they hurt others, hurt him, and need to be managed. Treatment also helped Darren to better understand and connect with his emotions. This meant addressing his developmental history and trauma and processing his feelings of abandonment, rejection, hurt, and loss. As this work progressed and he became more emotionally aware, sessions focussed on basic empathy skill development and teaching him to be 'other-oriented', that is gaining some ability to recognize how others might feel and how his actions can impact others. Treatment also focussed on healthy ways of coping and how to use his support system.

Treatment with Darren was painstakingly slow and challenging with many periods of him being highly resistant and returning to unhealthy and destructive forms of coping. He did however make some progress prior to his release. He became more self-disclosing about his personal and offending history, talked more openly about his sexual interests and arousal, and accepted responsibility for his aggressive and sexual offending behaviours, including the murder. There was a reduction in his acting out within the institution, with fewer incidents of being aggressive, hostile or inappropriate in his interactions with staff and other inmates. He developed some rudimentary insight into the factors contributing to his offending behaviour, was compliant with taking medication to assist in reducing his violent rumination, and demonstrated some progress in being able to challenge violent thoughts when they occurred. He identified a desire not to hurt anyone again and wanted to stay out of prison. Although encouraging, these treatment gains were fragile and in their infancy. He was still viewed by others, including myself, as being a very dangerous man. Risk management in the community was going to be very challenging. At the time of his release, police described him as a "time bomb waiting to explode."

Prior to Darren's release, a Section 810.2, Cause Fear, of *The Criminal Code of Canada* was applied for and he was released on a Recognizance/Bail Order. An 810 Order allows for offenders who are assessed as high risk to be placed on community supervision and compelled to comply with stringent conditions, which, if breached, result in criminal charges. What is interesting about an 810 Order is that an individual is charged for what they might do, based on their level of risk, versus for actually committing a crime. Although the fairness of this provision in the *Criminal Code of Canada* is certainly up for debate, these orders have been very beneficial for attending to risk management for many of our high-risk clients as they create a means for supervision, structure, accountability, monitoring, and support in instances where the individual would have been released from a federal penitentiary with nothing in place to provide structure, support, or to keep the community safe.

### *Community Risk Management: It Really Does Take a Village*

The day of Darren Smith's release was like an episode of a crime drama. There was significant coverage leading up to his high-profile release and the media were camped outside the prison. He was escorted from the institution to our downtown office by law-enforcement who whisked him away, delivering him to the back loading door of our building for an anonymous entry. The process of supporting him to safely integrate into the community was about to begin.

To support Darren's release to the community, a very comprehensive plan and multi-system approach was put in place. Input into the risk management plan was provided by the Manitoba Integrated High Risk Sex Offender Unit (MIHROU), a joint Winnipeg Police Service and RCMP unit; Manitoba Justice (High Risk Offender Prosecution Unit, the High Risk Offender and Sex Offender units of probation services); the Provincial Special Needs Program (PSNP), Community Living disAbility Services (CLdS) and Employment and Income Assistance (EIA) programs of the Department of Jobs and the Economy, and our practice. Roles were identified for each of the parties involved, a clinical intervention plan was laid out, and a commitment was made to work as an integrated team. Team meetings, which included Darren, were held on a regular basis to share information so everyone was working together to attend to Darren's needs and support community safety.

The Department of Family Services, a provincial department charged with providing case management and support services for intellectually disabled individuals, referred Darren for a psychological assessment upon his release to the community. The psychologist identified Darren as being at an "extremely high risk" to re-offend, and described there being "serious and grave" public safety concerns; the psychologist also indicated that he "absolutely required twenty-four-hour-a-day, seven-day-a-week supervision and programming." Although around-the-clock service was an understandable recommendation, it was not feasible. Family Services referred Darren to FPS and supported us to identify and develop a comprehensive treatment and support plan that would both attend to his needs, and address community risk.

Our practice is not your typical psychological practice. In addition to traditional psychological services, our practice offers a range of client support services, life skill and recreational programming, cultural approaches to healing, and residential supports with a therapeutic milieu. Over the years I have come to understand that talk therapy alone would not suffice in the management of high risk/high need offenders. Attending to the multitude of needs presented by this client group requires a holistic approach and a range of interventions that can assist clients take the information and skills gained in therapy and help them practice applying these in real world settings in their daily lives. Darren's community-based treatment started with him participating in two individual psychotherapy sessions per week and attending a weekly therapy group specifically designed for individuals with intellectual disabilities who had engaged in inappropriate and/or criminal sexual behaviours.

He also worked intensely with our Community Integration Managers (CIMs). CIMs provide practical life skill support to clients helping them with a host of practical needs (community adjustment, attending appointments, hygiene, budgeting, securing health care, accessing education, training, or employment), risk management needs (monitoring behaviour, confirming information shared to ensure accuracy/honesty, providing crisis intervention) and act as mentors and role models, assisting clients to learn to implement healthy coping skills. CIMs provide individual support as well as group-based activities designed to foster a host of positive life skills (social and interpersonal skills, problem solving and conflict resolution, frustration tolerance and delay of gratification, emotion management, empathy development). Client programming also serves to instill a positive set of life experiences and offers opportunities most of our clients have not had. Creating instances of inclusion in community events and activities, fun, celebration and success helps to sustain long-term risk management. As individuals develop positive memories, see themselves as more than the sum of their offending behaviour, and feel part of and connected to others and the community, they develop a reason to stay out of trouble, not hurt others, remain in the community, and be future oriented. Darren received thirty hours of CIM support per week and participated in individual support hours as well as life skill, recreational, and volunteer groups. Darren worked extremely closely with his first CIM, Bill, who was a tremendous support. Bill's patience, guidance, firmness, and caring significantly contributed to Darren's community integration, adjustment, risk managements, and transformation.

Housing presented a significant dilemma. The rent allowance allowed by social assistance placed significant limitations on where Darren could feasibly reside. Additionally a Community Notification alerting the public that Darren was a dangerous offender being released into the community further limited housing options. This resulted in an initiative to develop a specialized model of housing that was integrated into the overall treatment plan and offered independent but heavily supported and safe housing. Darren became the first resident of The Healthy Home model. CIMs and Residential Mentoring and Support Staff monitor the residents' behaviour in the home and deliver in-house life skill programming: budgeting, shopping, cooking, cleaning, laundry, recreation. Darren's days were highly structured, busy and productive. There were significant supports in place.

Our clinical and support team also worked, and continue to work, in a collaborative manner with the forensic psychiatrist from Forensic Services, Department of Psychiatry, Health Science Centre, who oversees pharmacological interventions to assist in moderating Darren's violent and sexual preoccupation.

Another important component of the risk management and community support plan was the engagement of Darren's family. Darren processed his past family of origin issues and wanted family connection. To their credit, most of his family were willing to support him to the best of their ability, in particularly his brother. Family members were invited to attend system team meetings, individual sessions, and CIM outings facilitating contact between Darren and his family members. Family were invited to Darren's celebrations; marking his anniversaries of being offence free in the community and his birthdays. His treatment team also spent time with Darren and his family to mark his mother and father's passing.

In addition to the multiple clinical services, other systems also provided key support. Darren received specialized, intensive and excellent supervision and support by Manitoba Justice's high-risk sex offender probation unit. He received comprehensive case management through PSNP and CLdS. He was further monitored by MIRSOU who conducted random curfew checks and surveillance, and encouraged him to stay out of trouble. This multi-system team met with Darren regularly for an extended period of time to review his progress, any concerns the team had, any concerns he had, and to continually evaluate his level of functioning and refine the risk management plan as required.

The mobilization of all these resources along with Darren's acceptance and active participation with his supports allowed for positive change. Darren adjusted and integrated into the community, progressed in treatment, and stabilized in his overall functioning and the management of his risk factors. He has maintained a strong commitment to not hurt anyone again; has demonstrated the ability to effectively use his supports, and allow, when necessary, limits to be set on him. He has also shown the ability to manage inappropriate thoughts and to recognize and remove himself from high-risk situations, while informing his team. He has become much more aware, in control, and appropriately expressive of his emotions; has improved his communication and interpersonal skills and has shown, caring, kindness, thoughtfulness and empathy for others.

As Darren progressed, the intensity of the interventions and supports he received were reduced. Individual psychotherapy moved from twice per week, to once per week, to bi-weekly. Today, I still meet with Darren for maintenance sessions, with these typically occurring once per month for a half hour. He completed the group therapy component of treatment and his CIM hours reduced from thirty to ten hours per week. He continues to receive individual CIM support time and participates in some group based CIM programs but to a lesser extent than he originally did. He continues to live in a supported residential placement. Team meetings are now held on an as-needed basis.

### *Shosana and Smokey*

With all the supports I have described, I want to highlight two very important and unique members of Darren's treatment team. These are Shosana and Smokey. Once Darren was assessed to be stable, it was strategically determined to assign him a female CIM to create a therapeutic opportunity to develop a healthy working relationship with a woman. For the last seven years, he has been working with Shosana and this has proven to be an extraordinary relationship with a significant positive impact on him. For the most part, Darren has been cooperative, respectful and appropriate in working with Shosana. He has verbalized his appreciation of her and the support she provides him. There have been occasions when Darren has become angry, resistant and stubborn with her, however he has never been aggressive nor sexualized her and is quick to take accountability and apologize for occasions when he has been difficult. The other important team member is Smokey, his cat, yes, his cat.

About ten years ago, Darren became adamant about wanting to have a pet cat. Obviously there were significant concerns about this given his history of cruelty towards animals. He had made significant progress in treatment by this time, had an extended period of stability and did not have legal conditions that prohibited him from having a pet. After significant deliberation, the team decided to support him to have a cat, with specific therapeutic preparation for this and a plan for close monitoring to ensure the animal's safety and well-being. Darren has consistently cared for and been loving to Smokey, his best friend, for over a decade. Smokey has provided Darren the opportunity to learn to nurture, care, be responsible, and to make amends for his past mistreatment of animals.

### *The Outcome*

This has been an extremely challenging case; one of the more difficult, resource intensive, and clinically complicated men we have had to manage in the community. The provision of clinical and support services has been long-term and supports of some kind will likely extend life long. Darren was released late winter of a year in the early 2000s. Later, during that summer, he stopped taking his medication and made a number of harassing telephone calls to police, upset about his conviction and incarceration. In the fall, he made threatening telephone calls to a nurse who treated him at RPC. For the commission of each of these offences he was sentenced to time served (a few days) plus three years supervised Probation. A few years later he was again detected making threatening telephone calls. One of these was a random call to a florist shop in the United States where he told an unknown woman he was going to sexually assault and murder her daughter. The woman, who actually had a daughter, contacted police. Police cautioned him but no charges were laid. So, are these behaviours indications of a treatment failure? In our business we refer to this as harm reduction. Although certainly not what we hoped for, and of serious concern, this was a containment of his violence.

Since 2004 Darren has had no new charges, has not been suspected of any additional offending behaviour, and is no longer under intensive police monitoring. In 2008, the fateful day occurred, Darren turned forty. He reminded me of the deal I made with him while he was incarcerated. He was in the community, offence free, and now I had to eat liver. He was thrilled! Strangely, this wager appeared to be a potent therapeutic intervention to support risk management. In making this bargain I had been quite confident that he would never collect. My thinking at the time was that he was so dangerous, the chance of him remaining in the community was slim and his self/health-care was so poor that his longevity was also in question. He however was very invested in seeing me eat his favourite food. I guess this is what you call taking one for the team!

As far as we know, Darren has been offence free for over twelve years. Not to say that there haven't been many challenges along the way, and these continue. At various times over the years he has perseverated on different females which required intervention, he has self-reported struggling with violent thoughts against women and identified using the coping skills he has developed to contain these, and at times we have discovered him gravitate to watching movies with violent or sexually violent content. During the writing of this chapter, Darren's father passed away and subsequent to this, his CIMs discovered he had downloaded a number of nude pictures of women on his smart phone, as well as images of dead women. This required an intensification of clinical intervention and support for a period of time until he stabilized. And so he, and we, continue to manage risk.

### *Concluding Thoughts*

What do we learn from Darren and this case? We learn that people who commit heinous crimes are not all evil. There is a life trajectory that leads to these tragic occurrences. Preventing such crimes requires early intervention for traumatized and acting-out children and adolescents. Would Darren's story be different if therapeutic supports had been put in place in his youth? Could harm have been reduced and a life saved?

This case also highlights the importance of strong correctional systems focussed on innovation and best practices. At the time of Darren's incarceration, CSC was an internationally recognized leader in research and effective approaches to rehabilitation. In the last decade these practices and this reputation has woefully eroded. Being smart on crime, practicing good corrections, and offering sophisticated mental health services make our communities safer. Being tough on crime and offering generic and simplistic programming does not.

Darren's story illustrates that entrenched deviant interests do not go away. They are persistent. At certain times over Darren's life, particularity during periods of stress/distress they re-emerge. However, they can be contained. Darren's case shows us that if necessary it is possible for dangerous offenders to be successfully managed in the community. It also highlights that if an atypical offender like Darren can be managed, safe community integration and risk management is not only possible but probable for the vast majority of offenders.

Darren also provides a remarkable example of the resiliency of the human spirit and how, if given the opportunity and support, even very damaged people can return to their true selves. For Darren attachments, joy and caring have replaced disconnection, rage and a desire for revenge. And the community is safer for this.

Finally, this case points to how we could benefit from shifting the way we think about and respond to crime. It is completely understandable to be shocked, angered and become punishment oriented when hearing about violent and sexual crimes. As a forensic psychologist, I orient to 'why' these crimes occur and strive to learn about the roots and effective responses. This is something, as a society, we might benefit from and do more of. So you might say, what about the victims? What about their rights? Who cares about and protects them?

In my clinical work, thoughts of the victims are front of mind and often haunting. These thoughts guide those in my profession to do the best work we can, as we understand and appreciate the stakes. These thoughts also contribute to coming to understand the pathway to the restoration of balance. An authentic way of obtaining restorative justice and community safety comes through addressing the origins of these terrible crimes, versus only punishing the man.

***The Honourable Mr. Justice Richard D. Schneider**, B.Sc., M.A., Ph.D., LL.B., LL.M., C.Psych. is a Justice of the Ontario Court of Justice, Chair of the Ontario Review Board, and Deputy Judge of the Territorial Court of the Yukon. He was previously a criminal defence lawyer and certified clinical psychologist. Counsel to the Ontario Review Board from 1994 to 2000. Certified by the Law Society of Upper Canada as a specialist in Criminal Litigation. Private practice was generally limited to the representation of mentally disordered accused. Also, Adjunct Professor, Department of Psychiatry, Faculty of Medicine and Faculty of Law, University of Toronto. Named Honorary President of the Canadian Psychological Association in 2002. Also, appointed Alternate Chairman of the Nunavut Review Board. A great deal of his time has been spent presiding at the Mental Health Court in Toronto. Major research interests are competency and criminal responsibility. Has published extensively in the area of mental disorder and the law. Recent books include:* Mental Disorder and the Law: A primer for legal and mental health professionals *(2006, with H. Bloom);* Mental Health Courts: Decriminalizing the Mentally Ill *(2007, with H. Bloom and M. Heerema);* Annotated Mental Health Statutes *(2007);* The Lunatic and the Lords *(2009);* Law and Mental Disorder: A Comprehensive and Practical Approach *(2013, with H. Bloom), all published by Irwin Law.*

# Mr. Justice Richard D. Schneider

## A Day in Mental Health Court

THE VERY FIRST THING I do at the beginning of every day as I am entering the courtroom, with the clerk's booming "All Rise!" and as I am in mid-flight up to the bench, and as the clerk bellows "the Ontario Court of Justice is now in session," and just as I am alighting on to my perch, to the clerk's "Please be Seated!" and on to my "Good Morning" to the court at large, I discreetly scan the room. Safely seated, I make my more particular overture, "Good Morning, Madam Crown."

"Good morning, Your Honour. Charles, initial 'M', for the Crown, we have a long list today."

I know that we have a long list—my docket is right in front of me!—but in a courtroom we say a lot of things that don't need to be said because we are always 'creating a record'. I am still scanning the courtroom; sizing up the situation. What kind of a day will it be? Will we get off to a fast start? Do there appear to be lots of accused ready to go? Who is here? Regulars? Problem cases? Will there be a school class to entertain at a break? Just how many pages are on my docket? How many accused are in-custody versus out-of-custody? What counsel do I see? The good ones? The bad ones? The fast ones? The slow ones? Who are my clerks? All of these variables are considered in answering the question: What kind of a day are we going to have? These are all things that are being reflexively processed in my brain in one-half a second or so as I sit down, open my bench book, and pour my first of many glasses of water.

Many of the individuals in the body of the court did not respond briskly, or at all, to the 'All Rise!' command. Some are wearing hats, some are slurping on coffee, some are eating something, some (measured by the distance of the nearest other customer) are malodorous, and some are talking to others, or themselves (normal court decorum, notwithstanding). But the court room constabulary take no notice. They are relaxed. The people attending 102 Court often appear wearing and carrying everything they own, including the last coffee they scammed with the last cigarette butt found tucked behind one ear. Here, traditional but unnecessary rules are relaxed considerably if not dispensed with entirely. This is mental health court.

"Alright, Miss Charles, what can we do?"

Sizing up the situation further, I see a handful of our regulars who will simply be remanded to another date, not too far off, after they have met with their court mental health worker. I see that, in addition to Duty Counsel, there are not yet any lawyers. Not a good thing. This means we will be 'holding things down' for counsel who will be arriving late—although counsel don't always appear for the regulars who are making frequent appearances. These regulars are working on 'diversion' with their court mental health workers, who have their offices next door. Diversion is a program where minor to moderately serious offences are withdrawn by the Crown upon the accused successfully completing a program of rehabilitation. And, for most of these appearances, it is not necessary that their lawyers appear.

Ah, yes, there are Mr. Hadley, Mr. Giovanni, Mr. Diabelo, Miss Perski, Mr. Kelly, Miss Galorme, Miss Johnson, Mr. MacNamara, Mr. Mercer, Miss Quade, the Arc Angel, Mr. Smith, Mr. McLaurie, and Princess Sophia. This group will move quickly, but there are forty others on the docket.

For this group the most important and remarkable part of their appearance is that they did appear. This is a fragile group of accused who have little in the way of community support and who report to the court regularly and frequently just so that the court can monitor their stability in the community. These are accused who would have had great difficulty in the regular bail court. Long criminal records, many breaches of court orders, no sureties, no support from the Toronto Bail Program, and sketchy community resources to tap into, all point to likely denial of bail in the regular bail court. But this is no regular bail court, this is courtroom 102.

"Miss Charles, I see that Mr. Hadley is here bright and early."

"Leonard Hadley!" is called out by Miss Charles.

Mr. Hadley is a small, slender, young man in his mid-thirties. He is scruffy, and unkempt. He looks like he hasn't had a bath in quite a while and his chronic state of 'under-dress' concerns me. I am aware that while he is required to stay at a shelter, the truth is that he spends many nights on the streets; sleeping over subway grates or vents on the sidewalks which are discharging foul hot air from large buildings. He'll show up in the winter wearing a t-shirt. I ask if he has a coat and he'll often say "no"... it was stolen from him at the shelter. A court mental health worker will then assist in getting him a coat from the Salvation Army office on the second floor of the courthouse. There is a large inventory of donated clothing at the courthouse for just such customers.

Leonard is on approximately eight bail orders at present. (This by itself is something that might well interest the Guinness Records people.) With each new arrest for each new nuisance type of offence, the Crown puts up a perfunctory (for the purposes of the 'record') pitch that this time Mr. Hadley must be detained, knowing full well that the court will probably release him yet again on bail. It is common ground that if Mr. Hadley remains in jail, any of the progress that he has made will be erased.

Mr. Hadley shuffles to the front of the court as his name is called. His movements are stiff; the product of cold nights on the streets and the side effects of the anti-psychotic medications that he is supposed to be taking. The streets have aged him greatly. He is a scrawny wretch reminiscent of a Dickens character and somehow, for all of his unattractiveness, ineluctably charming.

"Have you met with Miss Zabo?"

"No, not yet." Mr. Hadley is expressionless and barely audible. You have to look closely to see his lips move.

"Have you heard yet about your housing?"

Mr. Hadley has made an application for housing with the assistance of his court mental health worker, Miss Zabo, but has not yet had any word. Finding housing is a real problem for him given that he is facing charges of arson. Accused facing these charges are often not warmly embraced by prospective housing facilities.

"No, not yet."

"Miss Charles, on which days does Mr. Hadley report?"

"Monday, Wednesday, and Friday, Your Honour."

"Okay, we'll see you on Friday Mr. Hadley, but don't forget to check-in with Miss Zabo before you leave."

"I won't."

As I see Mr. Hadley turn around and shuffle out of the court, I realize that I'd just made the mistake I make too often. With Mr. Hadley you ensure that he has seen his court mental health worker, Miss Zabo, before he is remanded. Not that Mr. Hadley is necessarily trying to avoid his meeting with Miss Zabo; he is often in such a fog that he forgets within seconds and leaves the building. This, of course, is very frustrating for Miss Zabo who is trying to monitor his progress and get him plugged into community resources such as supportive housing.

Our court mental health workers try to ensure that everyone we put back on to the street is placed into an optimal set of circumstances. The court mental health workers are really the glue of the court. Until someone is placed back into the community there is not much that we can begin to do. So, we are very dependent upon the 'plans' that are created to ensure that otherwise unreleasable accused are released from custody and kept safe in the community.

I know that one day, after thousands of these judicial interim release orders, one will go terribly wrong and I fear that it will be taken as an indictment of our program at the mental health court.

### *Our Tiny Courtroom*

Our Mental Health Court, or 'Courtroom 102' as it's known, is on the ground floor of Old City Hall Court House in downtown Toronto. While our tiny courtroom is not at all beautiful, Old City Hall is a magnificent old building. It opened its doors in 1899 after a decade of construction and until 1966 housed all of the trial courts and city council. It remains one of our city's most prominent structures and was designated as a National Historic Site of Canada in 1984. The courthouse is located at the corner of Queen and Bay Streets, across from Nathan Phillips Square and the new City Hall in the heart of downtown Toronto.

Upon completion in 1899 Old City Hall was one of the largest buildings in Toronto and the largest civic building in North America. It was Toronto's third city hall. The building was designed by prominent Toronto architect Edward James Lennox in a variation of Romanesque Revival architecture known as Richardsonian Romanesque. It took more than a decade to build and cost more than $2.5 million; more than three times the original estimate. Work on the building began in 1889.

From the bottom of Bay Street looking north Old City Hall's clock tower dominates the view. The clock's face measures six metres in diameter and originally functioned manually, but was automated in 1950s.

So much for the magnificent building; what of its inhabitants? During the day, normal day-time visitors, lawyers, judges, clerks, reporters, secretaries, and maintenance people ply the halls of Old City Hall. But, what of the nights? Others are said to call the old building home. Stories abound as to all sorts of nefarious nocturnal ghostly activity. The rear staircase of the building is home to a mischievous poltergeist who seems to enjoy tugging at judges' robes. This resident is also heard walking up and down the stairs. Especially at night, the steps creak with each footstep. The cellars contain the holding cells for prisoners when the courts are in session during the days. At night the prisoners are returned to the various remand centres once the courts have concluded. And while there is a constant daytime din from the dozens of accused waiting in the cells, eerie moans are heard once the lights go out. The Northwest attic is also a spot where a 'presence' is felt, but no one is quite sure what it is. And, Courtroom 33 is said to be haunted by the spirits of the last men condemned to hang in Canada. This is where the spirits are said to be the strongest and it is a tradition for some member of the press to attempt to spend the night on Halloween. In John Robert Colombo's book *Haunted Toronto*, he tells of a pair of 'stout reporters' who almost managed to spend the night but gave in by four a.m. The reporters told of 'cool fogs' and weird noises that left them, at times, glued to the floor.

So, the old courthouse is a bustling spot, both day and night! I have an overnight stay in my judicial chambers on my 'to do' list.

### *Non-Adversarial*

Mental Health Court is not typically an adversarial courtroom. Most often, Crown counsel and defence counsel are more or less on the same page, as is the bench. The accused are, for the most part, individuals who inadvertently trip through the courthouse doors as a result of untreated mental illness rather than deliberate criminality. Our collective objective is typically to get these people back up on their feet and integrated back in to the community. The court's overall mandate is the 'decriminalization of the mentally ill'.

Mental Health Court, alternatively known as 'Courtroom 102', is now in its eighteenth year of operation. And, as mentioned earlier, it is housed at the 'Old City Hall' court house in downtown Toronto. Mental Health Court enjoyed a three-year window of fame as it was featured in a CBC series entitled *This is Wonderland*. It was the story of a young criminal lawyer learning the ropes in downtown Toronto. Mental Health Court factored into virtually every episode. Old City Hall is the busiest court house in Canada with close to thirty courts up and running every day. Toronto, as Canada's largest urban centre, is also home to the country's largest population of mentally disordered homeless people. Large urban centres, for a variety of reasons, are home to this population. The phenomenon is known as 'urban drift'. (You've probably noticed that there aren't too many mentally disordered homeless people wandering the leafy streets of the suburbs.)

With government's systematic closure of psychiatric hospital beds and the move toward 'community mental health care', the situation in Toronto was reaching a crisis by the early 1990s. Mentally disordered individuals were flooding the criminal courts which were, not surprisingly, poorly equipped to deal with this population. When mentally disordered individuals are shut out of the health care system as appropriate resources are depleted, they don't just disappear; they pop up in the criminal justice system. Left to their own devices their aberrant behaviour will inevitably attract the attention of the constabulary. Typically charged with low-end nuisance offences to moderately serious matters, they appear in the criminal courts and jam-up the system. Fortunately, for the most part, their offences are toward the less serious end of the continuum, however every now and then random psychotic violence can take lives though, for example, pushing people off of subway platforms or slashing strangers in unprovoked attacks with machetes, or stabbing people on bicycles with screwdrivers, or running over police officers with snowplows.

With questions of 'fitness to stand trial' and 'criminal responsibility' needing answers, psychiatric assessments ordered, and applications for 'treatment orders' made, the forensic mental health care system was, in turn, flooded. What was once an exotic commodity became, by the mid-nineties, mainstream business for the criminal courts. Inefficiencies were increasingly high, and delays embarrassing. Accused were spending inordinate time in custody while these matters were being resolved; often in respect of offences for which no custodial time would have been awarded had the accused pleaded guilty at first instance. It was decided in August of 1997 that a special court should be created to deal more effectively with the mentally disordered accused. Mental Health Court opened its doors in May of 1998.

The Mental Health Court has two principal components to its mandate. The first is the expeditious resolution of preliminary psychiatric issues, the most common of which is 'fitness to stand trial'. The second is an attempt to slow down the so-called revolving door. Under the old regime a mentally disordered accused would spend weeks sorting out his or her psychiatric status and, finally, when pronounced 'fit', after spending an excessive period of time in custody, would plead guilty. The sentence would inevitably be one of 'time served'. Then the accused would be released on to the streets of Toronto wearing an orange jump suit, with nowhere to go, no social assistance, no prescription, no identification, no other clothing, and no hook-up with out-patient mental health care services. Not surprisingly, 'survival rates' were not great. These individuals typically become unwell quickly, are re-arrested quite quickly and, as a result, cycle through the system repetitively. Hence, the 'revolving door'.

### *The Mentally Disordered*

Schizophrenia is by far the most common diagnosis seen at the mental health court. It affects approximately one per cent of the general population. This is generally true over time and from culture to culture. The rate is incredibly stable. Most of our customers are male—I would guess the percentage to be about seventy-five per cent. Most are homeless. Most 'self-medicate' with street drugs. Most have extensive civil mental health histories. Most are entirely disconnected from their families. After a time, exasperated families often give up on mentally disordered relatives who have not been able to access adequate mental health care or have, very commonly, refused. And, unless it can be demonstrated that the individual constitutes a danger to himself or others, the state will take no action.

Although there are many explanations for the disorder, the most likely is that we are all to some extent pre-disposed to schizophrenia but that our predispositions to actually manifest the disorder vary greatly as a function of our genetic makeup and the environments within which we find ourselves. It is likely, in part, a biochemical problem of the brain. All effective psychopharmacological treatments serve to, one way or another, dampen the activity of dopamine (a neurotransmitter) in the brain. The symptoms of this mental disorder include delusional thinking, hallucinations, disorganized or incoherent speech, grossly disorganized, bizarre, or catatonic behaviour, and flattening of affect.

Virtually every time I hear psychiatric evidence supporting a verdict of 'unfit to stand trial' or 'not criminally responsible on account of mental disorder' the diagnosis is one type of schizophrenia or another. It is the schizophrenic's propensity to misperceive his or her environment or the actions of others that is at the heart of these verdicts. The misperceptions can be caused by delusional thinking which would ascribe to others intentions or threats not actually present, or hallucinations which would have the neutral victim appear to be saying or doing things not actually said or done and cause innocuous situations to appear dangerous or threatening. Because of these perceptual distortions, the accused may be unable to conduct his or her own defence or instruct counsel to do so, rendering them unfit to stand trial. Similarly, at the time of the offence, this disorder may cause the accused to be incapable of appreciating the nature and quality of their actions or of knowing that they are wrong, rendering the accused not criminally responsible.

Mental health courts are the new 'in thing' in the criminal justice system in Canada. They started at about the same time in the late 1990s in Canada as they did in the U.S., okay, not so new anymore. The American mental health courts are based upon the model of the previously established drug courts. The American model, at the risk of over-simplification, requires the accused, who has volunteered to participate, to enter into a rehabilitative program. First, the accused pleads guilty. Then, when that program is completed, the accused receives a reduced or alternative sentence or, in some jurisdictions, the charges are withdrawn or stayed.

While these courts started in Toronto and Broward County, Florida, at about the same time, the paradigms are quite different. The basic approach in Toronto has been described earlier. What both of these so-called problem solving courts do have in common is the goal of decriminalizing the mentally ill. The philosophy driving the courts is based upon the principles of 'therapeutic jurisprudence'. That is the recognition that when individuals come into contact with the law they are directly impacted by it. While this may, at first blush, appear to be rather trite, it is worthy of some further consideration. The point is that this impact is not neutral; it is either positive or negative. Traditional responses by the criminal justice system to 'rule breakers' have not been shown to be particularly effective but are even less-so for the mentally ill who actually get worse as a result of these responses. The probability of recidivism is generally an inverse correlation of length of incarceration. Longer the incarceration, poorer the prognosis. With respect to mentally disordered accused, incarceration, in particular, is known to exacerbate mental illnesses. The objective of therapeutic jurisprudence is to get at the 'root cause' of the criminal behaviour and deal with that directly. The root cause is untreated mental disorder. Once we are able to stabilize the accused and get them settled in the community with appropriate supports the probability of re-offending plummets as the cause of it all has been addressed.

Once a mentally disordered accused is fit to stand trial the objective of the court is to (assuming the accused wishes to participate) get at the problems leading to the criminal conduct. It is often the product of addictions, untreated mental illness, homelessness, and poverty. The mental health court workers assist the accused in addressing these issues.

What we really didn't know when we began our mental health court project in Toronto was the extent to which mental health courts do what we think they are doing. For whom, under what circumstances, do the courts do what? While these courts were immediately embraced as intuitively superior to the old methods of doing business (there are now approximately three hundred around the globe, most in the U.S.) we really didn't have any 'hard data'. Early reports provided descriptive statistics, but measurable impacts were not recorded. Now, more and more sophisticated studies are confirming that the mental health courts are indeed accomplishing much of what we had projected at the outset. Recidivism rates go down, mental health contacts go down, stability in the community improves, employment rates rise, and substance abuse issues decrease, all as a result of participation in a mental health court program. And, further to recidivism rates going down, studies are showing that the sort of re-offending is different from the index offences. The re-offending tends to be less serious, less violent, and more often 'breach' types of offences.

### *Isabelle*

A scrawny wretch of a woman is in the prisoner's box. She has been brought up for a 'screen'. That is, she has been traversed from another court because that court had reason to believe that she may be suffering from a mental disorder that may have a bearing upon her fitness to stand trial. Her name is Isabelle Dusky. She is dishevelled. Her hair is matted. She has whiskers growing conspicuously on her face from unfortunate locations. But the important part for our purposes is that she has a scarf in her hand, cupped over her mouth. No one can hear what she is saying.

The natural suspicion, given the rest of her appearance, was that she was psychotic. So many street people are. Duty counsel start in on her, asking the standard questions. Do you know where you are? Do you know what you have been charged with? Do you know what so-and-so does? Do you know the pleas available to you? etc., etc. But no one can hear a word she is saying or if she is saying anything at all. And, what's with the scarf and the hand? She must be crazy.

At that point my clerk turns around, stands up, and whispers to me, "I don't think she has any teeth." I look quizzically at her and then the lights come on.

Well, who is the psychiatrist? Bang on. The little old lady had been apprehended and somewhere along the line had lost her teeth. She was apparently mortified to have anyone see her in such a state and consequently covered her mouth. Once the problem was rectified it was clear that she was not the slightest bit crazy. But the machinery of the state had almost missed it.

### *Incarceration and Recidivism*

The success of the mental health court is partly because of its design and partly, perhaps more than partly, dependent upon the personalities that are recruited to participate. For example, the Crown Attorneys assigned to the court must maintain their traditional eye on the protection of the public while at the same time subscribing to the basic principles of therapeutic jurisprudence. They recognize that the long-term safety of the public, as well as the most positive therapeutic outcome for the accused, is achieved where the court gets to the root cause of the criminality and deals directly with that. Getting at the 'root cause' is seldom (okay, never!) advanced through incarceration. Incarceration is now known to increase the probability of recidivism and exacerbate mental illness, thereby worsening prognoses. The literature is vast. It is clear that incarcerating accused with mental disorders does nothing to specifically deter them and nothing to deter potentially like-minded accused. As well, there is no rehabilitative gain to be made through incarceration.

Mental health court requires the Crown Attorney to adjust their approach. The hard-hitting prosecutorial mentality focussed upon obtaining convictions has no place in mental health court. As well, the litigious arena encountered in most trial courts is replaced with an environment that is less adversarial and more cooperative. In my experience with the mental health court, it is clear that some Crown Attorneys can make the adjustment whereas some cannot. It isn't for everyone. In our particular court there is a 'team' of two Crowns who divide the work. This is also good practice in that it affords a high degree of continuity. The Crown Attorneys get to know the accused and the accused get to know the Crown Attorneys and the accused come to view the court as a supportive rather than a hostile punitive environment. For many, the court staff are the only people who talk to them at all, ever. It is clear to me that most of the accused who attend mental health court view the court and their work with their mental health court workers as a very positive part of their day.

The same can be said of all of the participants in the mental health court. The duty counsel, while not getting paternalistic in their approach, recognize that having their clients sign-on for a therapeutic regimen is not only in their clinical best interest but will also produce the best legal results.

With respect to the bench, again it is a matter of personality. I always tell interested Judges from other jurisdictions that there are only three requirements for the job: 1) a sense of humour, 2) patience, and 3) an ability to read the *Criminal Code* in a very elastic manner. Some of my brethren can let go of the black letter law and embrace the principles of therapeutic jurisprudence; others cannot. Also, consistent with all we know about 'best practices', continuity is imperative and achieved best with one principal judge and a very few 'wing men'.

### *The Kennedys*

Today, Mr. Daniel Kennedy is back in court. He is a gentleman who had been charged with a variety of offences all having to do with threatening the Premier of Ontario and a Family Court Judge. He had been denied bail because of the fact that while he was clearly unwell mentally, the court did not have any psychiatric input as to his actual potential to carry out the threats. He was a forty-three-year-old man with no criminal record. But, his presentation in court was really quite alarming. His paranoid delusions were florid and his threats extraordinarily violent. A psychiatric assessment was eventually ordered under the Mental Health Act in order to assist the court with the matter of bail. And, while that assessment was incomplete, a further assessment order was made upon the Crown's application to determine the issue of his criminal responsibility (that is, his mental state at the time of the alleged offence).

The assessment report filed with the court revealed that, as discussed earlier, Mr. Kennedy had the fixed false belief that the 'system' at large was conspiring against him and was responsible for the removal of his two children, aged two and three years, into the custody of the Children's Aid Society. They were 'illegally' taken from him and his wife of three years as they lived in a 'family shelter'.

Mr. Kennedy came from a broken home and had difficulties both at home and at school. He failed both Grades 4 and 5 but eventually completed Grade 11. Eventually, he was placed in a residential program for children with behavioural or psychological difficulties. He remained there until the age of fifteen or sixteen years, at which time he moved to British Columbia to reside with his father. For approximately twenty years he had worked as a cook on barges and tug boats on the west coast. He and his wife had only been in Ontario a few years. He claims to have had no significant psychiatric difficulties prior to his arrest in respect of the matters presently before the court. Since his arrest, he has had contact with psychiatrists in the remand centres where he has been housed. He did offer that he had obtained a diagnosis of 'delusional disorder' as well as 'paranoid schizophrenia' in an unknown context in Vancouver. He claims to have never been treated with anti-psychotic medications. But, then again, later refers to having been treated with the drug Risperidone—an anti-psychotic medication. He also acknowledged a long-standing history of alcohol abuse.

It was apparent to the author of the report that Mr. Kennedy's delusional thinking was overt, obvious, and profound, of a paranoid, persecutory nature. Mr. Kennedy did not recognize this thinking as delusional but felt that it represented accurately what was going on in his life. He had apparently written a book which sets out, in elaborate detail, how the governments at all levels, police, Crown corporations, and virtually everyone else were conspiring to do him and his family harm. When pressed he indicated "....I have no proof, but I'm a victim of this." All of his harassing and threatening behaviour had been related to his attempts to regain custody of his children. He believed that there had been attempts upon his life and that people had hacked into his computer and left messages in his email. Apparently, the harassment began about the time he met his wife, who apparently believes all of the same things. "Before I was married," he said, "none of this happened ... it started at the time when I wrote the book and I got married."

His wife was in the body of the court on each and every appearance where I was presiding. She was a plain-looking woman of approximately the same age as Mr. Kennedy, wearing no makeup, who, in every respect, appeared to be 'normal' and unremarkable. She would wait quietly for hours for her husband to finally make his appearance in court. When he finally appeared, he would inevitably commence a discourse before any response was requested of him; one that he could not easily be diverted from. I could see his wife and a friend nodding emphatically as he rambled on from the prisoner's box punctuating his points with respect to all of those who were conspiring against himself and his wife. It was clear to me that as bizarre as Mr. Kennedy's rambling and sometimes-incoherent story was, his wife was completely and totally subscribing to the same set of beliefs. Obviously, she was as delusional as he was. If we are to believe Mr. Kennedy when he says that his troubles began after he was married, it might be the case that his wife exacerbated his condition and prompted him to take action upon his delusional thinking.

He denied hearing voices or experiencing any other hallucinations. All other clinical markers appeared to be within normal limits. It was his delusional thinking that was causing him the difficulties. His diagnosis was 'delusional disorder, persecutory type'. However, he claimed that he did not remember sending some of the more alarming emails. The view of the psychiatrist who assessed Mr. Kennedy was that the behaviour that brought him before the court, even though he was delusional at the time, was the product of the disinhibiting effects of alcohol and cannabis. The opinion was that he did not have a defence of 'Not Criminally Responsible' available to him. This was not challenged and Mr. Kennedy was therefore sentenced by me in the usual manner.

He had spent months and months in pre-trial custody. At the end of it all, I suspended the passing of sentence and placed him on probation for a period of three years. The key terms pertained to him maintaining psychiatric follow-up, which he agreed to do.

### *Complaint of Misconduct*

The Ontario Judicial Council hears complaints of misconduct made against judges. Fortunately, it is a body that most judges only read about. For most judges, just the mention of the name triggers a visceral response accompanied by a cold sweat, heart palpitations, and nausea. Whereas, courts of appeal deal with errors we might have made with the law or interpreting evidence that has been put before us in court, the Judicial Council deals with complaints of misconduct—bad behaviour.

One day as I was unpacking boxes during the course of my office move from the second to the third floor of the court house, Sarah, my secretary, brought the mail as she usually does. She pointed out a package that had obviously been delivered by a courier. Thinking not much of it I looked at some other opened material and then I moved on to consider the couriered package. It did not show a return address that I recognized. I opened the outer plastic wrapper and inside was an envelope. It was from the Ontario Judicial Council! Being totally unfamiliar with this body and their procedures I could only imagine that it was 'information' about the council ....or someone looking for 'information' (as I am often consulted). Then, as I opened the envelope I read ".....Re: Your complaint against the Honourable Justice Richard Schneider"

Well, let me tell you that this was a profoundly bowel loosening moment for me. As my viscera then tightened, I read on. Scanning it very quickly at first.

"The Kennedys!" I could feel my alimentary system resume its normal functions. The letter was from the 'Assistant Registrar'. I was being 'copied' with the Council's response. In reporting to Mrs. Kennedy that their (she writing on behalf of herself and her husband) complaint against me had been summarily dismissed, the process to date was summarized. The gist of the complaint was reviewed. Parts of it are as follows, "the judge's ruling was neither measured nor sagacious and he displayed a complete lack of objectivity or reason.... Moreover, Judge Schneider must support Justice 'B' (another judge who forms part of another complaint to the Judicial Council) who is a cruel and irrational judge..." The complaint had apparently concluded "Judge Schneider has a reputation for being an agreeable man but, unfortunately, I do not believe that a person can be pure and also participate in organized crime and mafia activities on the side." It was at this point that I was totally relieved and fully understood that the council was merely informing me of a complaint that had been made but summarily dismissed; being one that required no response from myself.

I am guessing that the Kennedys had lodged the complaint as Mr. Kennedy was being held for further assessments, ordered by myself, as described earlier. At some point they had apparently asked that the complaint be withdrawn—probably after he was sentenced by me and received no further jail but rather a period of probation. My guess, though, appears to have been accurate. That is, Mrs. Kennedy is clearly as unwell as her husband (or worse!). This could very well be what is known as a 'Folie à deux' situation. As described by Hinsie and Campell in their 'Psychiatric Dictionary (fourth edition)' this is a term applied when two persons closely associated with one another suffer a psychosis simultaneously, and when one member of the pair appears to have influenced the other. Remember that Mr. Kennedy disclosed that none of his problems pre-dated his marriage to Mrs. Kennedy.

I am strongly of the view that we probably and regrettably had the more stable one of the two in our court.

### *Miss Shaw*

People often ask me whether or not I find working in the mental health court as often as I do 'depressing'. In order to provide an answer beyond 'No', let me recount the story of Ms. Shaw.

One day not too long ago I noticed right away that Miss Shaw was in the front row of the court room looking very 'together'. She had been appearing regularly and I suspected that she was now close to being 'diverted'. That is, having her charges 'stayed' as a result of her successfully completing the program, which consists of 'getting better' and stable in the community.

Several months ago, fresh off the street, I had before me a very crazy looking Miss Shaw. She was wild, unkempt, unruly, profane, and abusive. She was wearing jeans, that were falling off of her very thin frame in a too revealing way, and a t-shirt. She was clearly in a manic state and completely out of control. She is a very attractive young woman in her early thirties; but was madder than a hatter. I can't recall what she was charged with. I just recall her desperate condition. Her uncle, Mr. Shaw, a lawyer, was with her apparently trying to sort things out, profoundly concerned but clearly out of his depth. I noticed him conferring with duty counsel, obviously seeking advice. He had the most minimal control over his niece. There was with him a familial entourage who were all struggling to contain her.

Later, I had heard that Miss Shaw was in hospital. I believe her family had obtained a Form 1 under the Mental Health Act which resulted in her involuntary hospitalization. Her uncle made several appearances on her behalf while she remained in hospital. And, I had really forgotten her once-wild appearance before me weeks before.

Then one typical day I walked in to court as I typically do, in my typical manner. This was to be one of my all-time most up-lifting 102 court experiences. There was nothing atypical about anything. Miss Shaw was certainly not on my mind. I scanned the courtroom as I typically do. I remember that I spotted the lawyers and organized in my mind who could be moved out most quickly. Lawyers representing clients out-of-custody who are simply being remanded queue-up as they have their matters called then move on to other courts to represent other clients. Sometimes young lawyers are a little timid (while the more experienced ones are certainly not at all). I try to look out for them and ensure that these young ones who are in court early don't get run over by the older others.

Shepherding is part of the judge's job. I recall that a few matters had been called and disposed of. Then, as I often do, I will turn to the polite, quiet ones, and ask if we can assist them. I noticed a nicely dressed young female lawyer with a thin valise sitting in the front row with a smile on her face. I asked if the court might assist her with her matter. Just as I had concluded, my question duty counsel popped up before the now-standing young lady had a chance to respond.

"Oh, Your Honour, this is Miss Shaw, could we hold her matter down? She is waiting for her uncle."

It took me a moment to make the connection. The wild and crazy Miss Shaw had not been to court for several weeks, or at least not while I was presiding, and I had completely forgotten about her. We sometimes have as many as eighty accused on a list in one day and many are quite unwell. So, while I was eventually able to recall 'the other Miss Shaw', she did not really stand out in my mind.

What stood out in my mind now was the contrast between the Miss Shaw presently before me and the Miss Shaw that I'd recalled from several weeks before. The transformation was remarkable. A completely different person was now before me. Once the dots were connected in my slowly grinding mind I was absolutely flabbergasted. The young lady before me looked like a Bay Street lawyer, almost too neat and tidy to have fit in well with the regular criminal lawyer 'rat pack'. I couldn't contain myself.

"Miss Shaw, I have to tell you that I recall you appearing before me several weeks ago and you now look terrific. Congratulations." She was beaming as was her uncle, who had by now arrived at her side.

"Thank you, Your Honour." They responded in unison.

I looked at our Crown Attorney, Miss Charles, who had apparently just had the same visceral experience I've just described. This was what the court was all about. While I appreciate that all of our customers cannot look forward to the sort of re-birth enjoyed by Miss Shaw, it is remarkable when transformations of this magnitude occur.

Miss Charles: "Yes, Miss Shaw, you are looking wonderful today... keep up whatever it is that you are doing." Both Miss Shaw and her obviously proud uncle were beaming, as was I.

Duty counsel: "October 25th, please, Your Honour."

"Yes, of course. October 25th, Miss Shaw." I was still in shock.

No, it's not a depressing place to work.

*Formerly Psychiatrist-in-Chief at Hamilton Psychiatric Hospital and Professor of Psychiatry at McMaster University,* **David Dawson** *MD FRCPC has for many years divided his time between clinical practice, writing and painting. He is the author of six published novels, three academic books, and seven plays. He has also written and directed several films and video productions. In 2016 two of his plays are being produced on stage. One is a small drama about his grandmother's life,* If There is a River; *the other is a two-hour production,* MacBush, The Musical. *He regularly blogs with Marvin Ross, medical journalist and advocate, on mental illness, mental health, and sometimes current events and politics. Dr. Dawson has also painted all his life, and is co-owner of Gallery on the Bay in Hamilton, Ontario. Writing and psychiatry inform one another. Writing is deconstruction, reconstruction, and dramatization of life in pursuit of truth, or at least verisimilitude, while clinical work is a process of listening to unstructured narratives while searching for patterns, causes, ways of understanding and helping. And painting? Well, painting is meditation, a way of damping down the incessant chatter of the left brain, and allowing the right brain to simply see and experience and perhaps capture something almost perfectly.*

# Dr. David Dawson

## Phil, Eddie, and Margaret

FOR TEN YEARS I held the position of Psychiatrist-in-Chief at a Provincial Psychiatric Hospital before moving to part-time clinical and consultation activities in order to devote half my time to writing and painting. As psychiatrist-in-chief or medical director I was inevitably brought in to help deal with problem cases: problems of diagnosis, of potential violence, legal issues, police investigations, clinical conundrums, poor response to treatment, clinician disputes, and politics. It was during those ten years that I met many of the people I write about. One of them was Phil. Another was Eddie. Yet another was Margaret.

My introduction to Phil came from a call from one of the wards asking for my authorization to use physical restraints. This would be the proverbial straight jacket or a more contemporary form of immobilization wear with a euphemistic name.

Phil had torn apart two seclusion rooms.

Though fairly barren and secure, these rooms did have radiators, ceiling tiles, and ceiling lights that could be destroyed by a particularly strong and energetic patient. Phil had done so to two rooms and the staff had run out of options. He could not be sedated with strong neuroleptic drugs because we did not know what other drugs were circulating in his system. A bad combination could be fatal.

I authorized physical restraints. But then came an odd pause. It seems nobody knew where they were stored. They had not been used in the first five years of my tenure at the hospital. Eventually an older off duty nurse was called and she sent us to the right closet. The restraints were dusted off and used to control Phil.

Phil suffered from a disastrous combination of a psychotic illness with bouts of mania, plus a penchant for all the wrong street drugs, particularly those that induced a state of psychosis and mania. On his frequent trips to the emergency department it was never clear at first whether he was suffering something that was drug induced and would pass, or not. Needless to say, he was not compliant on his prescribed medication between hospital visits.

Once, he had a wife and two children, long estranged from him, their address unknown to him. He often blamed a particular doctor and lawyer for this, saying that they fed his wife lies about him. And he was often concerned that I might be similarly keeping him away from his family. At other times his ex-wife was the villain in his stories.

When I knew him, his place of residence alternated between The Mission, The Salvation Army, the local jail, the hospital, and the street. He would wear out his welcome at one and move on to another, sometimes committing a minor crime simply to get off the street in cold weather and return to the jail. At other times, the crime would not be so minor. He needed long-term treatment and abstinence from drugs, but never stayed in hospital long enough for this to happen. And when he had recovered from his acute episodes he was not someone that any ward staff wished to have around for a long time. He had once held a nurse at knifepoint in an acute admission unit.

My relationship with Phil inspired the following short story. Though not written in the standard clinical form, it is as true as I could write it.

### *The Christmas Present*

On Christmas Eve one year, my secretary already home, Phil entered my office unannounced, and before I could so much as shift in my chair behind my desk, he closed the door behind him. Phil looked relatively clean, kempt, his hair combed, only day-old stubble on his chin. His prison issue shoes were black and substantial. He carried a large well-used shopping bag and put it on the floor beside the chair that he pulled up to the far side of my desk.

His eyes were worrisome as was his rictus grin. He had, as I had seen before, eyes that know a truth beyond ordinary human knowledge, eyes that flash intention, eyes that signal unwholesome intensity, a panel overload, a wattage barely contained, that odd manic combination of malevolence and ecstasy.

And sitting in the chair across the desk from me, Phil simply said, as he reached into his shopping bag, "I've brought a Christmas present for ya, Doc."

After all, I thought, one's life could end on Christmas Eve as easily as any other day, suddenly, unexpectedly, forgoing the pain and pleasure of family unraveling, the season of guilt. It was difficult to imagine any other purpose in Phil's visit, as I remembered the last time I saw him standing in shackles before the judge, professing his ingenuous intention to stay away from alcohol and cocaine, to attend a rehabilitation program, and to take his lithium. The judge had asked, "And when did you first learn that you have an alcohol problem, Mr. Dermid?" And Phil had answered, "Just now, your Honour. I hadn't realized it until just now."

But because I had stood on that witness stand before Phil's glaring eyes and had pronounced him very dangerous, especially when his mania was fuelled with alcohol and crack cocaine, the judge had locked him up, Phil's last minute insight notwithstanding.

A few days later I had picked up the phone in my office to find Phil on the other end, calling from the jail, calling from the cell block pay phone, with the voices of fellow inmates reverberating off the yellow hard walls in the background. Phil was using his brief allotted moment of semi-privacy to phone the doctor who had pronounced him violent and dangerous.

But on the phone Phil simply said, "You were a class act on the stand, Doc, a class act." And then he hung up.

And now, with Phil's right hand searching in his shopping bag, I imagined him reaching for a gun, no, not likely, a knife, more likely, a club, a simple rock, a weapon of some sort. We were three feet apart across the expanse of desk. My back was to the window. I did not feel young enough for this. Not young enough to react in time. I exercised stillness.

And Phil, for a moment the malevolence gone from his eyes, leaving only a neutral wattage overload, withdrew his hand, grasping a pen, a simple ballpoint pen, and placed it on my desk. He shrugged, grinned, ticked, and said, "Merry Christmas, Doc." It was the same voice as the phone call, the greeting laden with ambiguity, threat, prediction, sarcasm, even sincerity.

Phil left quickly, professing much to do, and the possibility of seeing the children he had given up several years ago for a chemically enhanced life on the street—the possibility of a Christmas visit.

I picked up the ballpoint pen, and noted, uncharitably, that it was a cheap thing, well used and chewed upon.

There is a footnote to this story, though an ambiguous one. It was some years later when, walking along a busy James Street with my wife, I saw Phil approaching. My instinct was to keep my head low, to avoid eye contact, but Phil saw me and veered in my direction. A psychiatrist never knows what to expect in these chance encounters, though usually I am pleasantly surprised, even by, at times, the friendliness and gratitude of someone who I sent involuntarily to a schedule one hospital a few months before. On this occasion Phil just said, "I'm still taking those drugs you prescribed, Doc, the lithium. And I'm doing okay." He knew I was no longer at the hospital. He wished me well, and then he was gone.

### *Eddie*

He was a big man of east European heritage but born and raised in Canada. And though he was born with a perfectly serviceable last name he legally changed it to Eddie Deersmith. He never fully explained that to me beyond the fact he liked the name, though perhaps part of the answer was apparent at a review board hearing attended by a brother and an uncle. They both spoke of their Eddie as a terrible, untrustworthy man and they were happy to see him locked up.

I believe I was testifying at the time that Mr. Deersmith did not pose a significant risk to the community if he stayed on his medication. And if he did not, well, it was predictable that something untoward would happen, but not predictable exactly what, nor how serious an event it would be.

Eddie was bi-polar, perhaps schizoaffective, and like a few others with this condition he preferred a state of hypomania over an earthbound and limited existence. And as long as the 'hypo' remained in place, he was fine. He could be funny and generous and entertaining, full of plans and hopes and dreams, though perhaps a little intimidating to others. His size, his enthusiasm and his loud voice could overwhelm. It was when the hypomania progressed to full mania that he got in major trouble.

He came to us, a psychiatric hospital of minimum security designation, after lengthy stays in first a maximum security hospital and then a medium security hospital. The charge had been a serious one when he was found not guilty by reason of insanity (the wording of the criminal code at the time): attempted murder of a police officer.

Here is what I know happened, though Eddie and the police differ on a few small points: Eddie was a car guy. What he drove or didn't drive was important to him. He could do some of the mechanical work and some of the body work and barter for parts. His limited budget meant that he was always rebuilding a wreck and looking for a garage in which to do it.

At the time of the 'index offence', Eddie was living in part of a rented house and he parked his car on the street. His car at the time was an old Jaguar.

Eddie never fully explained his motivation to me, even years later. As is often the case, someone acting in a manic state does not take the time to consider motivation, the probability of bad or good long and short term consequences, nor the logic of his urges.

But on this particular day Eddie was irked by his Jaguar. So he took a large axe and assaulted it. He smashed the hood, the windows, and the roof. A neighbour called the police. When the police arrived they saw a large enraged man wielding an axe and doing immense damage to a car.

I don't know what words were exchanged before a police officer shot Eddie in the ankle. He was charged with attempted murder in the hospital where his ankle was being repaired. I'm sure he waved the axe in a threatening fashion, and refused to yield, though as Eddie pointed out later, he was on the other side of the Jaguar and that's why they shot him in the ankle, under the car.

Years later he was fond of claiming that the bullet fragments left in his ankle were causing him lead poisoning. I think he meant it literally as a cause for his often ill health. He never considered that he was lucky the officers did not use lethal force but rather he would point out that the Jaguar was his and what he did with it was entirely his choice.

Two problems that exist on the uneasy boundary of the vagaries of mental illness and the absolutes of law have played poorly for Eddie. The first is the Attempt Murder charge, of a police officer. It stayed with him for life, and caused a long and cautious incarceration; the nuances, the context of the crime are not considered in the words 'attempted murder.' The second is that courts and review boards are more comfortable with absolute freedom or full incarceration than with freedom and an order to take medication.

There are many reasons for this but one is that the law is black and white and must assume humans to be, usually, rational beings with free will. While we know that humans are usually far from rational, that we live with shades of grey, and free will is a debatable condition.

So Eddie spent a long time on a Lieutenant Governor's warrant residing in three different hospitals and then he was fully discharged to the community with a promise to comply with treatment. At the time he promised he may have wholeheartedly intended to stay on his medication, but like the rest us us with our New Year's resolutions, our diets and exercise programs, his motivation slipped away within weeks of freedom.

I had promised to provide psychiatric treatment once he was discharged and so he became my difficult outpatient for a few years. He attended appointments but he chose his own medication. He would not take anything that he felt fogged his mind or brought him down. He had a particular dislike of lithium built mostly on some chemical theories of his own. He sometimes lived in his car, sometimes in rented rooms, sometimes shared an apartment. I could not keep track of his old friends he thought owed him money or his new friends who may or may not be cheating him, or the accusations toward his family.

I tried to keep him on some medication that might stave off a full manic episode. He would bring me findings, curiosities, at times, as gifts or to keep for him: an old film noir movie poster as a gift, a cumbersome antique to hold for him.

I hospitalized him on one occasion during that period. He had returned to the hospital grounds where he was found standing in the middle of a field, arms outstretched, facing skyward and whistling loudly. Two police officers waited with estimable patience beside their van while I talked Eddie into giving up his present enterprise and coming with me in the van to be re-admitted for a few days. He explained he was "whistling up a wind", something he had the power to do. He did not explain why.

He always had money problems and car problems and sometimes girl problems, but he survived for a while though he was usually at risk of drawing police attention to himself or being evicted. Still, it was only a matter of time. As I told the review board, "he was unpredictable in nature and severity."

He quite suddenly decided he was in love with a nurse who worked in a hospital two-hundred miles away. And that she loved him. He had, years before, spent some time in their medium secure unit.

He showed me 'proof' of her love in the form of a handwritten letter which may or may not have come from her and was of indeterminant age. But rational argument holds no sway with a delusion, especially an erotic delusion. He wrote letters to her but the fact she did not write to him only proved she was being prevented from doing so.

Unfortunately, he decided to pay her a surprise visit and demonstrate the extent of his devotion to her. He, quite literally, filled his car with balloons and headed down the 401, the major highway between Toronto and Kingston, Ontario to offer his hand in marriage. The car he drove at the time, with out-of-date plates and other infractions might have been enough to get him pulled over. Add to that a balloon-filled car speeding erratically, and it was a certainty.

The police pulled him over. They apprehended him and put him in the back seat of a cruiser. He resisted. He fought them. He kicked out a window in the cruiser. I'm sure when they checked their database they found the previous charge of Attempt Murder, police officer.

Eddie was found 'Not Criminally Responsible' for this assault and was placed back on a Lieutenant-Governor's warrant and sent to a medium secure forensic psychiatric hospital. He was forced to take medication there, and he became obese and developed diabetes. He wrote me letters which usually began well, but deteriorated into a diatribe against one doctor or another, and threatened law suits. I attended one of his review board hearings and offered the same opinion as before. Unfortunately, the medications by injection that he was forced to take had worse side effects than would have a voluntary regimen.

He was eventually placed in an apartment close to the hospital and his letters and Christmas cards continued. But his health was poor, and when not hypomanic he was often depressed. Despite his apparent good relationship with me, he once complained to the College of

Physicians and Surgeons of Ontario that I had refused to sign a form for him that would give him extra money for an exotic diet. This while he was an inpatient. I think he did it as a joke and to pass the time while contemplating other law suits.

In his small apartment he continued to write me letters, often of his ill health, his proposed lawsuits, his plans and wishes, one of which was to move to a bigger city.

His ankle continued to bother him, his weight increased. He had some medical emergencies he recounted in his letters to me after he was returned to his apartment.

And then the letters and Christmas cards stopped.

### *Accent on the Second Syllable*

Margaret is frugal. She takes great pride in this. In season, she survives on the edible fruits, berries, and mushrooms she finds in backyards and boulevards. She would like to teach her skills to mental patients. In the winter, she dresses in many layers and sleeps whenever and wherever she is taken in. She will not accept a boarding home. She defaces her family benefit cheques and does not cash them. These represent charity and are abhorrent to her.

She would like to see the Premier of Ontario, "a Highly Placed One," who could correct certain injustices, and reissue her cheques as salary. She is a woman of great dignity to whom God delivers explicit instructions, which she is expected to follow and convey to others.

She has spent a full weekend hiding in a closet in Queen's Park and when she talks of this she smiles and seems to recognize both the comedy and tragedy of her life. When, in the past, she was hospitalised and treated, treated against her will with injections of anti-psychotic medication, she spoke less about God, herbs, the Premier, and her conversation was easier to follow. But the moment she leaves hospital she stops treatment and recalls, bitterly, the needle, as a wrong and immoral act, an assault on her autonomy, her special-ness, and her humanity. At times she lives with her mother, a short, stocky German-speaking Romanian woman in her eighties, an ageing mother sure her daughter needs help, bewildered by our inability to make everything right.

During a very cold January I gave her fifty dollars to buy a pair of winter boots. She speaks to God for a moment and, apparently, He tells her it is all right to accept, for she takes the money and goes to the mall. When she returns she shows me the boots and gives me change, for she has found a bargain, which pleases her greatly.

Another day she arrives looking ill and tired, emaciated. I can smell acetone on her breath. She has not eaten for days. She is capable of foraging for food but this is a hunger strike, which only a word, a concession, from the Premier, the "Highly Placed One" will forestall. It is hopeless trying to convince her that I have no access to the Premier's ear. She has her own knowledge of how the world works. And in her world, within her reality, it is not so far-fetched that the Chief Psychiatrist of the Mental Hospital might stand very near the "Highly Placed One."

Now Margaret drops in unannounced quite regularly. She stays a while. Sometimes she sings a hymn. Sometimes she babbles incoherently. Sometimes her ramblings are interrupted with asides to God. Upon His silent instructions she continues or alters her current discourse. Sometimes she brings jars of liquid, which she claims contain all the nutrients any human should need. She wants to teach the patients of the hospital her survival skills, her nutritional knowledge. Sometimes when she has sung loudly I realize she is drunk. I am always fascinated by the way she constructs a sentence. She uses some combination of Germanic inversion and schizophrenic association.

But this time she is dying. Or will die within days if she does not start eating again. I take her to a hospital ward, escorted by nurses. I tell her I will be giving her a needle in the buttock and that she must start eating. She pauses for a moment, then looks at me, and shakes her finger, and says, "All right. But not as a husband to a wife." I can feel Freud smiling down upon me. She accepts the needle. She begins to eat immediately. She stays a few weeks gaining strength and a modicum of sanity, and then she departs.

It is another time, another year, and I find she has been cut off from welfare. Her purse is full of defaced cheques, yet some she has cashed and put in her bank account, which now totals, to my amazement, eleven thousand dollars. With a bank account that large she can no longer receive benefits. But she has no money to use. She is destitute, and again not eating. For the money in that bank account belongs to God. She cannot use it. She speaks to God for a moment and apparently He does not change His policy. On the telephone I explain to the Welfare Officer that Margaret has no money, that she cannot access the account of eleven thousand dollars. It belongs to God and God alone can release the funds. The Welfare Officer seems incapable of imagining parallel universes with different immutable laws.

It is the dead of winter once again, the mercury has dropped to twenty-five below. Margaret is on the street. She makes her way to my office and spends the day in a chair in the corridor keeping warm. She will not allow me to admit her to the hospital as a patient. She is not mental, she repeats. But when I broach the idea of sleeping at the hospital as a guest, not a patient, she accepts. The wards are full though, and the best we can do is to offer her a mattress on the floor in an empty room. The institution sputters here. Placing and making up a mattress is the job of Housekeeping, not Nursing, and the Housekeepers have gone home for the day. I say I will do it myself and this spurs the Nurses to agree to temporarily add mattress placement to their job spec. Margaret stays a few days. She behaves well. She is polite and tidy. When the cold spell dissipates and a thaw is in the air, she leaves.

Months later I am asked, by Union Officials, to write a letter absolving the nurses of any responsibility for allowing a non-patient to sleep on one of the wards. I write the letter, typing something like, "I and I alone did allow…..", while I contemplate the definition of insanity.

Margaret disappears for months at a time. Occasionally I might see her bent against the wind in her kerchief and multi-layered coats, making her way along an urban street. And then she would appear again, in my office, asking again if I would put her in touch with the "Highly Placed One."

I have been calling her Margaret in this writing, but my secretary and I never addressed her as Margaret. She would correct us. It must be Ms. followed by her last name. Ms. Rossal, accent on the second syllable. "Ms. Rossal is here to see you." In turn, she always addressed me as "Chief Psychiatrist Dawson."

When I left the hospital I had not seen her for some time, and I have not seen her since. But I did hear that she eventually accepted placement in a nursing home, though I think I prefer to remember her happily, with independence and dignity, foraging for edible roots and berries in the boulevards and parks of the city, in the good weather of course.

We have no doubt that Margaret is mentally ill (though she has her moments of great insight and good advice) and there are times she can be a terrible nuisance. There are also moments, during a hunger strike, when her life is endangered and we know, almost for certain, that we must take over and force her to drink and eat. There are also times when, through her craziness, a sense of mission, esteem and rightness shine, and other moments when she weeps about her circumstances. But she will never admit she is ill, or "mental", as she calls it.

Before 1960, we would have been convinced of our duty to satisfy her needs, as we perceive them, against her will if necessary, even if our means to do so were primitive. A sociologist might have pointed out other motives guiding our actions but we would leave these considerations to the academics and, as physicians, respond to the obvious, immediate human dilemma. This woman is ill. She requires protection and treatment.

Now our means to respond to her needs, as we perceive them, are not quite so primitive, but our society is no longer convinced we should, not without her permission and her cooperation. Individual autonomy is enshrined in our *Canadian Charter of Rights and Freedoms*. Exceptions are carefully delineated in our *Mental Health Act,* and monitored by forms, advocates, time limits, appeals and review boards. Today, we each have a right to become and remain mentally ill, and to lead eccentric lives, as long as we don't place our own and others' lives in immediate jeopardy. In the abstract, it is clear and commendable. Within the hard reality of the lives of individuals and their families, the struggle between freedom and responsibility continues.

When is Margaret's life really in danger? Should we allow her to base her choices on misperceptions and delusions? When does her loneliness, distress, and poverty outweigh her greatly prized freedom and dignity? What of the life she might have had with continuing treatment?

And what of her mother's pain?

***William Trudell*** *attended the University of Windsor's Faculty of Law, first graduating class. He is the Chair of the Canadian Council of Criminal Defence Lawyers and practices law in Toronto at Simcoe Chambers. He is a Certified Specialist in Criminal Law and often defends lawyers and other professionals before their regulatory bodies. He has served as a director of the John Howard Society, The Advocate's Society, and as a director and Vice President of the Ontario Criminal Lawyers Association. He is a Fellow of the American College of Trial Lawyers. He is a member of the National Steering Committee on Justice Efficiencies and Access to Justice and a member of the Steering Committee for the Annual Re-Inventing Criminal Justice Symposium. He represented the Canadian Council of Criminal Defence Lawyers at the founding meeting of the International Criminal Bar in Berlin. He was the recipient of the* Law Times *first Lawyer of the Year award. In 2012, he was named one of the Top 25 Most Influential Lawyers in the legal profession by* Canadian Lawyer Magazine. *He was the Law Society of Upper Canada's representative on the Judicial Appointments Advisory Committee and in 2014 was the recipient of the Law Society Medal. He is a frequent guest lecturer at continuing education programs and is often asked to comment in the media on matters involving the legal profession and criminal justice issues. He authors a quarterly column, Sidebars, in* Canadian Lawyer Magazine.

# Mr. William Trudell

## Defending the Mentally Ill
## There Must Be More To the Story

SHE HAD TUCKED her new young family into bed and after a typical busy mom's day and a chore-full night, she finally closed her eyes. The ominous sound of the phone shocked the silence of the night. It is a dreadful interruption of a parent's slumber to have the phone ring late at night. Her heart racing, she heard the quivering voice of her oldest child, who lived with her former husband. "You have to come and get me, something awful has happened, please!"

Propelled by fear and instinct, she found herself in her van racing through the dark city, the stillness only broken by shadowy lights from the lamp posts along the way. She realized she was not sure where he was, or where she was going. Suddenly sirens, racing police cars and ambulances seemed to be everywhere. Her pulse was screaming. Instinctively, she found herself in a police station and ran to the desk seeking information, "I'm sorry ma'am, someone has been killed, I can't help you now." Oh dear God she shouted to herself, not Troy, not my baby. Back in the van, she drove towards his father's basement apartment, when her phone rang again. "Where are you? What has happened?" she screamed.

She found him. White as a ghost, with his leg bleeding, he hobbled out of the darkness of the local high school. This was making no sense to her. He then said, "I want to go home…one more time, then I have to turn myself in." In a daze, she started to take him to his father's place where he basically lived, and her eighteen-year-old son murmured, "No mom, our home," and she headed in shock to her new family home.

An hour later, her son had surrendered to the police and was charged with first-degree murder. A policeman was dead. Her nightmare was just beginning.

Her son, a handsome young man, quiet, artistically talented, with absolutely no criminal past, would be on trial for the vicious murder of a police officer.

That Friday night, he had declined an invitation to accompany a couple of his friends, who that year had left him for university, to a movie, ironically called *Troy*. Instead, around ten o'clock, he found himself acting out a bizarre and dangerous plan, later, startlingly found in detail on the computer in his bedroom, a place where he shut out the world.

Equipped with his school backpack, filled with an altered shotgun owned by his father, a knife and ominous instruments to further his plan, he had walked a short distance from his father's home to a local abandoned hospital. He soon, wearing his ever-present hooded sweatshirt, stepped out of the shadows to meet the police whom he had summoned to report a robbery—a robbery that never occurred.

One officer left to further investigate, the other, with no conception that his death was imminent, began to question the young complainant. As they stood in the darkness, the officer said, "You know, I think you had better come down to the station to talk about this." Seconds later, slashed and bleeding from his neck, the officer un-holstered his gun and fired at the escaping young man, shooting him in the leg. The officer then collapsed.

The abandoned hospital parking lot was soon filled with the flashing lights of police cruisers, as chaos shattered the night. Hiding behind the trees, not far away, shotgun at his side, Troy watched the unfolding of his life and the ending of another. He began to run, through backyards, over sidewalks, his leg pounding in pain, until exhausted, he stopped. That is when he called his mother.

His nightmare had begun and I soon became a part of it.

### *Becoming a Part of It*

I was asked to defend him. A senior SWAT team officer called my home the next day. They had found Molotov cocktails and explosive devices in the shed behind his father's home. There were indications from Troy's computer that he was planning a suicidal rampage throughout the city.

In a strange and unique set of circumstances, police decided to ask the accused murderer's lawyer if he could assist to find out if there was imminent danger throughout the city. They had no idea how serious the situation could become. They needed to know. No one had any idea what they were dealing with. Not surprisingly, that included me.

The accused, then in custody, seemed in shock.

I was soon able to satisfy the police forces, assembled on high alert, that there was no further need for alarm. Whatever bizarre plan my young client seemed to be engaged in no longer existed.

The evidence against him seemed overwhelming, including a road map to chaos on his computer, and notes found in his backpack. However, something was wrong. The act was brutally real. An unsuspecting police officer was dead. It was surely a senseless killing, but it also made no sense. I immediately turned to mental health experts.

Before I could even consider addressing the 'why', there were immediate concerns for Troy's well being. I sensed that he, never having any trouble with the law, would have a very difficult time being locked alone in a jail cell. Facing horrible allegations, with only his mind as company, it was a realistic possibility that he could succumb to suicidal thoughts.

I was alerted to these types of concerns early in my career. Just days after meeting and agreeing to defend a man charged with a horrific crime, I received a call early one morning from the nursing station at the psychiatric hospital where he had been sent for an assessment by the Court. My client, when left alone ever so briefly, had killed himself.

And furthermore, I will never forget a haunting 'close call'. A client had been charged with sexual assault on young boys. Since he was prominent in his community, the media had loudly headlined the allegations. He was devastated. A series of meetings had taken place in my office but on one occasion he was unusually late. I phoned his wife to inquire and she, growing quite concerned herself, reported that he had left home "quite some time ago" and would have likely parked in the lot behind my office.

For some instinctive, perhaps fearful reason, I journeyed into the parking lot to check. And there I found him. He was locked in his car, bleeding from several self-inflicted knife wounds. With the help of others, I was able to quietly talk to, and urge him to unlock the door. He did, his life continued, and he was eventually able to deal with his charges.

Defence counsel are often witnesses to the horrors of depression and illness that precede, or are even precipitated, by criminal charges. Because some of the cases are so horrific, we, and all professionals involved, must be personally protective of our own mental health.

One of the most incredible and courageous examples of this is one of Canada's preeminent psychiatrists, Dr. John Bradford. He has had to explore into the minds of some of Canada's worst serial killers and sex offenders. He publically acknowledged living with acute Post Traumatic Stress Disorder (PTSD) after watching, studying, and listening to videotaped sadistic murders, complete with the haunting sounds of the victims as they died.

In October of 2010, Col. Russell Williams, the former commander of Canada's largest military airfield in Trenton, Ontario, was convicted of first-degree murder in the sex slayings of Cpl. Marie-France Comeau and Jessica Lloyd. Pursuant to a court order, Dr. Bradford conducted the assessment on Williams and viewed hours of horrifying graphic crime scene footage.

In the early 1990s, Paul Bernardo and his then-wife Karla Homolka were convicted of crimes in relation to the brutal rape and murder of two teenage schoolgirls, Kristen French and Leslie Mahaffy. Further to a court order, Dr. Bradford spent ample time with Bernardo and went through the crime scene videotapes at length, witnessing the disturbing and horrific scenes of the sexually motivated homicides.

Dr. Bradford has spoken openly and used his experience with Post Traumatic Stress Disorder to remind us of the possible effects and human cost to our own health in this line of work.

### *The Defence Counsel's Journey*

In considering the mental state of our client, we must immediately address the issue of fitness. Is the accused able to understand and comprehend the proceedings, to give instructions, to engage, and to knowingly take part in their defence? Unless they are mentally capable of engaging, the Court may find them actually *unfit,* and they are then kept in a psychiatric facility until they can appreciate the process.

Indeterminate hospitalization in a psychiatric facility is also a real concern in a very different scenario that raises ethical issues for defence counsel. If an accused shows signs of a mental illness, but the offence upon conviction might result in significantly less restrictions on their liberty, counsel must weigh raising the defence of Not Criminally Responsible (NCR), lest the client serve more time in a secure hospital facility than they might in a jail. A determinate predictable period of incarceration must be weighed in this circumstance.

Provincial Review Boards have been set up to conduct assessments of mentally ill offenders before he or she is released into the community, seeking a balance between treatment and public safety.

While an accused may be not criminally responsible for their conduct, the public may require protections and reassurance from further dangerous behaviour before their release.

Dr. Alan Leschied, Psychologist and Professor at Western University, and Psychiatrist Dr. Clive Chamberlain of Toronto, preeminent experts in forensic psychology and psychiatry respectively, especially gifted in the treatment of young people, agreed to assist me in Troy's case.

### *Defending Troy*

I retained them under the umbrella of my solicitor client relationship to help and report to me as to the state of my young client's mind.

We began to look for an explanation for Troy's behaviour, which clearly appeared to be suicidal in nature. A theory soon developed, that perhaps he was not going out that night with the intent to take someone's life, but rather to end his own. He needed to be provoked. He seemed to be fixated on his plan, on one outcome, but his rigid focus was interrupted by a police officer who had responded to his robbery complaint. This eighteen-year-old young man, in clouded thinking, had decided that the world would be better off without him. He needed to create an event.

A plea of Not Criminally Responsible was not available after the doctors' assessments. In the end, a jury, faced with the plan, and the apparent exact steps undertaken to complete it, found him guilty of first-degree murder. The evidence of isolation, depression, a splintered family, and the unravelling of judgement was not enough to reduce the charge. His flirtation with *The Anarchist's Cookbook*, first published in 1971, a book that contains instructions for the manufacture of explosives, rudimentary telecommunications, and other items, found online, filled a black hole in his mind and helped drive Troy to a fantasy that went too far. The officer, doubting his story, interrupted his bizarre behaviour with a shock of reality by suggesting they attend the station. But by then, the plan had become real, tragic, and too advanced for this young man to withdraw from.

Still, I urged, that if his plan was to kill police officers en masse, as was suggested, it made no sense that he watched from the seclusion of the bushes at the abandoned hospital, shotgun at his ready, and did not fire a single shot, although he had every opportunity. Instead he resorted to calling his mother.

It was described to me as a classic case of 'suicide by cop'. To this day, I believe he was ill, but despite the incredible help from the forensic experts, the jury found Troy guilty as charged.

### *The Experts*

The degrees of mental disturbances don't often reach the level of Not Criminally Responsible (NCR), or insane as we used to call it, where one fails to appreciate the nature and quality of the act. The courtroom debate is usually an attempt to fit the behaviour into an illness as defined by the *Diagnostic and Statistical Manual of Mental Disorders* (DSM).

In rare instances, the conduct is excused completely. In so many others, the degree of mental illness affects, contributes to, and is even causally linked to the conduct.

What separates many from crossing this line is a safety net in society, parents, family, friends, social relations, and treatment. So many fall through the cracks where there is no net and disaster and tragedy result. It is extremely difficult, if not cruel, to ask the wife who has lost her husband and father, the parent who has lost their child, the children who have lost their parents, siblings or friends, to try to understand that the perpetrator of their pain was ill.

Psychiatrists and psychologists are behaviour scientists of the mind. Their contribution to criminal justice is essential. Sometimes, however, their opinions may be mistaken and must be challenged. In this light, the role of Counsel, both Crown and defence, in cases involving mental illness, requires that we must ourselves become scientists to understand the behaviour in question. To call an expert witness, or to cross examine an expert witness, Counsel must never cross their fingers and pretend to understand. We, to some degree, must journey into the mind of the client.

Mental health experts are often retained to look at the issue from the Crown's side, to test an allegation of diminished or nonexistent intent.

In deciding which experts Counsel turn to, certain guiding principles exist. We need to be certain that the expert is indeed an 'expert experienced in the field', not simply generically skilled, that they are licenced by a professional College and, ideally, have been recognized as experts by the Court in other cases. It is always insightful to review examples of their previous testimony.

They must not be advocates for a position. They are there to help explain the science and be skilled communicators, educators, if you will, knowledgeable and respected by their peers. Whether they are called to testify or just provide reports, choosing and working with the right expert for the case is crucially important.

If mental health is the issue, it is often better to try to have the experts agree, rather than debate each other.

The widely respected former Chief Justice Patrick LeSage shared with me a case from many years ago (he was Crown Counsel at the time), where psychiatrists were retained by the Crown and the defence and the issue was whether or not psychopathy was a disease of the mind. The psychiatrists were invited to meet prior to their testimony and allowed to be in the courtroom when their colleagues were testifying. In a most unusual twist, the jury actually found the accused guilty of a series of offences, but insane (as it was referred to then) on others. The problem was that the series of sexual assaults were chronological. On the face of it, the verdict made no sense.

In a discussion with jurors after the trial (these discussions were allowed at that time), it became clear that their verdict was a 'practical' one as they saw it. The jury was concerned that the accused would be released too soon if they found him insane. They need not have worried. It has been many years now, he is still in a psychiatric facility and will likely never be released.

In the 2013 first-degree murder case of Richard Kachkar, he drove a snowplow through the streets of Toronto and eventually killed a police officer. The psychiatrists agreed that even though Mr. Kachkar did not fit neatly into an easy classification, he experienced a psychotic break from reality at the time. Three eminent and respected psychiatrists, Dr. Lisa Ramshaw, Dr. Phillip Klassen, and Dr. John Bradford, all essentially agreed with defence counsel, Robert Richardson's argument that Mr. Kachkar was, at the time, Not Criminally Responsible (NCR). Crown Counsel, Christine McGoey, relied on the equally experienced psychiatrists, Dr. Graham Glancy and Dr. Lakshmi Voruganti, who assessed Mr. Kachkar while in jail in the months after the tragedy, and found no evidence of Mr. Kachkar having a psychotic disorder at that time.

This was a remarkable case which featured highly regarded counsel for the Crown and defence, and an array of distinguished forensic experts grappling with important and vital questions of mental illness. Mr. Kachkar was found Not Criminally Responsible by the jury, in a singularly fascinating trial that captured the public's attention and became, for a time, a lightening rod in the debate between crime and illness.

***The Dilemma...Bad or Mad?***

What the hell is happening to our world?
How did we even get to this point?
I can't believe he did that!
It was her child for God's sake, how could she do that?
It just makes you sick, so senseless....
This can't be true, I know him....

The statements above are often the familiar background for defence counsel who take on a case with horrific allegations.

Actually, what keeps us going, perhaps even offers some comfort, is knowing that in almost every case, there is more to the story.

Often times, as the background unravels, the spectre of mental illness emerges as the key that unlocks the story behind the shocking conduct.

Defence lawyers instinctively know that 'criminal behaviour' is often times simply bad behaviour with a label, and our society resorts to a system to regulate and penalize the conduct that contravenes social norms.

An essential issue, however, that must never be forgotten is, as the saying goes, 'bad or mad?'

It is basic, that if someone is going to be sanctioned for breaking society's rules, they have to have intended to do so. Thus, there are two aspects that enter the microscope of the criminal justice lab...the act and the intent. It is incredibly difficult, especially in circumstances where the alleged crime seems so vicious and inhumane, to educate people that we are using the wrong label, that the accused is not a criminal, but is ill, a puppet actor to an uncontrolled mind.

Defence counsel are not qualified to give medical opinions, just as medical doctors do not give legal advice. The importance of mental health experts cannot be overstated in unravelling the obvious assumption that accompanies a horrible act and a visceral demand for retribution.

Criminal justice is often a catchment for many of society's failures. But herein lies the problem. The mentally ill need treatment, not punishment. The psychologists and psychiatrists become the vital interpreters of terrible mistakes, reminding us that we must not punish someone who is not accountable.

These experts are often Counsel's most important investment because as integral as the presumption of innocence may be, so is the inference that an accused intended the consequences of their act.

In many instances, asking a client who may even be delusional to tell you what happened is akin to opening a closet door to another universe. You do not know what will unfold.

But let's speculate about the responses one might receive from an accused who is suffering from mental illness.

"I don't know?"
"I don't remember."
"I didn't mean it."
"What did I do?"
"I don't believe it."

"Who are you?"
"I need my medication."
"I just lost it."
"I have been under so much pressure."
"I just can't cope."
"CAN YOU HELP ME?"

That last question is the unspoken first question for every defence counsel.

I think everyone reading this book recognizes that mental illness has become one of our society's greatest concerns and perhaps lurks just behind many closet doors. It likely won't surprise anyone that the large majority of clients that criminal defence lawyers see need counselling, if not therapy.

Defending the mentally ill is extremely challenging, but is perhaps the most important role a defence counsel plays in our society. One of the effective and indeed essential methods of defending the mentally ill is to encourage alternative ways of dealing with the obvious cases of illness. The criminal justice system is not where the mentally ill can or should be treated.

There is always more to the story.

# ACKNOWLEDGEMENTS

I am grateful to my wife Jennifer Briscoe, the Honourable Patrick LeSage, Dr. Alan Leschied, and my Executive Assistant and Law Clerk, Amanda Fernandez, for their guidance and assistance in my attempts to contribute to this interesting collection.

*— William Trudell*

Thank you to all my patients over the years who have enriched my life with their stories.

*— David Dawson*

I would like to thank all of the staff at the 102 Court at Old City Hall, Toronto, for the hard work and dedication that has resulted in a mental health court which many around the world have been modelled after.

*— Richard D. Schneider*

I would like to acknowledge my mom for teaching me every person is sacred; my wife for keeping me grounded and on my toes, and my daughter for the joy she brings. Thanks to my FPS colleagues, gifted people making a difference. Lastly, gratitude to my clients who have taught me many lessons and allowed me to be a part of their transformation.

*— Lawrence Ellerby*

I would like to thank my wife Celeste and my three children, Joshua, Lauren and Samantha who have supported me. I would also like to thank Vince Li for his willingness to have me tell his story.

*— Jeffrey Waldman*

I would like to dedicate my chapter to my life partner, Žarka, and our dog, Ragnar, both of whom rarely malinger. If Ragnar does malinger, it is fairly obvious.

*— Barry Cooper*

This chapter is dedicated to my best friend and partner in life, Kamil.

*— Jacqueline Kanipayor*

I would like to thank Katy Ross, and Bill Prestia.

*— Don Dutton*

# ACKNOWLEDGEMENTS


The chapter is dedicated to my wonderful parents Glynn & Carol Porter.

*— Stephen Porter*

I would like to dedicate the chapter to my parents, Bruce and Brenda Dilley, who have always supported and encouraged me to achieve more than I thought possible.

*— Tianna Dilley*

The chapter written is dedicated to all the women in South Africa who were in abusive relationships and who showed resilience and daring to get out of the relationship before it led to more devastating results. May they inspire and assist other women who are still caught in the web of abuse and join others who are working to make the dynamics and sequelae of abuse clearer to people in leading positions in the legal system and law enforcement system.

*— Louise Olivier*

To all who supported me and shared sage advice during this exciting and stressful stage in my career — many thanks.

*— Joel Watts*

Recently I spent thirty days on 'death-row' when a pathology report falsely diagnosed a cancer. When you are in that state you do a lot of reflection. No human can ever provide the intensity of support and love that a dog can. Thanks Beau.

*— Jack White*

To my clients and colleagues, for their patience with my many professional distractions; to my friends and family, for their understanding that sometimes work came first; to my wife, for her enduring love and support; and, to David, for allowing me to share a part of his amazing story, thank you so much.

*— Patrick Baillie*

When dealing with the unimaginably difficult, it is a gift to feel love for and from my six wonderful children; John, Jacob, Ellinor, Leonard, Elliot, and August.

*— Sven Å. Christianson*

# INDEX

# The 'True Cases' Series

**_Tough Crimes: True Cases by Top Canadian Criminal Lawyers_**

Book One in the True Cases Series

*"Tough Crimes demonstrates that Crown prosecutors and criminal defence lawyers do not escape unscathed from serious trials. The disturbing memories remain."*

*— Hon. John C. Major, CC QC, Retired Justice of the Supreme Court of Canada*

Tough Crimes is a collection of thoughtful and insightful essays from some of Canada's most prominent criminal lawyers. Stories include wrongful convictions, reasonable doubt, homicides, and community spirit.

Edited by C.D. Evans and Lorene Shyba

Price: $29.95 *Trade Paperback*

ISBN: 978-0-9689754-6-6

**_SHRUNK: Crime and Disorders of the Mind_**

Book Two in the True Cases Series

*"Shrunk's authentic portrayal of what mental illness is really like, and what it can do to people, sets it apart from other books of crime stories."*

*— Dr. Hy Bloom LLB, MD, FRCPC Consultant in Forensic Psychiatry*

SHRUNK is a collection of chapters by eminent Canadian and international forensic psychologists and psychiatrists who write about mental health issues they face and what they are doing about it.

Edited by Lorene Shyba and J. Thomas Dalby

Price: $29.95 *Trade Paperback*

ISBN: 978-0-9947352-0-1

**_Coming in 2017_**

**_Journo Tales: True Cases of Covering Crime_**

Edited by Colin Perkel and Lorene Shyba

Book Three in the True Cases Series

Trade Paperback | ISBN: 978-0-9947352-5-6

DURVILE PUBLICATIONS &

*UpRoute Bright Books with Bite*

# Other Durvile Titles

***5000 Dead Ducks***
***Lust and Revolution in the Oilsands***

A Novel by CD Evans and LM Shyba

*"5000 Dead Ducks is a masterfully crafted satire weaving together two of the hottest topics in Alberta (or Alberia) today: provincial politics and the oilsands."*
*— Daryl Slade, Calgary Herald*

*5000 Dead Ducks* is about a young environmentalist who finds herself teamed up with group of unscrupulous lawyers scheming a takeover of the Oilsands.

Price: $16.95 *Paperback*
Illustrations by Maxwell Théroux.

ISBN 978-0-9689754-4-2

***A Painful Duty***
***40 Years at the Criminal Bar***

A Memoir by CD Evans

*"Very rarely have I read a memoir or autobiography whose author had as overwhelming concern for truth and fairness as Evans displays in this book."*
*— Alex Rettie, Alberta Views*

In his memoir, Evans reveals insights into the practice and the characters of the Criminal Bar, with special tributes to the no-nonsense judges of the early days.

Price: $42.50 *Trade Paperback*
16 pages of colour photos.

ISBN: 978-0-9689754-3-5

***Milt Harradence: The Western Flair***

Foreword by Hon. John C. Major, CC QC
Retired Justice, Supreme Court of Canada

*"It should find a permanent home in every trial lawyer's library."*
*— Ron MacIsaac, Lawyers Weekly*

*In Milt Harradence: The Western Flair,* C.D. Evans perpetuates the legend of his flamboyant, larger-than-life colleague with whom he shared thrills, spills, brilliant courtroom spars.

Price: $30.00 *Trade Paperback*
16 pages of colour photos.

ISBN: 978-0-9689754-0-4

DURVILE PUBLICATIONS &

*UpRoute Bright Books with Bite*